GT
525
.J67
1986

Joseph, Nathan,
1922-

Uniforms and
    nonuniforms

$35.00

DATE		

Uniforms and Nonuniforms

UNIFORMS AND NONUNIFORMS

Communication Through Clothing _____

NATHAN JOSEPH, *1922 –*

CONTRIBUTIONS IN SOCIOLOGY, NUMBER 61

GREENWOOD PRESS _____

NEW YORK · WESTPORT, CONNECTICUT · LONDON

Library of Congress Cataloging-in-Publication Data

Joseph, Nathan, 1922–
  Uniforms and nonuniforms.

  (Contributions in sociology, ISSN 0084-9278 ; no. 61)
  Bibliography: p.
  Includes index.
  1. Costume—Social aspects. 2. Uniforms—Social
aspects. 3. Nonverbal communication. I. Title.
II. Series.
GT525.J67 1986   391   86-7677
ISBN 0-313-25195-9 (lib. bdg. : alk. paper)

Library of Congress Catalog Card Number: 86-7677
ISBN: 0-313-25195-9
ISSN: 0084-9278

First published in 1986

Greenwood Press, Inc.
88 Post Road West, Westport, Connecticut 06881

Printed in the United States of America

∞™

The paper used in this book complies with the
Permanent Paper Standard issued by the National
Information Standards Organization (Z39.48-1984).
10 9 8 7 6 5 4 3 2 1

Contents

Acknowledgments

I can hope to acknowledge only a few of the many whose advice and assistance made this work possible. Murray Hausknecht gave unstintingly of his time and sage advice throughout the long course of this endeavor. Nicholas Alex co-authored an early article on uniforms and performed the field work on occupations. Joseph Bensman read a previous draft and offered invaluable suggestions.

Frank Schubert, Historical Division of the Department of the Army, was most helpful and gave bibliographic data on the Old West. A. Godwin of the Royal Navy, Comdr. Hines, USN, Harold Langley of the Smithsonian Institution, John Munday of the British National Maritime Museum, Capt. Preuschoft of the German Navy, and George Tilton of the National Federation of Federal Employees furnished valuable information. I am also indebted to reporters of the *Navy Times, New York Times,* and *Wall Street Journal* who entered into correspondence. I should like to thank AMTRAK and the Visiting Nurse Service of New York for their cooperation in the interviews of staff members.

Herbert H. Lehman College aided by providing two Faculty Fellowships and a George Shuster Grant. The City University of New York assisted with a Faculty Research Award.

My greatest obligation is to my wife, Elaine, who labored indefatigably and prevented me from settling for second best.

Alfred Cohen, Edgar Joseph, Herbert Rosenbaum, my colleagues, and others provided essential words of encouragement. Needless to say, any flaws are attributable to me alone.

Abbreviations

GPO	Government Printing Office
HMSO	Her Majesty's Stationery Office
IHT	*International Herald Tribune*
IRA	Irish Republican Army
NLRB	National Labor Relations Board
NT	*Navy Times*
NYT	*New York Times*
SS	*Schutzstaffel* (Nazi Elite Guard)
WSJ	*Wall Street Journal*

(For additional abbreviations, see bibliography)

Uniforms
and
Nonuniforms

1

Introduction

Perhaps the best way to introduce the sociology of clothing is to answer the questions most frequently raised by laymen when they first learn of my interest, "What do jeans mean?" or, "How do you interpret the color blue?" My usual response is to indicate the ambiguity of the questions by pointing out that jeans have variously meant membership in such groups or statuses as agricultural laborers, civil rights movements, youth subcultures, or foreign communist elites with access to Western consumer goods. Similarly, blue has denoted English domestics, inmates of English philanthropic institutions, artillery officers in most eighteenth-century European armies, or police.

Clothing is very much a social artifact—a form of communication—which can best be understood by sociological concepts. My premise is that all signs derive meaning from their social contexts and may serve some function for individuals, groups, or institutions.[1] This study will explicate these contexts, emphasizing the dynamics of social interaction in the operation and, to some extent, the creation of sartorial signs. Clothing will be viewed as a system of signs that derives meaning from its context while enabling us to carry on our activities. In turn, changes in clothing serve as a means of accommodating and facilitating changes in their contexts.

Instead of attempting a complete account of the sociology of clothing, I have focused upon several strategic areas whose exploration may shed light upon the dynamics of sartorial signs. My entering wedge is that of uniforms. To indicate my rationale, I was once greatly impressed by the explicitness of nonverbal signs in a fable-within-a-fable. In his book on the Alhambra, Washington Irving tells the story of a vizier who warns his king of the approaching puberty of the princess by merely presenting his master with a ripening peach. This explicitness of nonverbal signs is reflected in reality by the precise and elaborate vocabulary of signs in the togas of some Ethiopian tribes which reflects emotional states, social status, and the desire for privacy (Messing 1978). If we are to study clothing as a form of communication, then the logical jumping-off point would seem to be where the rules of nonverbal discourse are most clearly stated.

Within contemporary society, the clothing that approaches such clarity and precision is the uniform which is used by various organizations, usually bureaucratic in structure. The uniform depicts specialized offices, hierarchical position, internal organizational relationships, and external relationships with the public more accurately than any other category of clothing. The precision and explicitness of the uniform render it eminently suitable for use as a means of bureaucratic control, reaching even into the status set of the wearer. The clarity of the message transmitted by uniforms makes them a model against which to assess other types of dress.

Implicit in the use of uniforms is an underlying mental set or cluster of values and norms which supports these relationships. Successful changes in uniform require concomitant changes in the accompanying norms and values.

As a first approximation to the definition of a uniform—the final definition itself will constitute an important discussion—the uniform is the legitimating emblem of membership within an organization. It does not refer simply to the similarity of dress within a group, a frequent error. Similarity of dress does not necessarily indicate such memberships and may at times be limited or even absent as we shall see.

The precision and explicitness of a uniform makes even small departures from the norm more obvious and meaningful to both wearers and audiences, thereby making the study of deviation much easier. Nonconformists in uniform are not merely expressing individuality or the sway of fashion but are also stating, usually consciously, their attitudes toward the organization. Nonconformity at times assumes the form of "overconformity", an extreme punctiliousness which carries its own message.

The characteristics of other types of clothing analyzed in this study vary sharply from those of uniforms. Occupational clothing, such as quasi uniforms, usually lack the legitimacy and explicitness of uniforms, thereby permitting the intrusion of extra-organizational norms such as those of unions or professional associations. Nongovernmental organizations usually exert less control over the status sets of their members through occupational clothing than do governmental groups through uniforms. Leisure clothing, the antithesis of occupational dress or uniforms, indicates the cessation of work and its obligations. Instead of asserting the presence of the social controls of the workplace, leisure clothing declares their absence. Finally, in contrast to uniforms, costumes deliberately obfuscate social position, indicate an "abnormal" state of affairs, or lend themselves to attempts at change.

To understand these clothing types, it is not necessary to analyze every example. I will not engage in, for example, an encyclopedic inventory of uniforms which are used extensively by, among others, the military, federal, state, and municipal services, schools, sports, occupational, and professional groups.

Fashion has long been a key topic in the sociological study of ordinary clothing, especially as a rapidly changing mode of class differentiation. However, it also characterizes the categories of clothing used in this study where it serves other functions as well. Fashion will be examined, where relevant, within these categories as a change in type and source of signs and in the degree of separation between groups.

Turning to the structure of this work, the first part consists of an examination of the several types of sartorial signs, their references to reality, and their frequent nonfunctional or ludic employment. The devices of metaphor and metonymy will explain the process of elaboration or development of signs. The physical basis of clothing, the vehicle for the signs, helps to explain some of the properties of sartorial signs such as the use of concealed signs, the impact of massed formations of uniform wearers, and the creation of economic relationships based upon clothing. Finally, expressive statuses such as wives, children, honor guards, domestics, and receptionists not only display and maintain signs for their group but also frequently serve as a source of symbols for the outer world.[2]

The second part applies the vocabulary of signs to an understanding of uniforms and explains why they are so desirable a means of control for bureaucracies. The uniform permits an organization to define precisely the types and degrees of membership within it. It further allows the organization to enlist the public's aid in enforcing controls upon its members since the norms and the deviations of uniform wearers are apparent to everyone. Because the uniform is above all a method of maintaining rigorous adherence to norms, departure from these norms—the actual mode of wearing uniforms—is an important topic. And so we shall spend some time on the types and causes of under and overconformity to uniform regulations. Sartorial behavior or the actual wearing of clothes, uniforms in this instance, is as important as the norms in understanding the use of clothing in any context.

As with any system of communication, distortions inevitably arise. In this instance they are due to the uniform as a category of perception with culturally determined values and biases, and the ideological use of dress. Clothing lends itself to manipulation and distortion as much as verbal signs.

The uniform has great importance for the public to whom it has provided perceptual categories or cultural personae such as the Minuteman, the Continental, and the Jolly Tar to structure and understand the social world.

The final section deals with sartorial contrasts to uniforms which will clarify the nature of uniforms and other types of clothing. The dress worn by non-bureaucratic groups of the past (patrimonial armies or liveried retainers) or the present (guerrillas or special forces) are read to indicate a set of relationships, personal or nonbureaucratic, that differ very much from those of contemporary organizations. Occupational dress, particularly the "quasi uniform", is an attempt to employ signs of organizational affiliation without the power of legitimating signs manifested by the state in its uniforms. Leisure clothing describes an array of relationships ranging from solitude, to aristocratic pastimes characterized by a stress upon the grace of the amateur, to the pursuit of sports with all the intensity of the marketplace, to attempts to alter the persona one presents to the public. Finally, costumes alter the routine types of interaction by removing the customary forms of responsibility and accountability for one's activities and facilitating spontaneity and easy sociability. They thereby enable the description of extraordinary states of affairs, permit moral holidays, and serve as a channel of catharsis or the expression of a desire for change.

To place this analysis within the perspective of other approaches, we may live in a cognitively structured world as the semiologists suggest but, instead of deriving the structure from the underlying constants of the mind, I suggest a sociological point of view in which the structure is derived from roles, statuses, groups, and institutions. Communication systems such as special clothing and other nonverbal media enable these components to carry out their functions. Clothing is not the sole channel of information but precedes and introduces other systems and provides a running commentary on them during interaction. Not all communication is germane to a group or institution, of course, for there may be nonutilitarian messages, intrusions from other groups, and individual communication. I do not rule out the semiotic approach; however, we need not always operate on the level used by semiologists to understand the workings of an institution.

The data for this work was derived from a variety of sources. Sixteen open-ended interviews were conducted with wearers of occupational uniforms.[3] For information on uniform wearers, correspondence was conducted with attachés and other officials of the United States, British, German Federal Republic, and French navies, Canadian Forces, and other military units.[4] Attitude surveys of servicemen in the navies of the United States, Great Britain, and the German Federal Republic were particularly useful. Transcripts of hearings before various labor relations and arbitration panels furnished an unexpectedly rich bonanza of information on dress codes and on conflicts between union and management on the wearing of occupational and military uniforms in private corporations, government agencies, and National Guard units. The *Navy Times* gave an inside picture of the serviceman's views on the long dispute over the abandonment of bell-bottoms by the United States Navy, the re-institution of the traditional uniforms, the "Pride and Professionalism" campaign, and other issues. The *Military Collector and Historian* provided detailed empirical data on contemporary and past military and naval uniforms. Not only did the *New York Times* and *Wall Street Journal* provide excellent data in many areas, but personal correspondence with some of their reporters added additional insights. Finally, I have relied greatly upon military biographies, histories of military art, and other secondary sources.

NOTES

1. I rely upon Durkheim (1947) and Raymond Firth (1973) in this area.

2. "Status" designates any socially defined position, including not only those derived from stratification, but also family, group or organization, gender, age, and other affiliations and memberships.

3. See list of interviews.

4. Data on naval uniforms was stressed because of the efforts in many navies to change from the traditional bell-bottom to jacket-and-trouser types of uniforms during the period of study, thereby affording the possibility of interesting comparisons.

PART ONE
BACKGROUND

2

Sartorial Signs: A Social Vocabulary

As with all systems of communication, the sartorial consists of signs, signals, and symbols which are borne by vehicles.[1] This chapter will analyze sartorial signs and their components, discuss their social nexus, and describe the formation of signs through the socially rooted processes of metaphor and metonymy. Examination of the abstract nature of signs will help to explain the use of clothing to suggest general attributes or qualities.

SIGNS: SIGNALS AND SYMBOLS

Clothing is a means of communication and communication is carried on through signs.[2] A sign is anything that stands for something else: a red flag for danger; free flowing hair as indicative of the immaturity of middle-class girls in the nineteenth century. Within the category of signs, there are two major subdivisions, signals and symbols. A signal is a simple cognitive link between things such as the green light instructing us to proceed or the redcoat designating membership in an army. A symbol is a more complex and abstract sign that conveys information about values, beliefs, and emotions. The American flag, the episcopal shepherd's crook, or the swastika painted on a suburban synagogue are all symbols. Sartorial signals and symbols are carried by vehicles, which are specific physical items of clothing such as blue jeans, military uniforms, or nurses' dress.

The line between signal and symbol is not absolute and distinct. For the citizen of Nazi Germany, the swastika on the armband of a uniform signaled the approach of a particular kind of policeman; what is a symbol in contemporary

America was a signal in Nazi Germany. Whether a sign is signal or symbol depends partly on social and cultural contexts. If the German citizen remembered the Weimar Republic, the swastika could have reminded him of the difference between the two political systems and aroused an emotional reaction. Who perceives the sign and how it is perceived also can determine whether at a given moment it is signal or symbol. But for the moment we shall lay aside these complexities to underline what is often overlooked; that is, clothing has important functions as a signal as well as symbol.

A given item of clothing may incorporate both signal and symbol or change from one category to the other. The apron, a protective and serviceable device which also indicated the desirable qualities of a housewife, was later incorporated into the wedding dresses and ball gowns of the eighteenth-century American elite to symbolize "housewifely duties and virtues" (Hicks n.d., 7). Its use by apprentice cooks and student nurses, on the other hand, signaled manual labor. A reduction in the size of the apron therefore accompanied a rise in rank to chef or British nursing sister (Cunnington & Lucas 1967, 390). Matrons, the highest rank in nursing, wore no apron (ibid., 321). The vestments of a contemporary female minister include both apron and clerical robe to denote the duality of her role (NYTM 14 Mar. 1976). By a process of stylization, a simple sign now symbolizes a variety of attributes as well as change in hierarchical position and function.

The distinction between signal and symbol permits the study of many questions of clothing which would otherwise be obscured. The meaning of the military uniform in international law stems from its role as a signal between adversaries; you must know your enemy as a prerequisite to fighting him. To see the military uniform only as symbol is to lose sight of its paradoxical function—the conveying of the minimal amount of information to the enemy essential for "civilized" warfare. To be sure, signals become suffused with emotion and turn into symbols; in World War I the very colors associated with the German military became anathema to the British (Fussell 1977, 77).[3]

The signal as advertisement is very important in a context of illiteracy as, for example, in the English statute fairs where job seekers literally wore their credentials in the form of occupational dress which indicated their background in farming, sheepherding, and other pursuits (Cunnington & Lucas 1967, 376–77). In a similar context, the distinctive garb of street vendors proclaimed their callings or wares (ibid., 380–86).

Within the complex urban setting, the occupational uniform often conveys only visual signals due to the ephemeral and casual relationships of the city where identification of another's position must be made within seconds and business completed within minutes. A railroad ticket seller reports that customers react to him primarily as the wearer of a red coat signalling his position, so much so that very often they cannot recall his face or even his gender a few minutes later (Int. 9). To label all signs as symbols assumes that all interaction occurs at the same deep and significant level.[4]

Whether a sign functions as signal or symbol depends upon the social context as well as the orientation and perspective they give rise to. In one occupational context, a uniform can be perceived in strictly utilitarian terms. When a chief steward was asked for the origin of cooks' uniforms, the explanation was entirely in practical terms of convenience and protection against burns from splashing (Int. 14).[5]

But in another occupational subculture, the uniform becomes an essential symbol. The attitudes towards military or quasi-military dress is often one of deep reverence as indicated in a discussion of the significance of the color of New York State Police uniforms.

The first thing the recruit is taught at the State Police Academy is that the very color of the uniform—gray—has meaning. . . . [Sgt. Roman said] "There's black thread for bad next to white thread for good, and together they make gray. The black stripe down the pant leg is in honor of our fallen comrades, and the purple hat band and necktie are because the Praetorian guards had a border of purple on their white togas." (NYT 5 Oct. 1971)

While not casting doubt upon the origins of the State Police uniform, it should be noted that the explanation was sought in symbolism—values and associations—and not availability of fabric, practicality and usefulness of design. The distinction between signals and symbols reveals two contrasting outlooks on clothing, a practical cognitive approach which results in signals, and an evaluative, at times ritualistic, one which results in symbols.

Signs function in interaction on several levels. On the simplest level, signs are used to validate one's claim to membership in a status or group.[6] Claims are made initially by one's appearance in the appropriate apparel, and their accuracy is later confirmed or rejected by subsequent interaction (Stone, G. 1962). Such initial interaction, following G. H. Mead, is usually described as symbolic interaction because Mead was primarily concerned with signs carrying emotional import for the person. The validation of claims to status is perfunctory or absent in much urban interaction. We accept the uniformed individual in the railroad terminal as a proper guide or source of information without investigation. We perceive the wearer of a habit on the street as a nun and behave toward her accordingly, greeting or avoiding her without ever being able to determine the validity of her garb.

SARTORIAL SIGNS AND THEIR SOCIAL BASE

Signs do not occur at random but usually acquire empirical referents in specific social and cultural contexts and very often serve some function. Our referent for clothing is the social reality represented by the structure and institutions of a society. Using stratification as an example, the English developed an elaborate system of indicating social class which was maintained in even incongruous circumstances. A nudist camp retained a hierarchy by dressing servants in short aprons to differentiate them from their nude employers (Graves & Hodge 1941, 263).

Class distinctions were also evident in the British army, as indeed they were in most. In the eighteenth century, the category "redcoat" actually comprised three different shades due to the varying grades of cloth used for officers, sergeants, corporals, and privates (McBarron et al 1974, 34). The military dandyism of elite Guards officers in the 1920's was expressed in their overconformity to norms (Green 1976, 203–4). Class distinctions persisted into the eve of World War II when Auxiliary Air Force pilots, generally of higher civilian status than other pilots, wore bright scarves and lined their jackets with red silk (Deighton 1979, 52). During the war, the deviation of British officers from regulation dress exceeded those of other armies and again indicated the claims of privilege.

Clothing cannot be explained entirely in terms of dramaturgy, image building, or impression management but instead is related to social reality. Attempts to propagandize, to distort the impression of the underlying reality by symbolic manipulation, may fail if they contradict that reality too sharply. The existence of the social structure cannot be ignored nor altered by signs alone. Recent attempts have been made to remove the unpleasant connotations of nurses' white uniforms by the use of pastel colors or street dress. However, as a student of nursing uniforms wisely remarked, the new uniforms may eventually become as unpopular as the old white ones if nurses continue to perform their unpleasant chores upon patients, especially children (Kornblith 1975, 26). On the other side of the coin, fee paying students of British schools in the eighteenth century requested permission to wear the academic dress used by the hitherto despised subsidized "scholars" when the latter proved to be of superior merit (Cunnington & Lucas 1978, 63).

The opposite approach which asserts that symbols have no autonomy but are complete reflections of the social structure is equally fallacious. To begin with, signs may not refer directly to an empirical base but rather to conventional understandings. Thus red does not intrinsically mean "stop" or green "go". Their meaning is derivable only internally within the symbolic system, syntactically as it were. Various colors and styles may not have any direct referent to the outer world but are explicable only esthetically. An excellent example is the "military" shirt, a popular civilian fashion several years ago, which was ornamented with a bewildering variety of insignia that made no sense and served only to form a decorative pattern.

A closely related use of signs is ludic or playful, a situation in which relationships to an empirical base are again complicated and cannot be interpreted directly. The ludic use is evidenced in sartorial punning as in Chinese dragon robes where bats connoted happiness (Camman 1952, xxxi); in charity clothing, the color sometimes reflected the donor's name (Cunnington & Lucas 1978, 33).

Conventional, esthetic, and ludic signs indicate that a symbolic system may become autonomous, need not always have external references, and need not carry out the work of society. In other systems, the theme of "art for art's sake" describes the same phenomenon; Simmel portrayed the joy of interaction for its own sake without any ulterior purpose (1950, 40–57).

Symbols may be so detached from reality as to constitute an autonomous realm of allegory and myth with few ties to an original base. An outstanding example is that of the American cowboy morality play which has developed an elaborate literature, style of life, and clothing that contrasts sharply with the hard life and often rough dress of the historical cowboy. From a different perspective, participants do not deal with fiction but with another universe of discourse with its own rules and functions.

In another form of dynamics, the original relationship between sign and base may be so greatly changed that the earlier meaning has been leached out. As political naifs, early members of the surfing subculture in California wore swastika medals without any ideological intent (Irwin 1977, 114). Arab keffiyahs or "PLO scarfs" were popular with European adolescents in 1977 and 1978, many of them seemingly wearing the headdress for apolitical chic (NYT 21 Apr. 1978). Similarly, antiuniforms changed from symbols of protest to yet another fad; the military insignia worn as mockery by antiwar protestors became the new "army look" of fashion (NYT 14 Aug. 1971).

The reading of the relationships of signs to their social base depends, in part, upon viewing audiences and their differing interpretations. One group of "readers" sees the swastika and the keffiyah in their original, political intent; wearers and other audiences perceive them in a later, decorative light. The effects of variation in audiences are also reflected in the caution given to amateur Kremlinologists visiting the 1980 Summer Olympics in Moscow against reading a pro-Western political orientation in the wearing of American jeans by Russians (NYT 3 July 1980). Instead, the reporter suggested that jeans indicated a privileged group with access to stores stocking Western goods, access to foreign visitors, and the ability to travel abroad. Jeans therefore reflected an elite with sympathy for the fashions rather than the ideology of the West.

THE FORMATION OF SIGNS BY METAPHOR

A distinctive mode of clothing assigned to a status may arise gradually, the military uniform, or be consciously created, the astronaut's dress, to fill the requirements of the status, not all of them necessarily utilitarian. My concern here is with two aspects of this formative process, how clothes derive their symbolism and how they become part of a system of communication.

The rhetorical device of metaphor describes the development of sartorial signs. Metaphor establishes a link between two items from different contexts so that the commonplaces associated with one item are applied to the other (Black 1962, 38–47, 236; Turner, V. 1974, 25). To call a man a wolf is to ascribe to him the qualities associated with that beast. The sartorial equivalent of metaphor consists of the borrowing of the social characteristics of another—status, relationships, and attributes—by adopting his dress. To dress a medieval nun in a widow's wimple is to transfer to her the nuances of asexuality, humility, and dependency.[7]

Metaphor is of necessity selective. When we speak of man as a wolf, we select among human traits. "Any human traits that can without undue strain be talked about in 'wolf-language' will be rendered prominent, and any that cannot will be pushed into the background. The wolf-metaphor suppresses some details, emphasizes others—in short, *organizes* our view of man." (Black 1962, 41) The metaphor is also selective of the wolf in that we are less likely to emphasize those associations of the wolf depicting it as friendly or helpful. It also follows that the meaning of the metaphor, the associations it evokes, depends upon the social context. The associations read into the metaphor vary with the group. Similarly in clothing, we use the metaphor in a selective manner which facilitates a romanticizing of the past or of other cultures and encourages ideological perspectives.

The questions guiding our analysis comprise: who is adopted as the model for the metaphor; who uses the metaphor; to what extent is the model adopted? The first two will be discussed simultaneously.

Models and Their Users

Although the use of clothing as metaphor is immediately observable to the viewer in terms of status, it can be understood only within an institutional or societal context. To explain the decline in the use of uniforms by British women despite their increased participation in a "man's world", Ewing did not resort to the immediate attributes of the gender role of women but rather to their changing position in society. With the decrease in discrimination, the male metaphor becomes unnecessary. "Women no longer need be uniformed aggressively in order to proclaim their presence or uniformed like men to demonstrate that they have a place in the man's world" (Ewing 1975, 146).

The church has long used sartorial metaphor. Religious orders and secular clergy, particularly of the Roman Catholic Church, have utilized clerical dress to insert themselves into social positions among laity appropriate to their mission, locale, and time. Nuns, priests, and monks have at various times adopted and converted into religious dress the clothing of peasants, widows, factory workers, 1923 flappers, and hippies (NYT 9 July 1975; Int. 1). In each instance, the wearers described themselves as humble, asexual, and powerless by equating themselves sartorially with those defined by the society as possessing these characteristics.

That undercover detectives often adopt the dress of their milieu as protective cover needs no comment. Of greater interest is the dress of police forces which use civilian attire as standard working dress and not as protective disguise. The social niches which they assume vary and may reflect the groups with whom they would identify. At their inception, the Texas Rangers wore the dress of Eastern farmers, and later, that of well-to-do Western ranchers (Jones & Elting 1977; NYT 5 Feb. 1978). The FBI under J. Edgar Hoover wore conservative business clothing. An agent who appeared in a newspaper photograph after capturing a dangerous criminal was chastised by Hoover for not wearing the required snap brimmed hat (Alpern 1980).

The military have similarly used civilian dress as metaphor. In earlier centuries, before bureaucratic exigencies became paramount, European and American officers dressed primarily in accord with their social class rather than their military rank (Carman 1957, 15–22, 59; Copeland 1973, 105; Lawson 1941, 2:9). The British midshipman was granted a uniform mainly to denote his position as a gentleman rather than to indicate rank (Lewis, M. 1948a, 221). To indicate the genteel origins of the purser in contrast to the plebian gunner, both warrant officers in the nineteenth-century Royal Navy, the former wore a top hat and the latter an ordinary seaman's cap (Masefield 1937, 107). Generals and admirals of the eighteenth and earlier centuries, before the advent of modern uniforms, wore a great deal of braid, not simply to indicate their rank but because that was the proper attire for gentlemen who were their civilian counterpart (Barnes 1951, 51; Jarrett 1960, 108).

To describe the role of the contemporary American naval officer, regulations now use the analogy of the businessman's dress; naval dress has shifted from a class to a bureaucratic referent. "The full dress coat, so long a tradition, was abolished in 1922. The Navy officers' dress had clearly left the trappings of the early 19th century 'gentleman' and its uniform now reflected the civilian fashion for business managers" (USN 1981, app.2 p.12). The reverse relationship, the civilian use of the military as metaphor, obviously occurs and employs military themes as motifs for fashion and the attributes of virility, adventure, and power.

A controversy over the substitution of modern for traditional naval uniforms of enlisted personnel has resulted in the widespread use of metaphor. A British seaman strongly prefers the traditional British uniform (horizontally creased and flap-front trousers) over the new version (vertically creased and fly-front trousers). "The old uniform is a recognised good run-ashore rig which every foreigner recognises as the British naval uniform. I am proud to be British, but the new rig looks like a lot of other naval uniforms. It also looks effeminate and I have not yet met anyone who likes it" (Munday 1979). The British sailor equates the traditional "old Navy" with masculinity, in contrast to the "effeminacy" of the outside world which includes other navies and perhaps the civilian world.

In the United States Navy, the proponents of the traditional bell-bottom uniform over the radically different modern type, the jacket-shirt-tie combination of civilian life and the army, compare the newer uniform with the dress of low status occupations such as bus drivers. In the West German navy, a jacket-type uniform was compared to that of a mailman (Preuschoft 1978). Proponents of the traditional bell-bottoms decry the loss of uniqueness, romanticism, and masculinity they regard as inherent in the uniform and are resisting the adoption of the civilian as metaphor.

However, the uniformed individual, especially in the military, usually has an elaborate set of role relationships (role set) requiring an extensive wardrobe.

Although the civilian image may not be acceptable as a metaphor in one capacity, it might well be in another. If the civilian suit is not a popular replacement for the service or ceremonial bell-bottom uniform, civilian dungarees are accepted for hard work in the navy. The baseball cap has become a naval "command cap", identifying the wearer with his unit, and a utility hat for hard work (Hines 1980).

On a societal level, an institution may become a model emulated by other institutions. In the late Victorian era in England, the popularity of the military order caused its uniforms to be adopted as a metaphor by churches (the Salvation Army and evangelical Protestant groups) and uniformed youth groups (Scouts and the Boys' Brigades).[8] The scientist's laboratory coat serves a similar function today, indicating the prestige of the profession.

Metaphor also crosses age lines. The young are under the control of adults who may draft them as demonstrators of cultural values. In Spanish graduation ceremonies boys have been dressed as admirals or fifteenth-century grandees, and girls as queens (Michener 1968, 61). The romantic Highland revival under Victoria put British youth of both sexes into tartans and kilts (Ewing 1977, 82–87). The metaphors adopted by the young themselves who possess power, contemporary youth, is of course another matter.

The dress imposed upon children, which describes them as miniature adults, sailors, asexual creatures, and Welsh fishwives is a metaphorical means for social placement. As miniature adults, children have been clad in reproductions of adult clothing down to corsets for six-year-old girls (Varron 1940). As nonsexual creatures, boys and girls have been dressed alike in long hair and skirts for the first few years of their lives (ibid., Aries 1962, 50–59). Each item of dress is part of a complex of social relationships and beliefs and not only helps indicate the appropriate social position of the child, but instills the desired attitudes in the wearer. Such dress also helps foster an image of the young or his clothier in the eyes of the beholder. The reverse, borrowing the attributes of the young by the no-longer-young, needs little explanation.

That the link between ideology and folk clothing for the young is neither inevitable nor eternal is evident in the history of a related symbol, the flag, which indicates that children have not been considered appropriate symbol bearers in all social contexts. Children did not wave flags to greet President Washington as they did later for General George McClellan. "Yet surely patriotism in earlier days was no less; children were simply not encouraged to infringe upon adult preoccupations" (Mastai & Mastai 1973, 200).

To express political, cultural, and romantic ideals, organized youth groups have often adopted the reconstructed dress of the past, for example, the "Saxon" clothing of the English Kibbo Kift Kindred (Finlay 1970, 53–55; Springhall 1977, 114).[9] The restoration of the medieval past as an ideology was similarly assigned to the German youth movement (Laqueur 1962, 133–43). This view stems from the definition of the young as atavisms or modern counterparts of their cultural ancestors—a perspective popularized by Rousseau, G. Stanley Hall, and others.

The selection of symbols by metaphor is not necessarily to be construed as conscious or deliberate by wearers who may take for granted their choice of an item as simply being more suitable to their purpose or as more indicative of modesty, humility, or respectability. They may have no awareness of the social implications of their selection. But whether or not the wearers recognize the import of their clothing, they are engaged in the manipulation of others' perception through assimilation to selected social positions.

Degrees of Metaphor

In adopting a clothing metaphor to project an image of a social status or position, one can express various degrees of identification with that position. At one extreme, the complete adoption of identity is desired, as with the imposter, the undercover police, or intelligence agent. Here, the assimilation of status extends beyond the symbolic and includes the iconographic. The intelligence agent does not want to suggest the appearance of an ordinary civilian but rather actually appear to be one. Indeed recognition of the masquerade as metaphor indicates failure. Espionage organizations go to great lengths in their attempts to insure authenticity in clothing worn in enemy countries, for example the placement and sewing on of buttons (Brown, A. C. 1976, 348–49). A suitable label is "total metaphor" which borrows symbols for their complete and literal designation of status.

Groups using a total metaphor must conform to much more rigorous standards of behavior and appearance than those originally wearing the borrowed signs. Whereas the individual who is what he appears to be can afford slight discrepancies of behavior, sloppiness which can be explained away if need be, the masquerader cannot afford the luxury of deviation. An Italian Red Brigades' manual uses respectability as a cover for terrorism.

The manual specifies, for example, that an apartment or house to be rented or bought must be "modest, clean, neat and completely furnished. It must appear from the outside as a decent house—curtains, an entrance light, a doormat and a nameplate." . . .

Since "strict discretion is absolutely necessary" if terrorists are to blend in with their surroundings, "every comarde must be decorously dressed and be personally well-kept: clean shaven and hair cut". (Time 1978, 34)

The total metaphor highlights the use of clothing as a prima facie indication of authenticity without relying on the back-up systems ordinarily used in daily life such as drivers' licenses or social security cards. All depends upon the first cast of the die, as it were, and therefore more scrupulous attention must be paid to first impressions. This is of course the often noted psychology of the urbanite who operates upon immediate visual impressions in city streets. On the other hand, when dealing with familiars, clothing is not as important in interpersonal perception (Knapp 1978, 178).

The total metaphor was used by those women of the seventeenth through the nineteenth centuries who disguised themselves as men to serve as sailors and soldiers. A notable example is that of Dr. James Barry who rose to the equivalent of major general in the British army and whose disguise was not discovered until her death in 1865 (Ewing 1975, 28–35). A failure to maintain the metaphor, "sloppy diction", occurred when U.S. Secret Service agents assigned to protective duty were easily spotted by inhabitants of a small town because of the agents' brand new overalls (NYT 31 Oct. 1975).

The assimilation of status by metaphor becomes an intense, almost full time, commitment by members of groups dedicated to recapturing the past. Many such groups have been created to reproduce the life styles of classical Greece and Rome, the Middle Ages, the American Revolution and Civil War. In one brigade of the American Revolution observed by me, the commitment involved all members of the family; children and wives of participants appeared in the appropriate clothing and prepared food of the era over camp fires. Much of the clothing, equipment, and weapons were handmade after research to insure historical accuracy. Metaphor becomes almost total; the assimilation of status is almost as complete as that of the imposter or intelligence agent. But it does announce itself as a symbol; dress is not a sign to convert wearers into actual Revolutionary soldiers or camp followers.[10]

A "partial metaphor" consists of the adoption of only some of the attributes of a status such as rank or relationships to others. A copy writer for a fashion magazine in the 1930's noted that when she left her office to mingle with other employees, she was directed to wear a hat to indicate her professional status (Barshay 1979). In this case, the earmark of a "lady"—the wearing of a hat indoors—was borrowed for its status connotations. The popularity of the military metaphor and uniforms for youth movements in late nineteenth century United States and Britain was not necessarily due to a desire to train the young as soldiers but rather to inculcate, among other virtues, subordination to adults (Kett 1977, 195–98). In this instance the uniform was an expression of aspiration to values rather than total identification with a social position.

Unlike a total metaphor wherein the identity of another is assumed in all respects, in the partial metaphor other symbols modify or qualify the claims of the metaphor. Neither the British Guards who borrowed the French bearskin, nor the American and other armies which adopted the Prussian spiked helmet lost their identity which was indicated by national insignia.

"Mixed metaphors" achieve parody by an internal contradiction of symbols, sartorial oxymorons. "Radical drag", for instance, refers to inconsistent transvestism, the wearer deliberately combining female attire with a heavy beard or exposed genitalia, thus presenting a picture of role incongruity (Humphreys' 1972, 73, 164). The "antiuniform" comprised military items combined with civilian clothing or uniforms worn in a very unorthodox manner. The ordinary transvestite will, on the other hand, engage in a total metaphor, attempting to eliminate all incongruities.[11]

Reversal and the "Broken Blade"

Metaphors can expand a symbolic system to express new situations or statuses. If death is seen as a disturbance of the ongoing scheme of things, then a deliberately created disorder symbolizes death. Accordingly, mourning aboard sailing ships was indicated by trailing rope ends, yards "a-cockbilled", and flags at half-staff (Baker 1979, 109). This device is also used to describe extraordinary positions such as honorific and stigmatized statuses.

The special status of military field musicians in the nineteenth and earlier centuries was signified by a special uniform (McBarron & Elting 1977b).[12] The use of a multicolored uniform immediately creates the possibility of reversing colors to designate special positions, a procedure very frequently followed for musicians. If the standard uniform for his unit was blue with red facings, the musician's would be red with blue facings (Carman 1957, 49, 54, 77).

The reversal of colors also stigmatizes a position such as that of military prisoner. Early in the nineteenth century, prisoners in one American garrison wore coats which were brown on the right side and blue on the left; trousers reversed the color scheme (McBarron et al 1977b). The difference from honorific reversal is that the stigmatized uniform is made grotesque within the contemporary symbolic context. In other contexts, such dress was acceptable as in the multicolored uniforms of the Vatican's Swiss Guards.

Reversability is also used in the literal turning inside out of coats as stigmata for military prisoners. This usage must of course be differentiated from a similar turning inside out of coats for fatigue duty, a *nonsymbolic* use of clothing stemming from a desire to preserve uniforms (Barnes 1951, 48). The turning inside out of coats in nonmilitary contexts often expressed a moral holiday. In various accounts of mumming and carnivals, the coat is frequently described as reversed to indicate a changed state of affairs in which standard rules were inapplicable, at least temporarily.

Since swords, spurs, and coats of arms denote prestige, their altered use signifies the reverse. Medieval knights were disgraced by hacking off their spurs and dragging their insignia in the dirt behind horses (Keen 1965, 54–55). As punishment in a German army during the early nineteenth century, "the majority of the Landwehr has been demoted to the second class, made to march past with their badges reversed, punished with hunger and beatings; the only thing left to do now is to have them shot" (Kitchen 1975, 54–55).

To distance oneself from a situation, one may incapacitate the relevant tools, the logic of the "broken blade". Heralds in the chivalric era and trumpeters in succeeding centuries filled important roles on the battlefield as intermediaries and negotiators between opposing armies (Barnes 1951, 99). They constituted an international guild which interpreted the rules of chivalry and proclaimed the winner of the day. To indicate a neutral status, vital to their function, heralds and trumpeters carried swords with broken-off blades until 1759 to declare their positions both as noncombatants and as gentlemen worthy of carrying swords.

The logic of the broken blade is also found in self-inflicted incapacitation to indicate surrender. In modern times combat planes indicate their surrender and willingness to comply with enemy orders by lowering their landing gear which also decreases their capability. Earlier signs of surrender included giving up weapons or reversing rifles.

THE FORMATION OF SIGNS BY METONYMY

Metonymy, another rhetorical device which describes the development of sartorial signs, is based upon the diachronic links between elements such as the components of a sentence, the courses of a meal, or the items of a dress ensemble (Barthes 1968, 62–63; Leach 1976, 48–49). In contrast to metaphor, metonymy operates within only one context or system; an item derives its meaning from its relationship to other parts of the system (Burke 1945, 506; Turner, V. 1974, 29). The part is taken for the whole; the crown symbolizes the king and ultimately the institution of monarchy because of its role within the symbol system (Leach 1976, 49–50).

In England, the neckband was part of ordinary dress before the Civil War (Cunnington & Lucas 1978, 28–29). After the Restoration, it was used by academicians, lawyers, and clergymen who seemed to form a single learned estate. Subsequently, only clerics wore it. Still later, the dress of boys in charity schools incorporated the neckband. In a display of metonymy, the neckband symbolized religious affiliation and, by extension, humility. Recipients of charity, especially the elderly, constituted a quasi-religious status whose appropriate activity was prayer and whose proper attitude was humble appreciation for kindness received (ibid., 29–30).

In effect, one symbol epitomizes or summarizes a set. The summarizing symbol organizes other symbols into foreground and background, thereby obviating the need to examine every item of an individual's attire in minute detail to place him socially. Instead, we take most of the attire of the other individual for granted, always with the proviso that the background does not thrust itself to the fore by some glaring incongruity or breach of norms but remains within the bounds of our expectations.

Background signs, when they do not conform to expectations, sometimes usurp the function of foreground items. Ordinarily, we identify an officer by such foreground signs as insignia of rank. However, when an enlisted Marine wore an officer's accoutrements such as nonregulation pistol, custom-made boots, ivory swagger stick, and binoculars, but without explicit officer's insignia, he was sometimes saluted by other enlisted men (Manchester 1982, 162, 236). Here, the background conformed to the signs designating an officer and was reacted to accordingly despite the absence of specific foreground insignia such as officer's emblems.[13]

Key or salient symbols, the "working symbols" in the foreground, structure both our perception of and behavior towards others whom we see and interact with as though their status was concentrated entirely in their outstanding symbols. Unmarried peasant mothers in Moravian Slovakia had to wear parts of married women's attire to indicate their position, focusing attention upon these functional equivalents of the scarlet letter to the exclusion of all other sartorial items (Bogatyrev 1971, 83–84).[14]

The general public may not read the uniform in the manner intended by the organization by focusing upon "inappropriate" salient symbols. When the uniform of a visiting nurse service was changed and the old symbols disappeared, salient symbols were in effect created by viewers who seized upon the familiar, unchanged bag as a ready means of identification of the visiting nurses (Int. 5). As we shall see, wearers often create their own salient symbols which differ from the officially designated ones.

Types of Salient Symbols

A very important type of salient symbol indicates legitimacy or certifies membership in formal organizations. They constitute the essential elements of uniform which serve as background to these indications of legitimacy. In American police uniforms, the badge is the salient symbol and receives special legislative protection. In Connecticut, the use of the familiar wide-brimmed hat—known variously as the Montana, campaign, or "Smokey the Bear" hat—is restricted by law to the State Police and its use forbidden even to local police departments (NYT 31 July 1975). In other types of uniforms, salient symbols include the public health nurse's organizational insignia, the hospital nurse's cap, and the soldier's emblems of rank and nationality.[15]

Another type of salient symbol, usually less protected by law, originates in the requirements of occupations and professions and includes the bag of public health nurses, the hat box of models, the intern's stethoscope, and the rule of the medieval carpenter. In medieval Europe, craftsmen were forbidden to walk abroad without some sign of their trade such as the baker's apron and the cooper's hammer, which became almost legitimating signs (Chevalier 1947, 2070–71). The waiter, otherwise indistinguishable from guests in his formal attire, is characterized by the napkin over his arm, a relic of the days when it served many useful purposes.

When different groups use similar dress, for example the contemporary coverall, then specific tools become convenient devices to distinguish the telephone linesman from the automobile mechanic. The several trades in a ship's galley and the various specialities in a printing plant also depend upon specific tools and items of clothing against a background of common dress for identification (Ints. 14, 15).

This use of tools as salient symbols is the rationale for including medical instruments, military weapons, and workers' tools as integral parts of uniforms and occupational clothing, for these often constitute the distinguishing marks for strangers and, at times, wearers. The stranger who has no other information identifies someone in terms of what he does and this may be more important than all other attributes. For wearers themselves, equipment and tools may become salient items for self-definition. The prominently displayed stethoscope enhances the self-esteem of medical students or interns (Coser 1962, 52).

In military organizations, a change of command is often indicated by the transfer of the implements of command, as seen after the wounding of an officer in World War II. "On leaving [Lieutenant] Williams, [Staff Sergeant] Price's first act is to hand map and compass (the symbols of leadership) to Technical Sergeant William Pearce whose seniority the Lieutenant has overlooked" (Marshall 1965, 63).

Weapons also denote rank. Frequently, officers or noncommissioned officers carry weapons differing in kind or quality from those of enlisted men (Bryant 1972, 26; McBarron & Elting 1977a; Todd 1955, 39–40). To illustrate the transmutation of tools into symbols, officers' weapons are often obsolete relics of preceding eras transformed into emblems. Changes in the role of the officer from fighter to manager were paralleled by their weapons.

This withdrawal [from direct killing] is symbolized . . . by the increasingly emblematic weapons which officers have carried; at the beginning of the eighteenth century, when the pike was losing its battlefield utility, a sort of miniature pike; at the beginning of the nineteenth century, when the sword was going out of use, an ornamental sword; at the end of the nineteenth century, when the machine-gun had asserted its dominance, a pistol, usually kept holstered; during the First World War, often, no lethal weapon at all, just a walking-stick. (Keegan 1977, 315)

The weapon often becomes the salient symbol of the uniform. The use of weapons as synecdoche becomes particularly important for the identification of guerrilla or conventional units in a state of rapid formation or decay, conditions when the uniform is in flux. Recently, pistols became the distinguishing emblem of Cambodian commanders when only they were trusted with them (NYT 2 May 1977).

The importance of weapons may derive less from their actual efficacy than their associated cultural values. The right to weapons has long symbolized the wellborn or even the ordinary adult male in a warlike society. When the kris was superseded by firearms in a Filipino Moslem society, the mystique attached to the sword was transferred to the gun which was then also described in very explicit sexual terms (Kiefer 1974). In seventeenth-century Europe, boys of one or two years of age, otherwise dressed identically with girls, were painted wearing miniature swords (Ewing 1977, 29–30; Varron 1940, 1138). Still later, swords were rented for the day at the entrance to public gardens to insure that gentlemen were well-dressed, much like modern restaurants which supply ties and jackets to the inappropriately dressed.

Within uniformed organizations themselves, an aura of high status and virility is similarly attached to weapons, especially pistols (Jones, J. 1979). The attraction that magnum pistols and shotguns have for policemen has less to do with efficiency, a problematic advantage at best, than the feelings of masculinity and authority they encourage. Even the police themselves are aware that these weapons reinforce the sense of power (WSJ 19 Aug. 1980). The shotgun, with its cachet of glamor, was proposed for the one-man cruisers in the New York City Police Department to compensate for the lack of a partner (NYT 13 Mar. 1980). Some of the latent fears at work can be glimpsed in the regulation that prohibited the first black naval officers commissioned in World War II from carrying sidearms (NT 3 May 1982); New York police officers deprived of their pistols and assigned to nonpatrol duties are described by colleagues as members of the "rubber-gun squad" (NYT 4 Dec. 1976). To emphasize the obvious, power and sex are close companions.

Metonymy and Stratification

Status symbols, more properly those of vertical stratification, are familiar types of salient symbols. In assessing the appearance of a stranger, very often we resort to a shorthand system of fastening upon a few significant clues to social position. Key signs of gentility such as gloves, hats, handkerchiefs, and umbrellas have demarcated the well-bred from the lowly; these key signs have in common an indication of the freedom from menial work or the ability to afford leisure. When the apparel of the upper classes becomes easier to emulate because of the decline of sumptuary legislation, the easy access to money, or the loosening of class lines, then recourse is had to other key signs that cannot be as easily emulated such as well-tended hands, personal experience, or speech (Pear 1935).

Key signs are also associated with pariah statuses such as membership in minorities (the emblems worn by Jews and Gypsies in medieval Europe and the various hats forced upon subject minorities in the Ottoman Empire), abhorred occupations (executioners, blacksmiths, leather tanners, and prostitutes), and the immoral or criminal (heretics, false witnesses, adultresses, and felons). Society comes to terms with these groups by a grudging acknowledgment of their existence while simultaneously voicing its disapproval. These key signs become the sartorial equivalent of a social distance scale by signaling varying degrees of permissible intimacy (Banton 1965, 77; Chevalier 1947; Robin 1964).

When an individual moves socially within a system, salient symbols become key indicators of change in position and the individual's own self-image.[16] Within the New York City Police Department, promotion from the probationary gray to the standard blue uniform is accompanied by the right to wear a gun, make arrests, and perform duties other than those of traffic regulation. The change in status is described as "moving up to the blues".

The salient symbol becomes a marking device for mobility and rites of passage for recruits and the newly promoted or retired. Typically, in military and quasi-military organizations, the complete uniform with the notable exception of the salient symbol is worn during these ceremonies. The conferral of the salient symbol is the ultimate marking of the rites of passage. In graduation from military academies, it is the insignia of officer's status and rank that is pinned on and in the New York City Police Academy it is the badge. Weapons also symbolize transition to full membership; SS recruits received daggers and in some police forces new officers receive bullets for their guns (Neumann 1942, 69; Van Mannen 1973, 417). When such ceremonies do not officially exist, they may be invented as in the instance of student nurses who conduct informal capping ceremonies in the face of official disapproval (Davis, F. 1972, 19).

Finally, retirees have attempted to retain some vestige of their former status by retention of its salient symbols. Legislation was recently sought to permit retired New York City police officers to keep replicas of their shields (NYT 29 Jan. 1976).

The drive for mobility may be overtly expressed by striving for the salient symbols of a higher status. The key to success lies in the ability to identify these symbols, a relatively easy task in a structured situation. The attempts of engineering and deck officers to achieve equality with executive officers in the Imperial German Navy before World War I were defined as striving for the sword and sash of the executives, the emblems which embodied the honor of this superior corps (Herwig 1973, 83, 99, 112–20, 136). Similar efforts at mobility were duplicated in other navies, such as the American and British, where staff corps strove for and eventually obtained the uniforms of the executive branch.[17]

Attacks on salient symbols express opposition to their wearers. In the revolutionary ferment after World War I, mobs literally seized upon the epaulets of Russian and German officers as targets. It was not until the nationalistic fervor of World War II that epaulets were reintroduced into the Russian Army (Mollo, A. 1977, 56–57).

Expulsion from uniformed groups has been accompanied by the destruction or removal of parts of the uniform during degradation ceremonies such as the sword denoting honor, the bars designating rank, or the buttons indicating legitimacy. A modern counterpart consists of depriving police officers who are on probation or under investigation of their weapons.

Minimal Symbols

A concept closely related to salient symbols is that of "minimal symbol" which asks, not for the most important symbol of a sartorial complex, but for the least symbol necessary to suggest a uniform, ethnic group, folk costume, or historical dress. During the Depression, the least part of a Boy Scout uniform that a poor boy in New York City could buy and still feel part of the organization was a hat (Gasnick 1976).[18] The perspective differs from that of the salient symbol in that we are inquiring into the results of a lack of relevant background.

Recent changes in nuns' habits raise a problem of minimal symbolism. If the traditional habit is abandoned, what is the minimal symbol necessary to insure recognition? Perhaps the ultimate in symbols is the purely personal reminder to the wearer, an outlook held by a nun. In the following, we can discern a problem of self-perception as well.[19]

But at the present time the sisters can choose to wear the traditional habit, or a modified habit with a veil, or they can wear contemporary dress with a religious symbol. Now there was some time spent with this religious symbol thing because it could be a veil, some thought we should have a cross or a pin that was typical of our community so there could be at least a little insignia of some kind. But we worked against this for a number of reasons because, again, how many people are going to be conditioned to recognize a little lapel pin and cross? You know you can walk down Broadway on the West Side and people are wearing crosses and all kinds of symbols like this. So we finally, and I guess it was a compromise, [decided upon] contemporary dress *with* a religious sign. Now, some of the sisters wear a cross or religious symbol of some kind with a chain around their neck or a ring, which I wear [sterling silver ring with a cross engraved upon it] or anything really that can be called a religious symbol. And I don't know whether this [ring] is particularly meaningful to anybody right now other than oneself. You wouldn't notice this as symbolizing anything. (Int. 1)

Minimal symbols are particularly pertinent to military organizations in the field where the identification of opponents through dress is vital. Analytically, such symbols clarify characteristics of the uniform. The perfectly uniformed and easily recognizable group is rare and most likely to be found, if at all, in a garrison setting with access to supply, maintenance, and a spit-and-polish discipline. In the field, these conditions are absent and deviations are the rule rather than the exception. The "imperfect" field uniform must then be relied upon as a means of identification. A minimal symbol such as a helmet becomes all-important.

The Geneva Convention of 1949 attempted to solve the problem of identification legally by defining broadly the minimal symbols required to qualify clothing as uniforms. To obtain recognition as lawful belligerents, individuals must have a fixed sign and carry weapons openly. The requirement for a fixed and distinctive sign is fulfilled by a military uniform, as with regular troops, or by an item that cannot be taken off instantly nor assumed at will, as with irregulars, but must be part of the clothing or sewn to it (Greenspan 1959, 59). The Geneva Convention recognizes the need for a minimal symbol but does not, as indeed it cannot, prescribe the details.

Turning to the definition of minimal symbols employed by the uniformed themselves, "uniformity of dress" emerges as a cognitive category. Since supply problems prevented the Frontier Light Horse of the Zulu Wars from maintaining their original corduroy uniforms, recruits provided their own variegated clothing with the significant addition of a uniform red band around their hats

(Morris, Donald 1965, 263). The band was a minimal symbol which met the requirements of uniformity. In these instances, the similarity of dress is far outweighed by dissimilarity but we have learned to look for the former in the military; we have learned to think in terms of uniformity as a minimal symbol. Parodoxically, uniformity is not essential to the uniform.

LEVELS OF ABSTRACTION

Abstractness is an important characteristic of signs which frequently may be read at any of several levels of meaning. Among the Ndembu, the milk tree on one level stands for matriliny, on another for tribal custom, and finally for tribal unity and continuity (Turner, V. 1967, 21).[20]

Through abstract metaphors, generalized positions are created out of specific statuses. Before 1830, Anglican clergy in New England used as street clothes the black broadcloth with black or white stock which indicated "the college graduate of genial disposition and liberal views" (McClellan 1977, 2:427–28). In the pulpit, Protestant clergy in general wore the black academic gown. In colonial New England, lawyers, judges, governors, and clergymen also had dressed alike (ibid., 1:113–15). The distinctive dress therefore denoted any educated individual, almost creating the category of a social estate.

Abstractions explain the derivation of cognitive categories from a social nexus. Metaphors may become abstracted to a degree where they no longer designate specific social referents but connote instead general attributes or qualities such as humility, bravery, or hierarchical relationships. The sartorial metaphor then expresses relationships that can be derived only from a societal level. Clothing derived from gender, class, or the military may suggest not the specific attributes of the original statuses but rather an abstract relationship among them. Thus, if a society conceives of men as "naturally" dominant, then transvestism in dressing may be used to describe, not perversion, but a belief in a world turned topsy-turvy where the woman is now dominant (Davis, N. 1978).[21]

Cowboy clothing, worn as fashion or costume by outsiders, is read on a specific level as romantic nostalgia for an Old West that never was. On a more abstract level, it indicates, not an actual historical scene, but instead the quality of laissez-fare individualism and virility. These virtues have been espoused by popularizers of the Old West from Owen Wister, Frederick Remington, and Theodore Roosevelt down to contemporary long distance truck drivers who seem particularly enamored of the legend of the Old West and its dress (Kett 1977, 220; Savage 1979, 49; Stern 1975). On an even more abstract level, the cowboy is merely one of many exemplars of a general image of machismo. He has been superseded by more recent symbols of ruggedness such as the soldier of fortune who has a rapidly growing periodical of the same name devoted to him (WSJ 15 Sept. 1981).

Borrowing a uniform in metaphor does not necessarily imply that one has any specific uniformed status or group immediately in mind. Instead, one may be expressing a generalized orientation toward the establishment, authority, or law and order. Accordingly, one may admire the uniform but abhor all specific wearers of it; admiration of the military as an institution in Great Britain or the United States was often combined with contempt for the enlisted man. We may admire the uniform but like only a specific uniformed group, the volunteers or militia, for example, rather than the regular army. Or, all uniform wearers—public health nurses, police, soldiers, and fireman—may be combined into a vast, generalized, and detested category of "they", which has occurred among dwellers of inner cities (Ints. 4, 7).[22]

Abstractness helps to account for the variation in meaning of the same set of signs for different audiences. In our own society, on a general level, one can recognize from her dress that a woman is a follower of high fashion and, with greater sophistication in reading dress, one may determine whether she patronizes Gucci or Vuitton, and whether she is of old or new money. Similarly, a layman may identify a uniformed member of a military or public health service organization, but only an insider, or one with equivalent knowledge, can describe the precise branch, years, and quality of service. Yet all rely upon the "same" overt set of signs.[23]

Outsiders may acquire a detailed knowledge of the signs of specific groups to obtain an advantage in interaction. Maitre d's of expensive restaurants learn the latest fashion signs in order to recognize elite customers upon first encounter. These outsiders may then become arbiters of fashion for the elite, or "symbol curators" in Goffman's terminology (1951).

The symbolic connotations also vary. Whereas the blue uniform may signify protection of property to the middle-class suburban white, to the ghetto black it may mean police brutality. Since metaphor involves the use of associated commonplaces, these associations will vary with the group as Max Black implies.

The same symbols may be used by very diverse groups. The American Indian and his dress have been used as a symbol by devout patriots, advocates of environmental preservation, very conversative students and alumni of an Eastern college, and East Europeans, the last to express anti-American sentiments. (NYT 8 Aug. 1977). In the same vein, a liberal politician protested several years ago the expropriation of the American flag as a symbol by the right wing of American politics (WSJ 22 Aug. 1975).

Abstraction helps explain apparent paradoxes and contradictions. General Douglas MacArthur wore flamboyant uniforms during the first part of World War II until he was informed of the modest dress of General Eisenhower, whereupon MacArthur also adopted a simple uniform (Manchester 1978, 360). Short of an unlikely transformation of personality, MacArthur's contradictory styles of uniform can be reconciled by including them under the abstract rubric of "showmanship" which includes both over and understatements.

NOTES

1. A discussion of clothing necessarily isolates sartorial symbols from related symbolic systems, often causing neglect of the interdependency of systems. The ornate

interior of the Schonbrunn Palace, the seat of the Hapsburgs, cannot be understood without visualizing it as the backdrop for equally ornate court dress (Fairservis 1971, 28–29). In turn, the court dress seems gaudy in other settings. Dress and carriage are also mutually dependent. The military uniform presupposes an erect bearing for its best display; the coat of the eighteenth-century gentleman required rounded shoulders and thrust-out stomach to hang gracefully; the dress of the flappers of the 1920's necessitated an aristocratic slouch (Hicks n.d., 14).

As a corollary, we compare clothing, speech, posture, and gait to determine the validity of communication. Guests who say they "must leave immediately" but linger in the foyer, make no move to put on their coats, and face away from the door may well have their statements doubted.

2. This discussion of signs relies greatly on Firth, R. (1973, 54–68).

3. To avoid overemphasis on the importance of signals, the communication of a uniformed organization can often be interpreted only on the level of "pure" symbolism as on ceremonial occasions whose primary function is to reenforce the emotive power of organizational symbols.

4. Accordingly, Banton opposes the indiscriminate use of the concept "status symbols" because "a big motor car is not a symbol of anything else; it is itself a sign [a signal in our terminology] that its owner is rich or enamoured of big cars" (1965, 69).

5. The steward's utilitarian explanation is contradicted by those who stress the importance of occupational dress as an indicator of status as well as a protective device (Cunnington & Lucas 1967, 386–92; Schramm 1960, 8–13).

6. On an intermediate level, the study of interaction consists of the examination of symbols for the operation of institutions such as uniforms for the military, occupational clothing for work, and leisure clothing. Study on a societal level includes the type of symbolic system used by a society, the formation or distortion of symbols in a society, and institutional changes such as the transition from a patrimonial to a bureaucratic army.

7. Metaphor and metonymy are not complete explanations of symbolism because they assume an already existent system of status positions with their associated clothing indicators, and then proceed to explain the further elaboration of symbols. The origins of the symbolic system is beyond the scope of this work. To reemphasize a previous point, metaphor and metonymy are not used in the structural sense to imply any underlying mental constructs but refer instead to meanings derived from interaction.

8. See the section on youth in chapter seven.

9. "Kibbo Kift Kindred" was a British woodcraft group, established shortly after World War I, which adopted "folk clothing" as a rejection of the perceived militarism of the Scouting movement. For British woodcraft movements see: Finlay 1970; Morris, B. 1970; Springhall 1971, 1977; Wilkinson 1969.

10. In an added refinement, a uniformed organization may itself use anachronistic uniforms as a metaphor to suggest historical continuity or evoke patriotic symbols. The United States Army employs a unit of soldiers in Revolutionary War uniforms as an honor guard. Paradoxically, one may become the prisoner of one's own metaphor. The honor guard in anachronistic dress must always wear neatly tailored uniforms. In reality, uniforms of the past were frequently slipshod, poorly dyed, and overly large to permit shrinkage of fabric and accommodate growth of the recruit. Even the total metaphor is selective and we must decide between the reality of the past and our romanticized view of it.

11. Willeford differentiates between dramatic disguises and satirical performances (1969, 54–55). In the former, players become those whose clothes and titles they assume;

in the latter, they rely upon the absence of illusion, the incongruity of being the opposite of what one half appears to be.

12. Field musicians held an essential position in armies before the middle of the nineteenth century in which they served as the counterpart of the contemporary radio operator by conveying messages from the commander to subordinates (McBarron & Elting 1977b). They also decoded the messages of the opposing commander to his own troops, signaled to the adversary for the arrangement of truces, and set the tempo of formalized movement in battle. Field musicians were often honorific retainers of the commander and other officers (Carman 1957, 11, 43–44).

13. The reversal of background and foreground is further evidenced by a retiring Marine sergeant who intended to embark upon a second career as physical trainer. To indicate his military expertise without illegally using a uniform, he wore a Marine-type shirt, slacks, and hat but without emblems, ribbons, or official chevrons (NT 16 July 1984).

14. Correlatively, the salient symbol, if repulsive, diverts attention from the rest of the wearer's symbols (Goffman 1963, esp. 43–62).

15. Indices of saliency in uniformed groups also include the following: U.S. Marine Corps regulations permit an officer to wear a sword inherited from his "father, brother, uncle, grandfather, or great grandfather" (USMC 1976, ch. 4 p. 31); New York City police may use the badges of their retired fathers (NYT 12 July 1982). Unlike other military insignia, heraldic items such as regular-sized decorations or service medals are not authorized for sale (USA 1981, ch. 2 p. 2). At a funeral service in Vietnam, the boots of dead paratroopers were arranged in formation, a use of honorific symbolism (Herr 1978, 23).

16. Anselm Strauss describes the importance of symbols in status passages (1962, 63–85). Salient symbols also focus visual perception so that Ian Paisley, the unionist leader in Ulster, "even knows when we fly the Union Jack upside down. I can't tell the difference" (WSJ 20 Apr. 1983).

17. Salient symbols are an effortless way for an outsider to express affiliation with reference groups. Ballet shoes, the focus of a ballerina's professional concern, are often sold as souvenirs when worn out (NYT 21 Sept. 1975). I was informed by a ballet aficionada that fans wear these shoes around their necks while attending performances or waiting on ticket queues.

18. For members of the British Boys Brigade in a similar situation, the minimal symbols consisted of cap, belt, and haversack (Springhall 1977, 25). The significance of symbols associated with the head is partially explained by the importance of the vertical dimension (Ball 1973, 23–30; Schwartz 1981). Barthes contrasts the "veristic" stage costume which reproduces the past by pedantic attention to detail, overwhelming the spectator in the process, with "good" costumes which only suggest the past. Whereas the former meticulously depicts every button on a uniform, the latter employs the "semantics of the soldier" through "clear forms", "severe yet bold colors", and above all, the "sensation of leather and broadcloth" (1972, 43).

19. The issue of public witnessing versus private affirmation of beliefs will be a recurrent theme in this work.

20. The level of abstraction is but one of the explanations of the ambiguity of symbols; the subtlety of cues, discussed in the next section, constitutes another. The importance of ambiguity rests in its explanation of the simultaneous existence of different audiences for symbols, each reading its own meaning into the same message.

21. See chapter eleven on status or role reversal.

22. Abstraction of signs has led to other instances of misperception and overgeneralization as when pedestrians obeyed the inappropriate orders of experimenters dressed in private guards' uniforms to pick up trash, leave bus stops, and deposit coins in parking meters for others (Bickman 1971). Some drivers refrained from illegal turns in the presence of an authority figure in a blue Air Force ROTC uniform without a badge, gun, or other police insignia (Sigelman & Sigelman 1976). See chapter nine on differential perception.

23. An analogous distinction is that between the symbols of prestige, the evaluation of a status in relationship to others by outsiders, and esteem, the evaluation of performance within a status by peers (Davis, K. 1942).

3

The Social Contexts of Sartorial Signs

Sartorial signs must be read within the social context from which they derive their meaning. The longer hair of a concentration camp inmate at Auschwitz meant that he was under someone's protection and therefore dared to depart from regulations (Friedrich 1981, 43). At other times, long hair has denoted artists, seamen, and political radicals. In the 1960's and 70's it suggested membership in the counterculture. In the 1980's, however, it means adolescent conformity to the standards of parents who had belonged to the counterculture; rebellious adolescents sometimes resort to short hair (NYT 7 Sept. 1980).[1]

The relativity of signs to their context will be established on the societal, organizational, and interpersonal levels.

THE SOCIETAL CONTEXT

Contextual Changes in Awareness

In interacting with others, we take for granted our ability to anticipate their reaction to our clothing. The assumption may be questioned when the context of interaction, especially if it is societal, changes. We may then become more cognizant of the impression we want to impart to others, be they "natives", enemies, or friends.

Washington made the facings of a Continental regiment's uniform identical to make the "best and most military impression on the French" allies (McBarron & Katcher 1974). Some British regiments in the Sudan campaign of 1895 wore scarlet coats to "render them more formidable in the eyes of the Dervishes"

(Barthorp 1983, 154). More recently, General Ridgway, in planning the capture of the Berlin airfield in World War II, included dress as well as field uniforms in the equipment of the attacking paratroopers to influence the "reaction of the German" by the "personal appearance of the individual soldiers" (Gavin 1978, 300).

Conversely, we may infer others' opinions of us by the way they dress in our presence, for example, the personnel officer's reading of the attire of a job applicant. Reflecting a frequently encountered point of view, the British felt that their defeat by the Boers was particularly disgraceful because of the latter's lack of uniforms (Farwell 1976, 380).

Obviously, in the instances cited above, the reaction by others to our use of symbols is imputed. The accuracy of the process depends upon the ability to empathize with others. As we saw, the attempts to determine the pro-Western sympathies of Soviet citizens through their wearing of American jeans proved defective. In a drastically altered context, empathy may be at least partially replaced by the projection of ethnocentric imagery as in the preceding instances. The awareness of projection with contextual change and its conscious manipulation may become ideology, or the use of symbols for purposes of persuasion or propaganda.

The Explicitness of Sartorial Signs

The explicitness of the links between sartorial signs and position, or the clarity of information given us by dress, varies with the society and institution. At one time or another, class distinctions have been conveyed by symbolic differences stemming from sumptuary legislation, clothing styles, and the use of hand-me-downs (the sartorial equivalent of the "trickle down effect" in housing). Occupational and religious categories have been indicated by subcultural differences in dress, legislation enforcing stigmata upon religious minorities and pariah occupations, or, as in medieval Europe, compelling workers to carry the implements of their trade as labels.

Explicitness becomes attenuated due to rapid changes in stratification, technology, and the dominance of institutions. Static societies are relatively more explicit in the relationship between sartorical symbols and societal structure. Generally, our society is not explicit in the information conveyed sartorially about class, religion, and, most recently, gender.

Some social areas are left vague, presumably because of the relative lack of importance attached to their internal differentiation as in contemporary religion. In our society, the links between class and dress have not been obliterated but instead obscured by the development of mass production and other factors, which have eliminated many of the qualitative differences among classes (Kidwell & Christman 1974). In turn, experts in symbols have arisen, for example, maitre d's who have learned to read subtle symbols of status such as designer clothing, and metasymbols such as designer's initials.

Our society is not devoid of explicit symbolic distinctions; they have, however, shifted to those embodied by bureaucratic organizations in the guise of uniforms. Other groups such as adolescents, hippies, surfers, and musicians have created their own symbols which differentiate insiders from outsiders. The inability of these groups to monopolize their symbols by law or tradition results in these symbols becoming public fads which lose their discriminatory power (Irwin 1977, 160–61; Sebald 1977, 278). The rapid diffusion and distribution of sartorial symbols leads to a lack of symbolic explicitness.

Organizational Dominance—The Organization as Metaphor

Certain types of organizational structure prevail in a society because of their efficiency, congruence with social values, or tradition. In modern society, bureaucracy has become prevalent in contrast to the dominance of patrimonial, feudal, and other types of authority in past centuries.

Organizations may also prevail because of their popularity, often resulting in the borrowing of their symbols rather than their structural features. Part of the context of symbols consists of the particular group that is widely selected as a metaphor, thereby imparting to a society a distinctive militaristic, scientific, or religious tinge.

Uniforms were adopted by the Salvation Army, not because it was particularly militaristic or fond of the military, but because it cashed in on the prevalent store of good will toward the army and its symbolism. British women invested heavily, both emotionally and propagandistically, in uniforms for various auxiliary and military forces during World War I to demonstrate their contributions to the community (Ewing 1975, 84–88, 94–97). Every uniform on a female worker or military auxiliary was a "blow for our side", an indication that women could serve outside the home. Uniforms were worn intensively even off the job. After the general acceptance of the role of women outside the home, about the time of World War II, the need for uniforms as a form of advertisement to the community was no longer essential. Postwar uniforms were restricted to the job and worn only where they were of some utility (ibid., 130–145).

Implicit in this discussion is the existence of a distinctive set of values for each type of organization. These values are either embodied in uniforms or assumed to rub off on the wearer. The extent to which they do so is related to the explicitness of the sartorial sign as an expression of value, function, or affiliation.

The Context of Safety

Informing others of our beliefs and affiliations is part of the everyday business of living. Under some circumstances, however, communication can be risky. As Simmel has pointed out, the occasions for complete frankness are extremely rare and potentially devastating to the ego, involving the peeling away of external protective layers (1950, 326–29; also Plant 1950, 256–59). As a practical solution to the lack of candor, we learn to expect minor departures from total truth and to test others' sartorial assertions of their social position (Stone, G. 1962, 101–4).

Under socially defined circumstances of physical danger, sartorial dissimulation of one's social position becomes appropriate. Travel, for example, has long been considered hazardous even before the modern era. Unobtrusive dress which did not indicate one's wealth was frequently used by travellers in classical and medieval times as protection against robbers (Braun-Ronsdor 1962, 12–17). The advent of the railroad resulted in the provision of a safe environment in which travellers were able to dress according to their true status and engage in conspicuous consumption.

The presence of danger creates two types of contexts: a hazardous environment in which one does not wear symbols of high economic status, membership in minority or pariah groups, and affiliation with disliked military or governmental groups; and a safe environment in which such symbols may be appropriately worn.[2] The pervasiveness of fear of the external world is revealed in a recent study which found that 60% of all Americans "dressed plainly to avoid drawing attention" when going out (Figgie 1980, 83). The accuracy of this perception is not relevant; what matters is the existence of the perception and its role in shaping the use of sartorial symbols. Not only do audiences vary in their interpretation of symbols but also in their degree of friendliness or hostility toward them.

The existence of these two contexts complicates symbolic systems. Many types of communication are possible only within a context of assured safety. One can let one's hair down only to familiar individuals within a context of privacy and intimacy. A dual set of sartorial symbols comes into play: those indicating one's "true" or desired status and attributes revealed only to friends; and the minimizing symbols used in the outer world to deprecate one's position and attributes.[3]

Conspicuous consumption and sexual display are admissible forms of symbolic interaction only when they do not endanger one's safety. Shabbiness or nondescript dress become the badge not only of urban poverty but of the wise traveller. City dwellers "dress down" to avoid unwanted attention. A man returning from a black-tie party stuffs his tie into his pocket on a dark street to look like a waiter; a woman en route to a party by subway wears a wrinkled raincoat, jeans, and sneakers, carrying in a shopping bag clothes into which she will change; jewelry is removed or concealed (NYT 3 Nov. 1980).

"They" need not be criminals but members of an oppressive majority or of officialdom. To illustrate the relativity of contexts, some contemporary Italians see New York City as a haven where they may drop the minimizing symbols employed in their homeland against the police as well as criminals.

One doesn't wear furs in Rome, they say, at least not showy furs. To do so is to invite robbery, kidnapping or the gaze of the policia tributaria.

"Those are the fiscal police who check to see who's not paying taxes. . . . The rumor is they dress up in tuxedoes at La Scala, like skiers at San Moritz and like gamblers at Monte Carlo." . . .

But here in New York . . . it is not so dangerous to walk the streets in fur. (NYT 23 Feb. 1977; also NYT 8 July 1977)

The functions of symbols vary. Besides concealment, they may also be used by "conspirators" for mutual recognition within a hostile environment. Secret service agents wear lapel pins, subtle cues to identify each other in a crowd. Homosexuals moving within a straight community have also used such cues (Humphreys 1972, 67; Lurie 1981, 258–60). As soon as outsiders recognize these symbols, they must be changed. The process is similar to the rapid obsolescence of fashion to avoid undesired emulation by others.

Even the visibility of uniforms and quasi uniforms, which is a great advantage within an organization, becomes hazardous in a hostile outer environment. The white medical dress of physicians which facilitates interaction within the hospital makes them affluent targets for muggers off the premises.

The killing of an off-duty physician reveals contextual changes in the reading of the uniform. Within the hospital, "there is a serene little garden at the center, where people eat lunch. Almost everyone wears the white coat and the identification tag that says, in effect, 'I am one of you'" (NYT 7 Nov. 1981). The attitudes toward the uniform manifested by a grateful patient contrast sharply with those of outsiders. According to the patient,

"I just can't understand it. I can't understand how anyone would go killing doctors, who only want to help people. You know it's a doctor you're killing, you can tell by the uniform." . . .

But down the street . . . two young men said people had to be realistic about such things. "It was wrong, that they killed the guy", one said, "but you know, doctors have money". (ibid.)

THE ORGANIZATIONAL CONTEXT[4]

The uniform is possible only after an organization has become permanently differentiated from other groups. Organizations also shape sartorial communication by their varying need for identification, the problem of visibility, and the changing requirements of organizational roles.

Organizational Differentiation—A Prerequisite for Uniforms

An organization can communicate sartorially only if it is a separate entity. Before an army differentiates itself from other groups by clothing, the environing society must be in a stage where armies are distinct organizations, a state of affairs that is not universal. In many societies, those who engage in warfare use special clothing or ornaments to achieve distance from other pursuits, much as an individual in our society demarcates work from leisure by the appropriate clothing changes. Not all societies, however, describe warriors as a separate and permanent group, the reading of the uniform when worn by the military. These strictures apply to other uniformed bodies such as police and nurses.

Where organizational differentiation has not occurred, group dress consists of livery, standardized clothing, or occupational clothing, but not a uniform. Differentiation occurred surprisingly late in the history of many uniformed organizations. Using the United States as an example, a naval force has existed since the Revolution.[5] Though the organization itself was permanent, the personnel was recruited, as in all navies, on the ad hoc basis of the ship's voyage. Recruiting was not centralized until the twentieth century but was carried on by the individual ship as the need arose. Most importantly of all, instead of training its own personnel, the navy relied upon the pool of skilled seamen in the major ports which served as a reservoir for both merchant and naval ships. The interchangeability of personnel was made possible by the similarity of skills for both services.

The American merchant and naval services did not separate in terms of personnel until the demand for naval seamen exceeded the pool of trained men due to the growth of the fleet in the late nineteenth century. The need for specialists created by technological change, especially those unique to the naval service, required expensive in-house training. Amortization of the cost of training led to an attempt to create a permanent enlisted force.

An important extension of symbols, separate and distinctive uniforms, occurs only after the establishment of an organization as a separate body. When merchant and naval seamen were undifferentiated, both used standardized dress—occupational clothing that follows a pattern set by informal pressures and the exigencies of work rather than explicit regulations. The modern naval uniform for enlisted men was not achieved until the middle of the nineteenth century (Lewis, M. 1957, 230–32; Lloyd 1970, 274–79).

The term "redcoat" could be used as a laudatory label or epithet, depending upon one's perspective, for the British soldier only after armies had evolved into national institutions in the eighteenth century (Corvisier 1979, 25).[6] Only then did uniforms become symbols of national identity. Prior to that, any European army included regiments of foreigners, often with their own identifying signs. As a result, there was no standardized uniform to symbolize the nation.

The uniform adopted by the London police in 1829 was patterned after civilian dress to differentiate the evolving police organization from the military which had previously performed police duties (Cunnington & Lucas 1967, 254–55).

On the other hand, the deliberate blurring of the distinction between the military and civilian groups, achieved in part by the shedding of distinctive uniforms and the use of ordinary civilian dress, is now used as a stratagem of war by guerrillas and special military forces.[7] The intentional elimination of organizational boundaries is possible only after those boundaries have been established in the first place.

The Sartorial Requirements of Organizations

Once an organization has been differentiated from other groups and becomes a distinct entity, then the reading of signs is related to the requirements of the organization, its statuses, and roles. The importance of varying organizational requirements can be seen in the different use of color in military and naval dress for unit identification and communication. Military clothing of the eighteenth and nineteenth centuries was colorful, not only to satisfy esthetic or ludic impulses, but also for visibility on smoke obscured battlefields (Martin 1963, 37, 60). When opposing sides used the same colors, errors occurred (ibid., 90). Two American Revolutionary units wore blue and red uniforms similar to those of the Germans and mistook each other for the enemy with resultant casualties (Katcher & Martin 1974). Color was particularly important for the identification of officers by couriers from commanders (Barnes 1951, 105). Drab and camouflaged uniforms arose when modern communication made visual identification less necessary, and improved observation and more accurate fire made color dangerous (Carman 1957, 153).

Early naval dress, on the other hand, did not require visibility to identify subordinates or differentiate opponents. Sailors, who were much more akin to laborers, wore occupational dress which was not as colorful as that of the military. Naval officers, whose tasks were not onerous in the days of sail, wore dress which was more ornate than that of enlisted men, but never as colorful as that of their land-based counterparts. Changes in naval technology and the officer's role led to the adoption of more practical dress by officers (Jarrett 1960, 124; USN 1981, app.2 pp. 11–13).

The reading of signs also depends upon the roles intrinsic to the group. In early warfare, the leader was likely to be a champion who led his followers by personal example. Military dress did not consist of a uniform in the modern sense but rather of occupational clothing, dress suited for the exigencies of warfare. Distinctive insignia marked the individual leader-hero rather than a group or unit and reached its acme in heraldry. The concomitant value attached to the role was personal courage.

In postmedieval linear warfare, leaders become officers who managed and led men from the front ranks. Their dress was a uniform which distinguished them as members of a unit and, within that unit, as an elite group of leaders rather than individual champions. The concomitant virtue was not individual prowess in battle but gallant leadership. Officers dressed conspicuously to inspire their men; a British general rode before his troops in a white coat to draw enemy fire away from them during the Sikh war of 1845 (Harries-Jenkins 1977, 15). The weapons of officers were less suitable for combat than those of their men and were often outmoded since they were used more as symbols than as tools. Whereas Roland or Arthur might carry a "super-sword" as befitted a paladin, an officer wore a sword or pistol rather than a rifle; his function was to direct others in inflicting violence. An officer did not kill an enemy at Waterloo but instead instructed a private to do so (Keegan 1977, 188).

More recently, the officer became a manager who usually operates from the rear. The uniform, with exceptions of course, is meant to minimize the difference in appearance between officers and enlisted men. While a general ought to spend time at the front, it should be to familiarize himself with the situation but not to draw enemy attention by conspicuous dress (Gavin 1978, 280–81). MacArthur's style of leadership was unwelcome to some subordinates who felt that the relevant role behavior was managerial efficiency rather than personal, personal, conspicuous bravery (Manchester 1978, 394–95, 480–81, 506–7).

Identical overt behavior changes meaning with the organizational context. The conspicuously dressed military leader in combat may be variously defined in different contexts as an adherent of the conventional norms of his period for which no special recognition is required, as a gallant officer deserving appropriate rewards, or as an egomaniac endangering his troops. The dress is similar in all instances, but serves different purposes, communicates different messages, and is read differently, all depending upon the institutional context.[8]

The organization also determines the range of others with whom the uniform wearer interacts in his role—his role set. As we shall see, a feature of the role set of a uniform wearer is its inclusion of the public as external enforcers of the organizational norms upon wearers, as an audience for uniformed group ceremonies, and as recipients and purveyors of metaphors and categories of perception.

Paradoxically, groups that require uniforms often include in their members' role set adversaries with whom they must interact. In controversial situations where adversaries meet with some frequency, techniques often evolve to mitigate the conflict. Lincoln Steffens described the efforts for the control of crime in his day as consisting, not of its elimination, but rather of its containment within acceptable limits, necessitating some modus vivendi between police and professional criminals. The same accommodation has been noted in professional sports and court trials. Similarly in warfare, in the absence of ideology to the contrary, techniques often arise to mitigate the rigors of war.

At various times, these mitigations have become institutionalized into a system of signs, partly through clothing. In the modern era, one's obligation to the opponent is to signal clearly the status of a lawful belligerent in order to preserve the state's monopolization of force and to ease the horrors of war. These obligations are spelled out most clearly in the Hague Regulations in conjunction with the Fourth Geneva Convention of 1949 for the recognition of irregular forces, and of course regular forces, as lawful belligerents. Basically, there is an obligation to inform the enemy, through fixed signs, of one's position as a legitimate opponent (Greenspan 1959, 58–60). Not only does the uniform serve as a means of internal communication, it also informs the opposing army that one is a legitimate enemy entitled to the protection of international law.

The uniform also honors the foe. The French were upset by the sloppiness of British infantry, in contrast to the Russian and Prussian troops, during the victory parade on the Champs Elysee after the defeat of Napoleon I. They felt it a disgrace to have been beaten by so shabby a foe (Brett-James 1972, 86). General

Gavin relates the evident care in grooming taken by a surrendering, threadbare German general who did not recognize Gavin's rank because of the latter's casual appearance (1978, 318–19).[9]

THE INTERPERSONAL LEVEL

Statuses and Power

Within any given social context, we read clothing, often unknowingly, in terms of social statuses and relationships. We would not think of complimenting the neatly dressed infant upon its appearance but instead reserve our congratulations for the parents. We postulate an obvious link between the child's dress and parental influence. These inferred relationships derive from our taken-for-granted knowledge of the social context. Describing some more complex relationships implicit in clothing will make our underlying assumptions about dress more explicit.

A basic relationship read into clothing is that of power, or "who controls whom" in the realm of clothing. The powerful, or controllers, include the parent of the child, the master of the servant, or the husband of the well-dressed traditional wife. The ponce or pimp of the British prostitute provides stability for her and "is also a gauge of her prestige. If she keeps him well in handmade shoes and black silk shirts, then her credit goes up among whores, and his among ponces. 'Mine's a good earner. Just look at this shirt' " (Young, W. 1970, 80).

The case of the ponce reverses the more common relationship between the conspicuous consumer and the producer of wealth. The ponce is a powerful consumer who controls the producer; in other instances the consumer lacks power while the patron both possesses power and supplies wealth.

Veblen's description of vicarious consumption in which an individual uses or wastes goods and services as the surrogate of another implies just such a relationship of power (Veblen 1934, 68–101). Taking domestics as an example, he asks us to read the clothing of the liveried servant as the expression of a relationship of power, of an inferior whose attire reflects favorably upon a superior. Without knowledge of this relationship, livery would lose its purpose. Therefore, the dress of servants is deliberately made anachronistic to clarify their position vis-a-vis their masters. As powdered wigs, knee breeches, and tricorne hats fell out of fashion with the elite, they then became the attire of domestics so that today's servants dressed in the height of yesterday's fashion (Cunnington & Lucas 1967, 178–80). The trend should not be construed as a cheese-paring, hand-me-down attitude, although that may well have occurred at times, but rather as a method of symbolizing the social inferiority of the wearer and hence the vicarious consumption of the servant. To avert the "very real hazard of mistaking the guest for the waiter", who wore ornate attire, "mistakes" were introduced into nineteenth-century servants' dress such as "the butler's striped trousers worn with an evening tail-coat" (Laver 1951, 128).

Power includes compelling wearers to dress in clothing not of their own selection and, significantly, to emit inaccurate messages. Employees have at times been obliged to adopt an occupational uniform which presented a desired image of the organization. In some instances, the message is that of sexual attractiveness or even availability, primarily of women, which was very often not the meaning desired by the wearer. The image may be irrelevant to the purpose of an organization as in the mandated use of "short-shorts" and short skirts in a supermarket (NYT 4 Aug. 1983). The discrepancy in communication, defined as sexual harassment, has recently caused much litigation.

Uncomfortable uniforms which severely constrain body movements are a constant reminder to their wearers of their lack of power. A British soldier of 1795 describes the agonies of dressing his queue ("pigtail") around a wooden plug which served as an armature.

When I was dressed for parade, I could scarcely get my eyelids to perform their office; the skin of my eyes and face was drawn so tight by the plug that was stuck in the back of my head, that I could not possibly shut my eyes; and to this, an enormous high stock was poked under my chin; so that, altogether, I felt as stiff as if I had swallowed a ramrod, or a sergeant's halberd. (Shipp 1894, 37)

Power and lack of power are relative terms, however, in that the powerless have some control over the powerful. An indication of low morale in the military is the deviation from uniform and other norms by enlisted men (Shibutani 1978, 7, 365). Power is a reciprocal relationship, implying responsibility on the part of both the more and less powerful.

In other contexts, the relationships of power are less apparent and, indeed, the definition of power must be changed to that of accountability or control of a situation. Who is responsible for the impression my dress creates on you, is it I the wearer, or you the viewer? Is the daringly dressed woman accountable for the thoughts she arouses in others or is it the others who harbor such thoughts? In such instances the imputation of accountability is socially patterned. In some puritanical contexts, the responsibility rests upon the shoulders of those who lead others astray by their dress and are therefore held accountable. Such was the judgment of St. Paul who ordered women to cover their hair in church, and of the advocates of the Islamic chador, which is rooted in the principle that the sight of women inflames men who are not responsible for their subsequent behavior. In a Jesus commune, a male accused a woman, modestly dressed by the standards of the outside reporter, of "stumbling" him, that is, of arousing lascivious thoughts by her dress (Harder 1972, 45). A judge recently absolved an adolescent of rape because he was inflamed by the sexuality purveyed by the media (NYT 26 Aug. 1977). Victimology offers similar examples of projection by attaching blame to rape victims who are accused of provoking attack by suggestive appearances. Though properly labeled rationalizations, they are derived, after all, from the prevalent patterns of accountability.

The literature on victims gives the reader the impression that, besides rationalization or projection by the rapist, the situation may also represent a misreading of symbols. The victim's attire often expresses the casualness of her reference group which is interpreted by her assailant as an invitation.

As noted above, a society often standardizes the attribution for sexual arousal. The chador obviously places the responsibility upon the female. An opposing view would hold that beauty, and undoubtedly lust, are in the eye and perhaps the heart of the beholder, which would place responsibility for impressions created by dress upon the beholder rather than the wearer.

Signs and the Situation

We may ask, "For whom does one dress, oneself or the viewer?" After one's credentials have been established in the eyes of others, the continued use of symbols may be questioned. If the relative statuses of masters and servants, officers and enlisted men have been defined, then livery, formal dress, bars, or stripes seem unnecessary.

Very often indicators are not worn in these circumstances. For a long period, female English domestics did not wear livery because they were either of high status or worked back stage unobserved by outsiders. Servants of both sexes at times wore clothing that could not be distinguished from their employers' (Cunnington & Lucas 1967, 156, 172–73, 195; Hecht 1950, 119–21, 209–11). In the Pacific campaigns of World War II, the practice arose of not wearing insignia of rank, which created problems when the custom spread to the European theatre and made it difficult to reorganize battered units (Gavin 1978, 116). If indicators are used solely as signals, signs that inform, then they are unnecessary in a group whose members know each other. They are still essential within large organizations, vis-a-vis outsiders as in a hospital, or for police on city streets.

Sartorial signs continue to be used even after credentials have been established because of their function as symbols. They remind others and oneself of the norms and attitudes relevant to a situation. Male domestics in England wore livery because they were more likely to be seen by others in the front regions of the house where the norms of conspicuous consumption and formality held sway (Ewing 1975, 56). Similarly, an amateur choir wore tuxedoes when appearing before a blind audience (WSJ 9 Dec. 1976). Formal dress enhanced the dignity of the occasion in the minds of the singers. The first Zionist Congress demonstrated the importance of formality very clearly.

That is indeed the point of armies, discipline, uniforms. Men who feel lost and defenceless in their original condition are transformed into brave and disciplined fighters when they are given a brand new cause to fight for. . . . Theodor Herzl knew what he was about when he compelled his bewildered followers at the first Zionist Congress to wear the most formal possible dress in order to rise to the dignity and historical grandeur of the occasion—an occasion which was to lead to their spiritual and material metamorphosis from a collection of disorganised individuals into a national movement. (Berlin 1982, 259–60)

In some circumstances, one may act as if one is "above" the requirements of the situation and need not conform. Hence the phenomenon of the eccentric British aristocrats who take liberties in dress, furniture, and other symbols unthinkable for the middle class (Perrott 1968, 236–39, 257–69).

Signs are the property of the relationship or situation, not of any given individual. One dresses for the requirements of an event.

Expressive Statuses

In examining the clothing of groups, especially uniformed organizations, one is struck by the ornate dress of some members—military aides and musicians, honor guards, and airline stewardesses in hot pants—which singles them out from the rest of the group. While all statuses symbolize their groups, especially those of uniformed organizations, some are more symbolic than others. These are designated as representatives or expressive statuses who indicate the power, wealth, or values of their group through dress. The "super visible" clothing of expressive statuses often functions primarily as symbols intended to project a desired image of the group, rather than as signaling devices in the practical operation of the organization. The description of the uniformed status as purely a control device does not suffice to explain fully these expressive statuses. We are thus forced to visualize an organization's symbolic structure comprising statuses and subgroups in their capacity as curators or promulgators of symbols. We must distinguish the underlying social operative structure from these expressive statuses presented by the symbolic representatives of the group. This approach is suggested by Veblen whose concept of vicarious consumption becomes meaningful only if we can infer the relationship between the peacock and the patron in the background.

Veblen describes expressive statuses, such as wives, liveried retainers, and domestics as those upholding the values of status positions (1934, 78–83). Applying his outlook to uniformed organizations, their expressive statuses maintain values common to the organization, such as honor or group pride, and are centered in the important group insignia. These positions derive their importance not from personal enhancement but rather their relationship to these symbols which in turn embody group values.

Expressive statuses and their associated symbols may also operate as repositories for values cherished by external groups such as the nation. They safeguard the unifying national symbols embodied in military cemeteries, historical documents, battle flags, and saintly relics.[10]

Understanding expressive statuses requires an examination of their sources and functions for the group. Not only are statuses derived from the internal dynamics of a group but they also emerge from external sources. Since the internal statuses of an organization may not suffice to express all of its appropriate characteristics, the group may therefore borrow external statuses to describe its desired images in toto or in part. It may also be charged with expressing the values of a larger group. By metaphor and metonymy, the group extends its vocabulary to project these images.

As has been often pointed out, the external status may take the form of an animal whose attributes are borrowed by the group as in bearskins, eagle feathers, or the contemporary animal mascot. Even the attributes of an opponent may be assumed; the British Grenadier Guards adopted the bearskins of their French counterparts after Waterloo. Fictional statuses which do not conform to the contemporary reality of the institution are derived from the organization's past as in the use of United States Army color guards and bands in Revolutionary uniforms for ceremonial occasions.

External statuses, such as those of women and the young, may be temporarily assimilated as a metaphoric device to borrow the attributes which are lacking in the organization's indigenous vocabulary. Women have, for a long time, been widely used by military and civilian organizations as externally derived expressive statuses for ship's launchings, the making and presentation of flags, and homecoming queens for colleges and service academies. Their presence added the connotation of innocence and purity to the newly improvised "traditional" ceremonies for the creation of the Cambodian national flag in 1970 (Firth, R. 1973, 347–48). This function may well be derived from the widespread role of women as the custodian and promulgator of morality (Lane, Robert 1959, 212– 13). In the past century, women were part of a romantic complex surrounding the military (Cunliffe 1973, 403–4). The integration of women into contemporary uniformed services has led to a corresponding use of them as part of the array of honorifics. Accordingly, one of the companies of the cortege for the state funeral of an American president consists of servicewomen (Mossman & Stark 1971, 391–99).

Symbol bearers are at times obliged to wear the awkward costumes of the past. The burden is often thrust upon the young to symbolize generations, national myths, or arcadian legends because of the characteristics of purity and idealism frequently associated with them.

Uniformed institutions of learning often perform their socializing mission by incorporating symbols of the past into their structure and surrounding the young with them. Service academies in the United States and elsewhere function as repositories of old battle flags, dead heroes, and military memorabilia (Ellis & Moore 1974, 6–7, 208). Archaic uniforms for cadets accentuate this association.

Similarly, the grizzled veteran—the ancient patriarch in the "Spirit of '76"— or the venerable retainer may be used in expressive contexts that reverse the age/time order. At the other extreme, the uniformed pensioner becomes the custodian of symbols. Great Britain maintains retirement homes for veteran servicemen who are given special uniforms, subjected to military discipline, and who participate in ceremonial events and parades.

Symbolic statuses perform many functions for the groups they represent and have many institutional locations. The "external receptionist" or "symbolic gatekeeper", a status drawn from within the group, portrays the desired group image to the public entering the front region (Goffman 1959, 22–30). The array of lavishly uniformed doormen, domestics, receptionists, and airline stewardesses constitutes the organizational representatives with whom the public initially interacts. The exaggeration in dress of these symbolic gatekeepers provides additional information beyond the statement that they are legitimate members of a group. It also informs us that they are vicarious displayers of attributes which vary with the context and historical period.

English livery reflects a transition from the function of servants as indicators of power to that of the instruments of vicarious consumption. In the eighteenth century, when servants still denoted the master's power, neither the upper ranks of male domestics such as butlers or stewards, nor female servants of any rank wore livery (Cunnington & Lucas 1967, 194–95; Hecht 1950, 66–67, 119–21). Lower ranking males such as footmen were liveried not only to display the master's wealth, but also his power—a function better filled by a male. Liveried servants were a symbolic relic of the feudal, often armed, retainer who was a pawn in power struggles. Servants of higher rank, on the other hand, were removed from the area of display, the front region, and therefore did not have to wear livery. Female domestics had not been retainers and did not indicate power.

By the nineteenth century, old English families had to abandon all vestiges of the definition of the servant as retainer. Instead of dressing their servants in livery of traditional family colors which had been customary for retainers, they were forced to change to vivid colors, selected primarily for display, in order to keep up with parvenus who attired their servants entirely for ostentation (Hecht 1950, 120–22).

These symbolic gatekeepers were vital for the class position of the well-to-do Victorian English household. By this time, female domestics could be used for this function. "In [nineteenth-century] women's magazines, for example, there is constant reference to the fact that the first appearance of the footman or parlourmaid at the door reflected the family's rank and quality. . . . Such 'front-stage' servants were deliberately chosen for height, good looks and clear speaking voice" (Davidoff 1973, 88).

A patrimonial leader very often has a band of personal followers subject to his complete discretion, apart from the broader group of personnel to whom he has some accountability. This band included musicians in military organizations, and the captain's gig (small boat) crew in the days of sail who served for the personal glorification of the leader. These statuses were of honorific liveried retainers, a function they filled long after it lapsed among their civilian confreres.

Another important function, filled largely by internal statuses, is that of reenforcing the symbols vital to the group's self-conception. The group witnesses not only for outsiders but also for itself. This function first comes into play with the arrival of the recruit who is subjected to the socialization of an "internal receptionist". The adjutant at Sandhurst Military College conveyed at least the external patterns of an officer's role to the cadets after their arrival.

The lordly Adjutant, beautiful beyond belief with his dark blue hat, red face, glassy boots, and golden spurs, strode slowly around our scurrying squads, communing in silent scorn with some Coldstream deity who hovered a hundred feet up in the air in front of him. Before his feet steps became level ramps, doors opened, potholes were filled, walls vanished. He never tripped or stumbled and he never looked down, round, or about. (Masters 1968, 41)

The secret of the superhuman adjutant was later made manifest to the author when he too assumed the post in the course of time. It consisted of preliminary observation of the scene by the adjutant and the discreet promptings of his aide (ibid., 283–84).

Since an essential component of a group's image is derived from its history, symbols of the past are often incorporated into the dress of internal receptionists as in the revival of the archaic campaign hat for the sole use of the drill instructor of recruits in the United States Army and Marine Corps (USA 1981, ch.11 p.4; USMC 1976, ch.4 p.11). The expressive statuses of color guards and standard bearers also reenforce symbols for the group.

Some statuses are concerned primarily with the custody or maintenance of an organization's key symbols, a function often overlapping that of receptionist. In nonmilitary organizations, the large public or private bureaucracy, the key symbol may center around corporate headquarters, particularly the offices of the chief executives. These shrines may be accentuated not only by lavish materials but also by important trophies and guarded by custodians such as receptionists and secretaries. Although a great deal may be explicable as status symbol, much of the grandeur of the office can be better explained as the custody of key group symbols.

In military organizations, the key symbol may become sacred and, therefore, to be protected against profanation. The operation of the expressive status can be understood better by the examination of two constellations of symbols widely used by the military, the flag and the cemetery. Expressive statuses do not occur at random but are connected to essential clusters of symbols.

Through metonymy, a military unit's self-image, conceptualized as its honor, centers on key symbols such as flags. Accordingly, the loss of flags in battle was disgraceful. These insignia were treated as veterans of many campaigns, decorated with streamers or other emblems to commemorate past victories, and became the repository of the unit's honor (Wise 1978, 26–27).

Uniform wearers acted as custodians and protectors of these symbols. The bearers of the flag, or the equivalent standard such as the Napoleonic eagle, were specially chosen men of rank who were deemed worthy to defend the sacred emblem (Grose 1812, 51, 135–36; Rogers 1977, 67–68). Flags were surrounded with religious ceremonies from their original consecration to their retirement in treasuries of symbols such as churches (Wise 1978, 26).

Another major complex of symbols centers around military cemeteries, which are more than graveyards and function instead as treasuries of past symbols (Barber 1949; Mosse 1979). Military cemeteries, especially the tombs of unknown soldiers, are similarly honored by appropriately uniformed elite guards. In a related complex of symbols, the military funeral, the calculus governing the size of the escorting cortege is based, not upon the force required to protect the remains against marauders, but by the quantitatively measured honor meted out to the deceased. In 1965, the cortege for official American funerals varied from the three bands, sixteen companies of enlisted men, and one company of enlisted women for the state funeral of a President to the solitary band and single platoon for officers below the rank of colonel or navy captain (Mossman & Stark 1971, 391–99).

The association of uniformed statuses with the flag and cemetery complexes, especially the latter, may be explained as the dramaturgy of ritual. These symbols are not presented in a cognitive fashion but as part of a choreographed pattern in which the expressive statuses play the essential role. The national flag, the dead soldier, the religious symbol are not merely presented to the public, but are guarded by bearers of expressive statuses and honored by being so flanked, preceded, and followed. These symbols are preceded in a procession by expressive statuses and accompanied by lesser symbols such as music, and swords, or unloaded rifles as protection.

NOTES

1. Social context is a key to understanding the degree of conformity to norms. During the American Civil War, Confederate naval officers who were stationed abroad were able to obtain regulation uniforms and maintain them properly (Wells 1971, 85). Upon return home, however, they would give some of their uniforms away or change to old faded ones, to conform to the standards of fellow officers who suffered from the blockade.

Deviance is also contextual. A young Hassidic husband forbade his wife on grounds of modesty to exchange her short skirt for the longer length then coming into fashion because the lowering of the hemline indicated an undue concern with the dictates of contemporary fashion (Mayer).

2. The original Scottish plaid was not a heraldic device which identified family or clan. "Remembering the continuous clan feuds and the consequent state of more or less perpetual hostilities, a recognizable clan plaid would have been a positive danger to the wearer when outside his own territory" (Lawson 1941, 2:61). Instead, a Scotsman had a wide selection of patterns (setts) from which to choose (Dunbar 1964, 14–21).

3. The antinomy of external-unfriendly and interior-friendly contexts has been noted in the analysis of regions by Goffman (1959), the discussion of the public sphere by Sennett (1978), and the attitudes toward strangers by Lofland (1973).

4. This section will focus primarily upon formal organizations. See chapter ten on leisure for an examination of communication outside of formal organizations.

5. The discussion of the United States Navy in this and succeeding paragraphs is based upon Harrod (1978, 4–18, 35–39).

6. As in many symbolic systems, the red coat became a symbol partly as a result of

oversimplification which in this instance ignored the international use of blue coats for the artillery and green for riflemen and rangers.

7. See chapter nine on guerrillas.

8. The explanation of color in uniforms was not couched in terms of flamboyance, an ethnocentric and pejorative outlook, but from the perspective of the functional requirements of roles within the historical context of an institution. Epithets often designate inappropriate role behavior or attempts to revive obsolete role definitions.

9. Honoring opponents pertains to an older definition of the officer's role as a knight who was a free professional independent of membership in an organization. In strong contrast, the modern officer has a position only as a member of a bureaucratic profession. Accordingly, knights were bound by a common code which transcended loyalty to nation, superior, or any organization. Henry V of England executed a French knight who had surrendered a castle to him in violation of the rules of chivalry (Keen 1965, 46–47).

10. Expressive statuses are the keepers of the collective representations of a society described by Durkheim (1947, 16–17). In time, these statuses may themselves become cherished values.

4

Vehicles: The Visual and Physical Framework

The vehicle, clothing, gives sartorial signs some of the properties which distinguish them from other forms of communication. This chapter examines the influence of the visual and physical aspects of clothing upon messages and the creation of multiple audiences, including the self. Finally, the effects of scarcity upon social relationships, the economic factor, will be examined.

CLOTHING AS A VISUAL MEDIUM

Visibility

Clothing is a visual system of signs that, unlike speech, projects itself by its very presence. To use an analogy of David Riesman's, it is akin to a perpetual radio transmission, whereas speech is more like radar to which one responds only when probed. The wearer of clothing has committed himself to the statements they make. To change the message, he must remove or conceal them; he cannot remain mute as in speech. The crusader's cross is an early and outstanding example of this principle of visibility.

The symbol was unquestionably an innovation. The historical precedent of "crossing oneself" may of course be invoked. But this was only a fleeting gesture, while now a durable, visible emblem had come into being. Contemporaries must have been deeply impressed, for the sources are much concerned with it. Medieval history offers no earlier example of a company of laymen adopting a distinctive emblem for their clothing; we need only consider how widespread this custom would become—it survives to the present day—in order to realize the decisive significance of its invention. (Erdmann 1977, 345–46)[1]

Visibility prevents private communication. Whereas we may confine our conversation to a private discussion with a solitary other, clothing makes the entire viewing world a reader of the sartorial message. If clothing embodies behavioral norms to which the wearer is held publicly accountable, as in the uniform of a police officer or school child, then all onlookers are enlisted as norm enforcers.

Visibility permits group statements in a manner not available to speech. These statements may demonstrate political beliefs, parade the power of a group or the state, or pay ceremonial homage as in the procession of bridesmaids or honor guards. A verbal analogy is the shouting of a mob, the cheering at a political rally, or the singing of a congregation. The appearance of an entire group in similar dress such as military uniforms, the colored shirts of political movements, gang colors, or ethnic dress affirms a common value or belief. Appearance is made all the more impressive because of its silence. The importance of silence, or alternatively the higher regard for visible symbols, partially explains "witnessing", the display of symbols as testimony of one's beliefs, and "massing", the group display of symbols, themes we shall encounter repeatedly.

Visibility in clothing is a social rather than physical property. We respond not simply to the physical appearance of the clothing but to the information it provides about wearers' statuses or affiliations, the norms to which they are held accountable, their degree of conformity to them, and whether they are in the appropriate context (Merton 1957, 319; Stone, G. 1962). The distinctive dress of the domestic announces the low status of the wearer and creates invisible men and women who fade into the background (Goffman 1959, 151; 1972, 302–10).

Visibility is relative; indeed, the seemingly high visibility of uniform wearers leads to invisibility if they are immersed in a sea of identically dressed individuals. In the Civil War, the colonel of the 23rd Massachusetts Regiment, a unit noted for its theft of turkeys from neighboring farmers, ordered his men to abandon their distinctive Zouave uniforms in favor of standard uniforms so that they could not be identified in their forays (Haythornthwaite 1976, 128).[2]

Witnessing

The high regard for visible symbols in our society enhances sartorial witnessing. "Propaganda-of-the-deed" is far more persuasive than verbal propaganda; the former does not bear the opprobrium and cynicism attached to the latter (Merton 1946, 89, 92, 145; Osanka 1971, 410–11). "Doing something" is more desirable than mere discussion or contemplation. When yellow armbands and ribbons were worn to show sympathy for the Americans held hostage in Iran, one participant said that "wearing the armbands shows that you're not taking business as usual—it shows you care" (NYT 6 Dec. 1979). He described his participation as "doing something" and therefore more sincere and indicative of his true feelings than mere words. The wearer is not simply voicing his opinions but is giving them greater visibility for all to see. In effect, he is wearing his heart on his sleeve.

Witnessing becomes a key to the revelation or concealment of deeply held beliefs. Basically, we may follow one of two strategies in adherence to values. We may engage in bearing witness, the bold declaration of beliefs even in the face of hostility. In religious contexts, an outstanding contemporary advocate is the Salvation Army whose uniform "not only identifies the wearer as a member of a world-wide evangelistic movement, but is also a silent witness that the wearer is a Christian. The manner in which the uniform is worn should be an evidence of the inner personal relationship with Christ which it is presumed to represent" (Salvation Army n.d.). The ill-treatment accorded wearers of the uniform is accepted proudly. "No Salvationist has any need to be ashamed of his uniform; indeed, he should wear it as an honor. There was a time, admittedly when it was scoffed at, sneered at, besmirched with rotten eggs and fruit, soot and what-not" (Kitching n.d.).

Witnessing by dress may also promote group cohesion; members of a group can identify each other and draw comfort from knowing that they are not alone when all wear the same distinctive dress. In the late 1960's, dashikis were critical in "distinguishing those who were with you from those who weren't" in the Black liberation movement (NYT 17 Mar. 1976). As the dashiki and other styles of African origin became less of a political statement, they were assimilated into ordinary dress and became less dramatically visible.

An opposing strategy urges the privacy of beliefs, for the "truth shall prevail" and external or visible confirmation is unnecessary. Margaret Fell, an early and prominent Quaker, "did not, however, approve of the subdued attire [of Quakers]. She thought that women should dress 'in pleasing fashion' and in bright colours, arguing in support of this that outward conformity was the enemy of inward righteousness, which was based on the freedom of the individual" (Ewing 1975, 27).[3]

Subtle Cues

In his *Guide of the Perplexed,* Maimonides wrote simultaneously for a broad audience which read the work on a manifest level, and for a limited group able to perceive the subtle cues in his writing (Strauss, L. 1963, xvii–xxiv). How is Maimonides' feat duplicated when one wishes to communicate sartorially with a limited audience? To switch metaphors, we seek the sartorial equivalent of the whisper, the sealed envelope, or the classified file. "Subtle cues" are signs that try to solve the dilemma of the visibility of dress and the desire for relative anonymity.

Subtle cues are of strategic importance because they explain the existence of a plurality of audiences for the same sartorial symbols. These cues change the relationship of a clothing wearer to his audience. Although all symbols may be interpreted differentially by audiences, subtle cues are a deliberate effort to focus the transmission of symbols upon a selected audience and to obscure the meaning for others. The advertisement of some products such as jeans, cologne, and cigarettes is couched to reach both homosexual and heterosexual audiences while not alerting nor offending the latter (Stabiner 1982). In a safe context one may be interested in being read primarily by a significant reference group, but interception of the message by others is of less concern. The overt is not merely the visible; what is visible depends upon the context, and an understanding of the context reveals the visible.

The first type of subtle cues is those intentionally directed toward limited audiences, for example, those used by marginal groups such as homosexuals in the days of the closet and the slight raising of skirts by Victorian prostitutes as a proposition toward prospective clients (Huggett 1977, 122; Humphreys 1972, 67). Secret Service agents and others frequently wear colored lapel pins to identify themselves to each other in a large crowd. Similarly, much of understated fashion depends upon its readability to a limited audience, the unobtrusive but expensive dress. The significant aspect of this type of communication is its occurrence within the context of a larger, unknowing audience.[4]

Other subtle cues are unintentional and consist of instances when we give ourselves away, for example in the perpetual warfare between criminal and police, or spy and counterspy, where each group ''smells'' the other out. Street criminals are detected by their frequent touching of trouser waistbands to reassure themselves of the presence of a revolver, a lack of shoe laces which is a carryover of prison habits, and, in 1950, the wearing of sneakers then dubbed ''felony shoes'' (NYT 1 Oct. 1981; Rubinstein 1973, 248–49). Street demonstrators identified members of the police ''red squads'' by ''posture, the manner of using their hands, the shine of their shoes or the color of their socks'' (Humphreys 1972, 67–68).

In World War II, allied secret agents behind enemy lines attempted to avoid detection by careful attention to minute details of clothing, for example, the sewing on of buttons in a parallel rather than criss-cross manner, properly enscribed suspender buttons, and appropriate inside pockets (Brown, A. C. 1976, 348–49, 382). Despite their care, agents were nevertheless recognized by the Paris Gestapo because of their identical wristwatches. The agents were also able to identify each other because of the similarity of the clothing and suitcases provided by their home base.

Plainclothesmen may be detected by outsiders because of a frequent uniformity of dress, raincoats or the ubiquitous black leather coat of Central and East European plainclothes police (NYT 12 Jan. 1977; 21 Dec. 1979). The surprising similarity of dress, physique, and walk between Israeli and Egyptian agents during Sadat's visit to Jerusalem made it difficult to distinguish between them (NYT 21 Nov. 1977). This suggests a professional deformation that cuts across national and cultural boundaries.

These observations indicate that a very frequent subtle cue is the uniformity rather than the nature of an item. Unintentional uniformity arises from the difficulty of deliberately reproducing in clothing from a single source the range of differences invariably found in clothing from multiple sources. A statement made by contemporary Guatemalan civilians illustrates the problem of obtaining a random sample in a purposive manner. "The army intensified its patrols in the area. . . . the soldiers were invariably dressed in civilian clothes. 'Sure we recognize the soldiers. . . . They go around in groups of 20 or 30 dressed as peasants, but they all have the same boots and the same weapons' " (NYT 15 Sept. 1982).[5]

Split Signs

Cross pressures are a familiar phenomenon of everyday life; the young, middle-class professional, whose working-class parents swore by FDR, attracted by the blandishments of Republican candidates. The sartorial analogue is the split sign that indicates mixed affiliations or dual statuses. The precise interpretation of a set of split symbols can be made only in light of the context. My concern is not with the meaning of such symbols but with their sheer existence and their use to transmit information about cross pressures which they both express and reconcile.

In nineteenth-century England, outfits for women engaged in yachting, hunting, riding, and shooting took the form of mannish attire above the waist and skirts below (Cunnington & Mansfield 1970, 105, 116–25, 203–6, 294–95). Queen Elizabeth follows the same style when she reviews the troops on horseback. Today, the adoption of blue jeans by both sexes has not abolished the split sign but merely changed the body zones where gender symbols are expressed. "Ninety percent of middle-class and college students of both sexes are now identical below the waist, though above it they may wear anything from a lumberjack shirt to a lace blouse" (Lurie 1976, 72).

Split signs designate the duality of military and other affiliations such as race, ethnicity, or gender. A familiar example is the combination of the British tunic and the Scottish kilt. The importance of the duality to the wearers is indicated by the mutiny in a Highland regiment in the eighteenth century after the abolition of the kilt (Enloe 1980, 35). The Samoan battalion in the United States Marine Corps wore a khaki lava-lava (skirt) and a Marine undershirt (Gero & Thompson 1979).[6]

The use of split signs must be differentiated from instances in which individuals wear pieces of discarded uniforms as ordinary clothing—refugees or camp followers who use them out of need. In contrast, an example of split symbolism qua symbolism is that of the newspaper reporter who so closely identified with the police that his working attire often included a police sweater (Bernstein & Woodward 1974, 15).

CLOTHING AS A PHYSICAL MEDIUM

Marshall McLuhan's "the medium is the message" made it impossible ever to forget that medium and message are not wholly separable. But, even earlier, G. H. Mead pointed out that, because the speaker could *hear* himself speak, the spoken language could influence the development of the self (1934, 65–66). What is true of speech is also true of clothing, and so we must explore how the physical characteristics of clothing shape communication. We must be alert, therefore, to the dangers of oversubtlety and remember Freud's dictum that sometimes a cigar is just a cigar. Not all properties of clothing can be ascribed to its use as a communicating device. Some may derive entirely from its physical aspects or its utilization as a tool or practical device.

In gay bars these days, the men's costumes, with their coded signals, are so elaborate that even habitues are beginning to get confused. Keys dangling from a belt over the left hip generally signal a desire to be sexually dominant; on the right, a passive disposition. . . . An expert on left-right symbolism . . . warned of a further possible misunderstanding. If they are on the right side he said, it may just mean that the wearer is righthanded. (Time 8 Sept. 1975)

General MacArthur's reaction upon meeting General Wainwright, after the latter's release from three years of brutal wartime captivity, illustrates the relationship between vehicle and meaning.

The General [MacArthur] was equally moved. . . . Something in the dining room reunion troubled him, and he couldn't put his finger in it. Then it came to him. It was the brown walnut cane with the curved handle. He had given it to Wainwright in prewar Manila, expecting him to use it as he had used his own—as a commander's stage prop, a swagger stick. Instead it had supported the dwindling weight of a whipped man, suffering torments of shame through those years of humiliation when he had been unable to lean upon anything else, not even pride. (Manchester 1978, 525)

The pure symbol had been transformed into a tool, becoming an entirely different symbol, that of age and weakness rather than panache.

Layers of Signs[7]

Multiple layers of clothing enable varying levels of communication, each transmitting to a potentially different audience and perhaps presenting a different image of one's self. With the outermost layer, we are addressing a general audience or public. Successive layers are directed to more intimate groups until, finally, we are interacting primarily, but not solely, with ourselves or, more precisely, the view of ourselves derived from society.

Since the signs transmitted by each layer may vary, the wearer often carries different and, at times, contradictory messages—conformity and rebellion, middle and lower class affiliations, male and female gender roles. The concept of partial transvestism, in which the messages of different layers are at odds with each other, must be enlarged to include class, politics, religion, and other modes of passing as well as that of gender with which transvestism is usually associated.

Beginning with the outermost layer, the Muslim veil in its many forms has been used by women to conceal Western dress from disapproving clergy or other censorious males (NYT 8 Apr. 1975; 30 May 1980; WSJ 11 July 1975). Cloaks to disguise class or identity are a standard ploy in tales of the Caliph Al-Rashid, the plays of Shakespeare, and by the traveler in dangerous areas.

At an inner layer, West Point cadets expressed their defiance of authority by wearing concealed ragged shirts and shoes with holes in the sole (U'Ren 1975, 26). Eighteenth-century Japanese merchants evaded sumptuary laws mandating plain kimonos by weaving gold threads into the lining (Richie 1973). Under Mao jackets, Chinese women in the early 1980's often wore colorful blouses with sleeves cut short to prevent accidental exposure; flowered patches sewn on the lining were "flashed" at friends (NYT 11 Mar. 1981).

In the revolutionary 1840's, German students concealed ribbons indicative of tabooed political beliefs beneath their coats (Feuer 1969, 67). Over a century later, Poles, after the imposition of martial law, also wore their Solidarity Union buttons hidden under their lapels (NYT 28 Dec. 1981).

As will be seen in the following section, underwear bears its own distinctive message.

Finally, even a solitary layer of clothes and skin allow for divergent messages. Walzer contrasts the messages presented by the sight of the nude and the uniformed enemy (1977, 138–42). The former is revealed as a human with whom one has much in common and who is often spared, or at least killed reluctantly which of course ameliorates the situation. On the other hand, revenge is very often wreaked upon the dead by despoiling them of their uniforms, equating their nudity with humiliation rather than humanity. Concealed tattoos reflected the Bohemian attraction of the lumpenproletariat or underworld for European royalty and nobility.

Our bodies may turn into battlegrounds between those group affiliations and self-images we prefer for ourselves and those to which we are socially bound. We may conform at one level, but deviate at another. We are our own audience and the signs we extend to ourselves of ourselves do matter, even when the external world is not cognizant of our statements. The divergence in perspectives toward the concealed is yet another reflection of the perennial antinomy, repeatedly encountered in this analysis, between external witnessing to others and the internal adherence to personal beliefs. The external and the internal, the public and the private are expressed in these attitudes toward layers of dress as they are toward layers of the self.

Multiple layers allow the differentiation of attitudes toward the self. Thomas à Becket was discovered upon his death to be wearing a verminous haircloth shirt beneath his rich outer robes, a frequent and effective mode of reconciling divergent statuses or the world and one's conscience (Turner, V. 1974, 88). The heterosexual transvestite may wear masculine clothing over feminine dress which "symbolizes that the entire sex-role behavior is a role—an act. Conversely, stage impersonators sometimes wear jockey shorts beneath full stage drag, symbolizing that the feminine clothing is a costume" (Newton 1972, 101). In all instances, the individual proclaims to himself that he is not what he outwardly appears to be. The audience for whom we dress includes ourselves, and the advantage of a hidden layer is that we may effectively exclude all others from participation. The innermost closet self is fantasy made safe by an outer anchorage of convention and respectability.

The innermost persona may be the "true" self which cannot be exposed for many reasons. Split views of the self may stem from resistance to norms or authority and comprise a self which outwardly bows to the demands of religious or political control and a self which discreetly declares one's real feelings. To express his complex, counterrevolutionary views, Floyd Dell, the radical author, wore silk BVD's beneath "blue-flannel proletarian shirts and corduroy trousers" because he "liked them, but also, no doubt, as a symbol of the leisure-class part of my nature" (Aaron 1961, 235). His clothing also indicates his cynical views on radicalism.

The use of inner layers expresses an evaluation of the concealed. In Renaissance France, children, even of the highest classes, wore underwear of cheap and coarse fabric in sharp contrast to the rich material of their outer dress (Varron 1940, 1138). The reasoning is impeccable and based upon sound common sense; why waste expensive material and money on the unseen? As soon as they are revealed, then the newly visible items should be made of better material as happened to petticoats when skirts were gathered up and when revealing crinolines became fashionable (Born 1943, 1676; Varron 1940, 1138). Only the audience reached by the outer layers is significant.

The logic is impeccable until we consider the opposite strategy, the use of expensive and ornate materials in concealed places precisely because they *are* concealed. Moss Hart, the playwright, used monogrammed gold collar stays; Cripps, a London dandy, commuted regularly to Vienna for fitted underwear; Russian peasant women had rich embroidery inside the back of their skirts; and a fashionable New York woman owns a gold evening bag with her name spelled out in diamonds on the lining (Frazier 1967, 209; NYT 6 Jan. 1977; 10 Dec. 1978).

Secret defiance of repressive norms may be revealed by displaying the concealed layers to others. Even our secret redefinitions of our selves and group memberships need reenforcement from others. As Simmel put it, there is a strong tendency to betray a secret in order to reveal that we possessed it in the first place (1950, 333–34). The epynomic flasher derives gratification by revealing the nudity beneath his raincoat. The Japanese in his modest kimono with lavish lining, the Chinese woman whose Mao jacket conceals a flowered blouse, and the Russian peasant with embroidery on the inside of the back of her skirt, all display their sartorial secrets at one time or another. Female impersonators skillfully mingle, visually and verbally, simulated female and actual male roles (Newton 1972, esp. 101). Flashing by these performers is also made an act of defiance by the disclosure of deviation. They deliberately smear their masquerade by allowing a masculine element to intrude such as a beard beneath make-up or a sudden baritone comment. Messages conveyed by the intermingling of several layers have a special connotation for the viewer—the provocativeness of forbidden fruit, the voyeuristic view of the tabooed.

In addition to being seen, clothing may be heard, felt, and smelled. Concealed layers may therefore be heard even if unseen. The hidden Victorian underskirt or petticoat was revealed aurally by its "frou-frou", regarded as provocative, which indicated the use of expensive silk (Mansfield & Cunnington 1973, 20).

Deception in communication may occur not only in the message but in the physical vehicle. Cheap fabrics which simulated the sound of silk made aural counterfeiting feasible. Visual counterfeiting included the dickeys or stomachers which simulated shirts (Bultzingslowen 1957a, 16; Cunnington & Cunnington 1975, 68).

Underwear and Hidden Signs

The discussion of multiple layers of clothing inevitably involves underwear, the final buffer between the privacy of the nude and the public outer layers. Yet even nude, we are not fully private persons, for society in the guise of the internalized other performs as a voyeur.

The intrusion of society is indicated by the social origin of concealment which is an interplay of the physical and social aspects of symbolism. Concealment is desired when the body is seen as visually contaminating and therefore to be hidden not only from others but one's own self (Cunnington & Cunnington 1951, 22–23, 151). In this context, underwear functions as the physical equivalent of a superego. Essenes never saw themselves nude but always bathed in a shift; an English girls' school some decades ago enforced the same behavior (Edwards 1977, 22, 62).

Properties of the body, actual or alleged, are often transferred to clothing. The shoe becomes a fetish because of the foot; underwear also exemplifies transferred eroticism because of its concealment of other erogenous zones (Cunnington & Cunnington 1951, 12–17; Rossi 1976, esp. 171–94). Therefore not only the body but also the underwear itself must be concealed since it in turn becomes tabooed. In the girls' school mentioned above rules prescribed an elaborate procedure to hide used underwear.

Concealment and its connotations foster the use of underwear for erotic fantasies (edible female bikinis or sexy male shorts), transexual identification (underwear of the opposite sex), or identification with another economic class (expensive lingerie under the cheaper dresses appropriate to one's station in life) (Lurie 1981, 260–61; NYT 17 May 1973; Newton 1972, 52). On the other hand, one eased the economic strain of keeping up with the Joneses in Medieval and Renaissance days or during recent recessions by the use of much cheaper underwear or no underwear at all (WSJ 3 June 1975).

In puritanical eras, underwear, even if seen only by the wearer or perhaps because it was seen by the wearer in the absence of an external censor, had to be kept devoid of erotic connotations. In nineteenth-century England, women's underwear was white, simple, and unattractive to avoid lustful thoughts (Cunnington & Cunnington 1951, 151).

Underwear may also be concealed because it reveals our use of props such as bras and corsets to enhance our public image (Gross & Stone, 1964). An attractive persona adheres to the social convention that our images are genuine and not supported by artifice.

The innermost body need not be seen as contaminating and the associated clothing need not be abhorrent. Clothing of the priests in ancient Judea was used as lampwicks for the Temple because of the transferred holiness of the garments (Patai 1947, 145–47).[8] Similarly, intimate clothing carries the connotation of sincerity since it is associated with the "true" self. In medieval Europe, the shirt or its detached sleeves was an emblem of one's self; the blood-soaked shirt of a fallen knight was often worn by his widow (Bultzingslowen 1957a, 13). Medieval penance was performed in one's shirt as a sign of humility; the surrender of a fortress was made by its inhabitants in shirtsleeves to indicate sincerity (Bultzingslowen 1957b, 27; Renbourn 1964, 7). An executive in his shirtsleeves is a sign of commitment to work, a person who "does not fool around on the job".

CLOTHING AS AN ECONOMIC MEDIUM

Clothing is an economic fact of life. As a commodity with scarcity value, it is intertwined with a distinctive set of social relationships comprising initial distribution and, because of its durability, frequently a subsequent secondary distribution after owners tire of their wardrobe or die.

The Initial Distribution of Clothing

In the United States and Western Europe, the modes of obtaining and distributing clothes have included custom-tailoring, homemade clothes, ready-made clothes, and secondhand clothing. These modes denote, depending upon the context, relationships among classes, between organizational staff and inmate, or parent and child.

One of the most important sets of relationships described by clothing is that of stratification which was much more clearly expressed in previous periods by the assignment of well tailored custom-made clothes to upper classes and secondhand or less skillfully tailored homemade garments to the lower. Ready-made garments were of inferior quality and intended primarily for seamen and slaves

(Aries 1962, 59; Copeland 1977, xiv–xv; Kidwell & Christman 1974, 19–31, 227–29; Schramm 1958b, 9).

The clothing revolution of the nineteenth century greatly increased ready-to-wear clothes, removed the stigma, and correspondingly decreased custom-made clothes. Several changes in the sartorial symbols of classes ensued. Previously, the dress of different classes was sharply differentiated, while clothing differences today form a gentle gradient. Furthermore, in contemporary United States and Britain, it is easier to be decently dressed than housed, fed, or doctored (Orwell 1961, 83). "America has the best dressed poverty the world has ever known" (Harrington 1972, 13). Earlier, deprivation was defined not only by malnutrition but also by the lack of clothing (Cunnington & Lucas 1978, 1).

The distinction between lower-class ready-made clothing and upper-class custom-tailoring is reflected in the procurement of uniforms in many armed services. Enlisted men are issued their uniforms; officers usually procure theirs, ready-made, from outside agencies. Ironically, British female officers were expected to obtain their uniforms from civilian custom tailors after World War II when the decreasing number of these tailors and the abandonment of such clothing by upper classes had already made the practice anachronistic (Ewing 1975, 139).

Not only is the mode of distributing clothes important, but also whether or not it conforms to the prevalent pattern in society. Total institutions like armies or prisons very often rely upon standardized clothing or uniforms to control their members or inmates. Being unable to select their own clothing, inmates are denied a symbol of responsible adulthood. Were the prevalent social pattern that of distributing clothing through gifts, the deleterious effects would probably be much less. Nowadays, some reaction to the traditional pattern of total institutions may be observed. Mental patients are taken on shopping trips as a therapeutic device and convicts obtain clothes other than prison dress through purchase or barter (Stanton & Schwartz 1954, 49–50; Strange & McCrory 1974).

Modern uniforms are possible only under certain economic and social conditions. First, enough surplus must exist within a society to clothe, as well as feed and equip, a large body of men not engaged in primary production. Additionally, there must be an effective system of distribution which permits the group to assume responsibility for clothing members. Only in fully rationalized bureaucratic systems do uniformed organizations like armies take care of their own. Failing these conditions, men may clothe, as well as feed and even equip, themselves as in the Colonial era, the American Revolution, the English Civil War, and many other instances.

In earlier periods, the military assumed responsibility only for needy members who could not afford clothes and equipment. During the English Civil War, cavalrymen, who usually provided their own clothing since they were recruited from the wealthy, dressed more ornately than the poor infantry who received free dress (Carman 1957, 19). Sailing ships' slop chests offered standardized work clothes, rather than uniforms which were not provided until the mid-nineteenth century, only to those without suitable clothing (Lloyd 1970, 235). Those who boarded ship with proper attire continued to wear it (Masefield 1937, 139–41).

Early military clothing regulations arose more out of a desire to insure the well-being of troops than to maintain dress standards. For a long period before the modern era, colonel-contractors were delegated to raise troops for whose upkeep they would be given a yearly sum. The warrants of Queen Anne, one of the earliest sets of British regulations, were intended to safeguard the troops against the rapacity of colonel-contractors who profited from scrimping on clothing for their men (Barnett 1970, 143–44). Note that these groups are being provided with standardized clothing to obtain the economies of large scale purchase, rather than with uniforms in the modern sense.

On the other hand, a large inventory of clothing makes the adoption of new types of uniform more difficult. A decade after the American Civil War the army had to make-do with Civil War clothing and equipment (Rickey 1963, 34–35). An unwanted backlog may be disposed of to some hapless group, especially the ornate uniforms for which there is a ready market. The Graustarkian uniforms of the White House Police under President Nixon have since become the property of Iowa high school bands (NYT 16 May 1980).

Durability and Secondary Distribution

A good part of the structuralist theories of communication rests on the distinction between *langue* and *parole*. The former is what we ordinarily call language, the abstract rules and conventions that organize any given utterance or text. *Parole* is a specific utterance and is ephemeral; once made, it disappears. An item of clothing—gown, uniform, or business suit—is roughly analogous to an utterance but is hardly ephemeral.[9] Clothing is durable and any item may persist long after the death of its owner; a century-old pair of leather breeches was used continuously by an English farm family (Cunnington & Lucas 1967, 35). The physical durability of clothing is therefore a constraint that must be taken into account in a manner that the spoken word is not. Something must be done with the clothing. It must be worn, stored, or disposed of in some manner; it will not vanish of its own accord.

Since an item of clothing is not only a physical vehicle but also carries a freight of signs ranging from the profound to the trivial, it cannot be disposed of without reference to its meaning. Where the symbolism is sacred, the garment may not be disposed of at all, or else only with special consideration. One does not merely discard a wedding gown, baptismal dress, or clerical robe. Where the garment, though not sacred or ceremonial, has inappropriate symbolism for the new owner, redefinition must occur, for example, clothing given by a master to a domestic.

Sheer longevity may itself engender ritualistic significance both secular and religious. A wedding gown or baptismal dress that is merely identical to the one worn by forebears does not carry the same symbolism as the original garment which provided additional values, the mystical properties adhering to the touch of ancestors. Burial in a wedding suit or gown depends upon the survival of clothing for its symbolic effect.

What does one do with leftovers from an orgy of conspicuous consumption? At Versailles, uneaten food was sold at the palace gates (Braudel 1981, 203). Similarly, there must be some mechanism for the disposal of clothes that accumulate as the result of conspicuous display.

The solution to the sartorial legacy of the past year or century lies in secondary distribution, the transferral of used goods. Secondary distribution involves a system of relationships which may be classified by the mode of disposal, each involving perpetuation or reinterpretation of the symbolic freight of the vehicle. The relationship may be a personal one in which the donor is aware of the recipient. When clothes are an expensive commodity and do not incur rapid obsolescence, they are frequently inventoried in wills and bequeathed. This procedure was prevalent in the United States and Europe in former centuries (Aries 1962, 57; Cunnington & Lucas 1978, 1–2; Deetz 1969). Used clothing may be transferred as a gift to servants (Hecht 1950, 115–16). On an impersonal level, secondary distribution in contemporary society involves a network of clothing discarders. A thirty-eight-year-old executive with a very large "big label" wardrobe sells unwanted clothes periodically to a store specializing in such transactions because "he likes to change his wardrobe seasonally, he needs the closet space and he hates to throw or give away expensive clothes" (WSJ 17 July 1978). Other participants include rag dealers and eventually often foreign purchasers in areas such as Afghanistan which rely upon the system, or did, as an important source.

NOTES

1. I should like to thank Murray Hausknecht for this quotation.

2. Zouave uniforms were gaudy and very popular in many armies. Derived from North Africa via the French, they included fezzes or turbans, baggy red or vertical striped trousers, elaborate embroidered insignia, and ornamental jackets (Haythornthwaite 1976, pls. 18, 24, 26, 52, 54, 55).

3. The very need to assert one's loyalties may be interpreted as casting doubt upon them. Whereas in most British regiments of the Victorian era the first toast after dinner in the officers' mess was to the sovereign, some units refused to make the toast since the regiment's loyalty had always been unquestioned (Farwell 1980, 63). The analogy to the controversy over loyalty oaths in the 1950's will be apparent.

4. Goffman described the techniques used by spies to contact each other and exchange information while remaining unnoticed by the public (1972, 214–20). The secrecy of the subterranean conflict between spy and counterspy clashes with the desire to accord overt symbols of honor to CIA agents killed in the line of duty. A memorial in CIA headquarters includes seventeen anonymous stars for covert operatives (NYT 22 Apr. 1983; 26 Apr. 1983).

5. One solution to the problem of randomness, although perhaps not consciously intended for this purpose, was to steal the wardrobes of refugees going through U.S. Customs in World War II, with suitable though indirect compensation, in order to equip O.S.S. agents (Stevenson 1976, 205–6). This solution substitutes the random statistical distribution of a multitude for the inevitable centralization of one or even a few guiding individuals.

6. Gypsies divide the body into a clean upper half and a polluted lower half (Kephart 1982, 14–17). Orthodox Jews make the same distinction with waist cords or sashes. The body as the source of cognitive categories for structuring our perception of the world has been discussed by Douglas, Durkheim, Hertz, and others. For a summary, see Polhemus (1978).

7. Upon finishing this section, my attention was called to a similar discussion of layers of symbols by Allison Lurie (1981, 245–46).

8. The tassels denoting Judaism were originally worn externally (Milgrom 1981). In a later era of persecution, these salient symbols were transferred to inner garments and attached to the hem which was the extension of the wearer's person and authority—the ancient counterpart of the seal. Mormons receive a special set of underwear to be worn at all times, with embroidered symbols reminding wearers of their temple obligations (Kephart 1982, 262).

9. *Parole* consists of specific items from a vocabulary of words, foods, clothing or other symbols to form a sentence, meal, or suit of clothes and is drawn from the complete verbal, culinary, or sartorial "menu" or *langue* available to us. The acceptable use of *parole* is delimited by the context, such as the social affiliation of the wearer, and by the occasion. A breakfast menu would be out of place at dinner; the sartorial range for a formal upper class-banquet would not fit lunch at a student cafeteria. The appropriateness of specific menus and their degree of interchangeability are determined by norms and are most severely restricted for uniforms.

PART TWO
UNIFORMS

5

The Uniform and Control

The uniform lends itself to a variety of controls. It enables an organization to establish strata of memberships to which admission becomes a carrot. Uniforms enlist the public as external censors to enforce organizational codes. The precision of uniform regulations permits cycles of permissiveness and strictness to indicate changes in policy.

The uniform not only mediates routine interaction but serves as pure expressive display. It is the outer manifestation of inner grace or, in secular terms, the means of inculcating and displaying loyalty to an organization. When wearers of uniforms feel it unnecessary to witness externally their inner commitment to the organization, then the expressive quality of the uniforms may lead to a rejection of control.

The dynamics of the uniform are transformed when it is displayed by a group simultaneously instead of in a one-to-one interaction between wearer and viewer, and its use as a control device is concomitantly altered.

After a definition of the uniform and an examination of its components, the several types of control over uniformed individuals and groups and the import of witnessing and massing will be analyzed.

THE DYNAMICS OF CONTROL

Thus far, I have described some of the key components of clothing, especially those pertaining to uniforms. Integrating the components will be done by examining their dynamics, their fitting together in action. Before doing so, the properties of uniforms must be explored.

Characteristics of the Uniform

The uniform identifies group members, helps insure that organizational goals will be attained, and orders priorities of group and status demands for the individual.

The uniform enables a group to exert a degree of control over its members who must carry out the goals of the organization. Both colleagues and public must be certain that the activities of the police officer on duty will be consistent with the needs of the department and not the result of personal whim or external affiliations. At the same time, individuals must reconcile the often conflicting demands imposed by their affiliations and statuses. To understand how uniforms function as a means of control, let us start with the characteristics of the uniform.

The Uniform is a Group Emblem. The uniform designates a group. One does not simply wear blue, white, or khaki; instead, one's dress indicates membership in a police force, hospital, or military unit.

Because of its association with a group, the uniform assumes the properties of a totemic emblem and embodies the attributes of that group. In a peculiar sense, the uniform becomes the group, and the uniform rather than the group can become the focus of thought and affect. Thus, an individual's behavior may reflect favorably or unfavorably upon his uniform rather than his group and, in extreme instances, one may disgrace the uniform. Reciprocally, the uniform may enhance or diminish the honor of the wearer.

As with other cultural artifacts, the uniform seems to have an existence independent of the group or its wearers. In the old army saw, one "salutes the uniform and not the man". The uniform is not only an emblem but also a reminder of the behavior appropriate toward this emblem; it becomes a third factor in the interaction between wearer and other. It is an impersonal objectification of the group. The identification of the uniform with the group reaches its epitome in the *ehrenkleid* of Germany—the uniform as an "honor garment" that transfers to its wearer the accrued glory of an organization or nation. To win support of the masses, Hitler granted them the right to wear uniforms and "proclaimed that 'he returned honor to the German laborer'" (Vagts 1959, 444).

As with any symbol, the perception of the uniform depends upon its audience. Accordingly, the police uniform in the black ghetto has often signified all the hated manifestations of "white power" and this attitude overcomes even the common bond of skin color (Alex 1969, 172–79). Black police officers complain that they are not considered human beings in their own communities by their neighbors. The effect of the uniform depends, therefore, upon the relative degree of prestige of the group it objectifies. Minorities usually accord lower prestige to police departments; southerners in the United States usually grant higher prestige to the military services.

The Uniform Reveals and Conceals Status Position. The uniform is read as the indicator of a single status, that of membership in an organization.[1] The uniform makes the wearer's position or status much more visible than do other types of dress; it minimizes the possibility of confusing members with nonmembers. Its importance as a differentiating device is indicated by the often severe sanctions against imposters. Ironically, the explicit symbolism of the uniform facilitates its counterfeiting. It was much easier for the cobbler from Kopenick to assume the status of captain in the Kaiser's army than for Liza Doolittle to simulate membership in the English elite. The cobbler's status claim was implemented by his appearance in easily identifiable and guaranteed symbols while Liza's claim had to be legitimated by appropriate behavior as well as appearance.

The explicitness of the uniform as a status indicator depends upon its monopolization. While one is in uniform, indicators of all other statuses are suppressed. As an extreme example, army regulations have discouraged officers in uniform from carrying packages, the ultimate indication of domesticity. The devices used by ordinary citizens to express their attitudes are denied to the uniform wearer—political buttons, religious insignia, and symbols of individual esthetic or ludic preferences.

The definition of a master status is a cultural variable. The Jesuits clad both male and female converts in a Paraguayan mission in the same clothing since the sexual distinction was unimportant compared to the difference between Christian and heathen, an ordering of priorities that is not universal (Banton 1965, 84).

The importance of the master status and its influence upon the attitudes of the public toward uniform wearers is reflected in the experiences of a wartime sailor who described the results of being taken out of civilian statuses and clothes and put into conspicuous uniforms. "By the mere act of donning the uniform, thousands of civilians, a good proportion of whom had never been in any vessel larger than a ferry boat, were presumed to be sea-faring men. The public's naive attitude was 'You are in the Navy now, so of course you certainly know how to splice rope' "(Warren 1946, 204).

West Point cadets are more likely to be influenced by their uniformed officer-instructors, especially those with combat decorations, than by their civilian counterparts, even though the latter might be more qualified in the academic specialty (Ellis & Moore 1974, 132; Masland & Radway 1957, 205). The uniform confirms the master status, officer, at the expense of the status of instructor.

The Uniform is a Certificate of Legitimacy. The uniform is read to discern the relationship between wearer and organization. The very existence of a uniform implies at least a two-tiered organizational hierarchy, wearers and superiors who have granted them the right to wear the group uniform, and who supervise conformity to group regulations. By permitting the use of its uniform, a group certifies an individual as its representative and assumes responsibility for his activities. The uniform is a symbolic declaration that an individual will adhere to group norms and standardized roles and has mastered the relevant group skills. Failure to meet these standards will result in penalties, and, in extreme cases, discharge and deprivation of the right to wear the uniform.

For the uniform to function as a certificate of legitimacy for its representatives, the public must learn to recognize it as an indicator of a special status. The proliferation of uniforms may, however, result in public confusion. New York City police complain, in effect, about the lessening of the significance of their uniform as a certificate of legitimacy when they protest its adoption by other municipal services such as the Transit Authority and Department of Sanitation police officers and by private agencies (Alex 1969, 176). Evidently, the public recognition of the Department's uniform tends to decrease when it is blurred by imitation, a social version of Gresham's Law. Police officers complain about fixed posts because they are often confused with private guards while occupying them.[2]

At times, the legitimacy of uniforms becomes complicated. For some police functions, the symbolism of the uniform is a hardship and has been replaced by that of less provocative civilian or quasi-civilian clothing. A crucial test of uniform usage occurs when police hostage teams face the dilemma of having to avoid uniforms in order to placate the hostagetakers, while requiring some identification for other police officers to pass freely into the "front lines". Nassau County police officials use a jacket with distinctive insignia on the *back* to allow access to the "inner perimeter of operations where only negotiators and Precision Firearms Team members are allowed" (Maher 1977). The jacket is not worn during face-to-face negotiations. The New York City Police Department has also experimented with unbuttoning jackets and removing ties to eliminate barriers in the handling of domestic disputes (Kornblith 1975, 25–26).

Another testing of uniform legitimacy occurs in the massing of uniform wearers. When a platoon of police, a fire company, or a battalion of soldiers appears on the scene, one does not bother to question their legitimacy. Onlookers are in a position to do so only if they possess superior power. Though the uniform is essential elsewhere, it is unnecessary as a badge of legitimacy when power in the form of massing is manifested.

The Uniform Suppresses Individuality. The uniform suppresses individual idiosyncrasies of behavior, appearance, and sometimes physical attributes. One nun described how her former habit revealed only a tiny portion of her face and nothing else (Int. 1). The uniform may lead to total depersonalization when individuals are picked for an organization merely because they fit the available attire as occurred to page boys in the Canadian Parliament and cocktail waitresses (NYT 22 Sept. 1973; WSJ 7 Apr. 1976).

At the other extreme, conformity imposed by a uniform stems from its symbolization, and individual deviations from norms are much more visible when the individual is in uniform. A detective asleep in a car arouses far less notice than a uniformed police officer engaged in the same practice of "cooping". A sleeping uniformed police officer is incompatible with our expectations of vigilance and alertness but the norms for an apparent civilian, the sleeping detective, are much more ambiguous.

Standardization of dress is itself a source of group imposed conformity. Were uniforms to deviate widely from standards, their ability to demarcate members and to serve as certificates of legitimacy would be diminished. The range of permissible variation in uniforms differs depending upon alternative evidence of legitimacy. We accept police officers in shirtsleeves occupying desks in a precinct house; their presence in headquarters implies awareness and acceptance by other police officers. But deviation in the uniform often entails tampering with the legitimacy of symbols. One impugns the sacredness of group totems and ultimately of the group itself. One also implies that the group cannot control its own certification.

Deviation from uniform standards stems in part from the ludic element which expresses itself in many ways, not the least of which is personal adornment or self-enhancing modes of dress (Huizinga 1950, 183, 192–94; Sapir 1931, 140–41; Simmel 1957).[3] It influences the selection of ordinary dress and especially costume. Note the scorn attached to the uniform-like quality of some types of ordinary dress, for example the gray flannel suit of Madison Avenue in the 1950's. However, the successful maintenance of the uniform as a device for group regulation requires the suppression of individual variations. Although resistance to conformity exists in all groups, the problem looms larger for uniformed groups because uniform regulations are usually much more precise than other types of norms. The distance between chevrons and shoulder seams can be defined and enforced more precisely than academic grading for example. The slightest deviation from prescribed wear can be defined as being "out of uniform".

Control through Definition of Membership

Given these characteristics of the uniform, we can now see how it functions as a means of control. The process starts with the decision by the heads of the uniformed organization to extend or refuse the privilege of the uniform to some or all of its personnel. The first mode of control through uniforms is, therefore, that of permitting or forbidding members to exhibit their organizational affiliation through clothing. At times, an organization may best achieve its goals by concealing or minimizing the relationships of group power and individual responsibility stated by the uniform. The very existence of a uniform gives an organization these options, denied to nonuniformed groups, which can become powerful tools of control. In effect, the group allocates individuals to various categories of membership and determines whether or not to make these subgroups visible. While some students of visibility have described its function for the operation of organizational statuses, I am posing a prior question. Under what structural circumstances is visibility desired?

One condition is safety; invisibility may be the better part of valor in unsafe conditions. In recent years, the use of uniforms by American military personnel was restricted or prohibited in unsafe areas due to political unrest as in Kuwait, Turkey, Puerto Rico, and Iran of course. In other circumstances, the very presence of a uniform makes explicit the affiliation of an individual which the organization prefers to obscure by making him less visible. Military personnel in the United States space program wear civilian or NASA clothing (NT 1 Jan. 1979). Certainly no denial is made of the military background or rank of astronauts, but they are not highlighted and, instead, the scientific dimension is emphasized. Each of the armed services maintains liaison officers—discreet lobbyists in civilian dress with offices in the Senate and House of Representatives—as a two-way channel with their organizations (NT 8 Feb. 1982). In the United States in 1939, army officers were forbidden to wear uniforms even when on duty in Washington, D.C. (Ambrose 1972, 3). With the current stress on rearmament, military officers on duty in Washington, D.C. have been ordered to wear uniforms full time.

Categories of membership and their uniforms describe the degree of acceptance accorded individuals within an organization ranging from begrudging acknowledgment to ordinary membership to elite status. As an example of peripheral membership, the first uniforms mentioned for the 33rd Regiment of U.S. Colored Troops during the Civil War consisted of red coats and red trousers in contrast to the blue uniforms of white troops. Later, blue coats and red trousers were worn; eventually the standard uniform was issued (Sturcke & Gero 1977). "The red trousers were never well liked by officers or men, and the regiment was pleased to hear General Hunter . . . promise them blue trousers, Springfield rifled muskets and full pay" (ibid.).

Similarly, various "invalid corps", units fit only for limited service due to wounds or other infirmities, have been established. During the Civil War, the Invalid Corps of the Union Army was given a distinctive uniform which was "extremely unpopular as the members of the Invalid Corps disliked such obvious distinction from the 'real soldiers' fit for active service" (Haythornthwaite 1976, 163). Eventually, they were issued standard uniforms. The special uniforms of elite units require no discussion.[4]

As a variation, the elite of a uniformed organization, for example the detective force of a police department, may wear civilian clothes. Attitudes may then be displaced from the uniform to civilian clothes. As a student of the New York City Police Department noted, detectives took care of their civilian clothes and dressed fashionably, unlike plainclothes personnel in sloppy attire and officers who were indifferent toward their uniform (Niederhoffer 1969, 82–83). Anticipatory socialization, expressing the hopes of the uniformed for promotion into the ranks of the detective force, took the form of neatly worn civilian clothes.

A seemingly analogous, but actually sharply different situation, is that of the decision of a uniform wearer himself to assert or minimize his organizational affiliation. Admiral Rickover has appeared before congressional committees in civilian dress to dissociate his views from those of other navy officials (NYT 13 July 1975). Rickover had a sufficiently elevated position in his organization to have the option of civilian dress.

Organizational control extends to the type of uniform worn. The uniform reflects the role set of the wearer and must be changed to conform to each interaction or relationship. British Army regulations prescribe fourteen orders of dress for officers based upon climate (temperate or tropical) and occasion (ceremonial, service, or combat), with numerous subcategories for each (UKMD 1978, 7–11). Tables for officers' ceremonial dress prescribe appropriate uniforms for six court functions and seventeen other occasions including reviews, investitures, balls, weddings, funerals, and court-martials (ibid., 27–27A).

An organization may prefer to have its personnel visible to outsiders in only certain types of uniform, certainly not the work uniform. One of the reforms instituted in the early 1970's by Admiral Zumwalt of the United States Navy to bring it into line with contemporary society was to ease the restrictions on the wearing of work uniforms in public. The efforts to tighten discipline in 1981 included reimposition of these restrictions. Probably one reason for the change stems from the evaluation of the Navy's role as symbol provider for society. Allowing the sailor to be seen as a laborer tarnishes the cultural image of the service.

Restrictions on uniforms apply also to nonmilitary uniformed organizations although they may lack a large wardrobe of uniforms. Nuns have informally adapted habits for kitchen work by pinning up sleeves (Int. 1). Senior nuns act literally as gatekeepers to the outer world to insure that nuns will return to the formal use of habits upon leaving the kitchen.

Under some circumstances a uniform wearer remains primarily an individual rather than a representative of his group. Walzer collected instances of the nude soldier, where the enemy's essential humanity or kinship to an opponent outweighs the labeling of his uniform, thereby averting his being shot (1977, 138–43). These cases include being caught nude in a bath in the open; performing an essentially human act such as smoking, chatting, or drinking coffee; or when one is obviously in a revery. The repugnance at killing the individual detached from his unit was formalized in Union Army regulations during the Civil War which forbade shooting sentinels, outposts, or pickets (Baxter 1951, 343; Walzer 1977, 143).

On the other hand, despoiling the enemy of his uniform, and thus reducing, or perhaps elevating, him to his essential humanity, has been frequently engaged in as an act of hatred and revenge. In the context of a war that is intensely ideological, the detached uniform wearer may be precisely the desired prey.

Control through Interaction

The uniform is a dramaturgical device which provides a symbolic medium for interaction. Its use enables the actor to define group boundaries, achieve organizational goals, and resolve priorities in dealing with the significant others in his status set.

Although it undoubtedly mediates in all stages of social interaction, the influence of the uniform can be most readily seen in the social placement of the other. Only after this initial question, "With whom am I dealing?", is answered does the actor enter the discursive process of interaction described by G. H. Mead. When dealing with a uniformed stranger, the question is answered clearly and almost instantaneously. The uniform wearer is a one-dimensional man who announces only the status he wears on his sleeve. The ambiguity ordinarily attached to strangers in modern urban society is absent for uniform wearers whose group membership, and perhaps rank, seniority, and prior achievements are proclaimed by their apparel.

The need for legitimating symbols is greatest in the city which simultaneously creates conditions leading to distrust of such symbols. While the uniforms of service groups such as the police, information clerks at transportation terminals, and public health nurses connote safety in an often hostile urban environment, the same environment may engender distrust of these very uniforms. Symbols may actually be what they seem and uniforms are then perceived as indicators of an oppressive group, often the relationship between police and minorities. Symbols may be misperceived or distorted; public health nurses are sometimes lumped together with other wearers of blue into a category of hated authority. Symbols may not be what they seem; due to imposters in the inner city, public health nurses may make preliminary phone calls to reassure clients whom they intend to visit (Int. 3).

The second process of social placement is the assessment of the status claimed by the stranger. We know who he purports to be, but can his assertion be verified? Again, the uniform provides an apparent answer. It validates the claim, by being an emblem and a certificate of legitimacy.

During a door-to-door search by the police for a missing child, I once noted that a plainclothes officer was accompanied by a uniformed officer who reassured residents of the identity of the detective. The reluctance to admit a stranger to one's apartment in the early morning hours was obviated by the sight of a uniform; the uniformed officer wore credentials for both.

In contrast, when an individual asserts membership in an upper social class by expensive attire, no comparable procedure of validation exists. In an anonymous urban society, the self-definition of prestige claimants has to be accepted at face value in lieu of detailed knowledge of their background. We are much less likely to doubt the authenticity of a man in a police uniform regardless of our attitudes toward the police. Correlatively, exposure of an imposter in uniform is usually more devastating, both to the wearer and the other, than the exposure of one in mink as a nouveau riche.

As a result of these two processes of placement, which may occur simultaneously, the uniform solves the problem of group boundaries. We know the identity of the stranger at the door, and we can recognize our peers in a uniformed group. But, we do not know that the uniform wearer will conform to group norms; the uniform wearer must also settle his own dilemma of multiple statuses. The answer to the latter two problems requires the examination of the dynamics of interaction in more detail.

Everyone who recognizes the uniform to any extent becomes an other who has some expectation of how the uniform wearer will behave and manifests these expectations in interaction. Obviously, though others may recognize a uniform, they may not be completely accurate in their knowledge of the duties or behavior of the concomitant status. At an extreme, even though they may not be aware of the type of occupation performed by an individual in a work uniform, they are aware of his membership in a service occupation and have formed some conception of his status and duties. Everyone, then, becomes an other and reacts primarily in terms of the wearer's master status, the principal clue he offers to his social identity.

The uniform provides only one set of norms in evaluating the wearer. With strangers in ordinary dress, several sets may be applicable, none as explicit as the single set pertaining to the police, for example. This is to say that the wearer does not have the protection of the status anonymity of the modern urban stranger. Wearers become closely identified with the uniformed status and only with this status. To escape their obligations as members of the group they often must remove their uniforms. The police may wear civilian dress when going to and from work to avoid being on public call. Uniformed individuals may remove their uniforms while engaging in pursuits which might disgrace their group, such as frequenting bars off-duty.

Philadelphia police were "forbidden to appear in public wearing only a portion of their uniform. This rule is designed to discourage a man from taking off his shirt or jacket and slipping into some place for drinks or some private business. This is also why some police trousers have wide stripes down the seams" (Rubinstein 1973, 446–47).

Whereas the Philadelphia police employ the uniform to insure accountability, in contrast, as previously mentioned, a Civil War colonel ordered his regiment to replace their distinctive Zouave uniforms with standard uniforms so that they would not be identified as turkey thieves (Haythornthwaite 1976, 128). In each instance, organizational heads employed social visibility as a tool, the former to enforce norms, the latter to evade them by submerging the unit in the anonymity of a common uniform.

The interaction of uniform wearer and viewer rests upon the unambiguity of the relevant norms and the casting of the viewer in the role of the other and judge. These norms may not always arise, however, from within the organization but may be created by outsiders and then adopted by the group. Kipling's image of the military was adopted by the army as a model. "Life very much imitated art in the Victorian-Edwardian army because, in discovering how Kipling saw them, or wished them to be, its members learned how to play themselves" (Keegan 1980, 36). Outsiders are not passive participants but have initiative and a stake in interaction with the uniform wearer.

Two patterns of disagreement between the wearer and observer emerge over the norms governing uniforms. In one instance, wearers view their uniforms in instrumental terms as tools to be changed as expediency demands. Outsiders, on the other hand, may see the uniform as subject to ceremonial norms and want it to be preserved intact as symbols of the organization for the outer world. Accordingly, the proposal to replace the traditional "bells" in the contemporary West German Navy with trouser-and-jacket uniforms was strongly opposed by nostalgic civilians, especially veterans.[5] In another situation, the roles are reversed, outsiders advocating an instrumental approach and wearers a ceremonial approach toward uniforms. Benjamin Franklin favored a simple military uniform patterned after Indian dress; the military have favored ornate and traditional uniforms. In both instances, the issue is the conflict between instrumental rationality and tradition.

The uniform influences wearers themselves; everyone with whom they interact is an other who proffers the same mirror. Since no other statuses, nor any touch of individuality, are recognized in the uniformed individual by others, wearers are encouraged to act primarily as occupants of their uniformed status. In one famous experiment, college students absorbed the demands of the uniformed statuses to which they were arbitrarily assigned. Half the group assumed the mock status of prison guard and wore the appropriate uniforms; the others became "convicts" and were given demeaning, effeminate smocks. Both types of clothing greatly reinforced the respective behaviors and internalized assertiveness or dependency (Zimbardo 1972).

The definition of one's status and duties may vary between peers and public, but both groups will agree on the key social position defined by the uniform. For organizational peers, the uniform underscores a common membership, allegiance to the same set of rules, and the probability of similar life experiences. To outsiders, the uniform stresses differences in status, norms, and way of life. The uniform serves, then, to bind the wearer to his peers and to separate him from outsiders.[6] These processes of segregation from the outer world and integration within a group are powerful forces which help to explain a great deal of the effects of uniforms. Additional and often unintended forms of segregation may be applied internally to achieve other distinctions within the group. Externally, others may attempt to borrow some of the attributes of the uniform wearer to achieve the benefits of such an identification or association.

Two sources of ego gratification are granted uniform wearers by virtue of their dress. From their own group, they will obtain self-esteem through conformity; from other groups, they will obtain self-regard by conflict.[7] From the former, they win approval and see themselves as "good" by living up to others' expectations. From the latter, they obtain autonomy and derive a sense of potency by opposing the demands of others. Although these processes of identity validation are available to all groups, the relevant groups are much less subject to doubt for those in uniform.

Because uniform wearers are encouraged to order the priorities and demands of the various statuses in their status sets in accordance with the group perspective, they may, in addition, very often flee to the safety of their uniform to avoid the anomie of ordinary life (Lyman & Scott 1970, 210–11). For these individuals, the multiplicity of the demands imposed by modern society is simplified by collapsing the status set to a single dimension. To the extent that uniform wearers have internalized the norms of their group, and to the extent that these demands are instrumental, organizational efficiency is thereby assured. But even where internalization has not been fully accomplished, uniformed individuals are subject to constraints by peers and outsiders who are aware of the norms to which they are expected to adhere.

The Context of Control

The uniform as a control device is based upon the existence of certain societal contexts. These are especially relevant in Western society where there emerged the modern bureaucratic structure and its concomitant ethos, the reliance upon a market economy and modern technology, a widespread division of labor, and urban anonymity.

Conditions may change within these broad contexts and render the uniform less effective as an instrument of control. Bureaucratic institutions, after they achieve dominance, may become "less total" in response to greater demands for individuality and lessen their control over members. The result may be reflected in the decreased stress upon membership in the institution as the master status—the departure from the traditional nun's habit, the reforms of Admiral Zumwalt which permitted the possession of civilian clothes aboard ship by all ranks, and the movement away from traditional prison uniforms.

To complicate the picture, however, uniformed individuals may at times reject the decreased emphasis upon uniforms and insist upon making it more of a master status than the institution requires. One of the objections to the uniform innovations in the United States Navy was precisely that they made the wearers less distinctive and merged them into an amorphous mass composed of other armed services and even uniformed civilians. Men who strongly identified with the army and their role as combat soldiers voluntarily wore uniforms off-duty, while those who rejected the military, headquarters clerks for example, were more likely to wear their civilian clothing under similar circumstances (Moskos 1970, 73–74). The increased use of uniforms among these individuals may be explained as a use of the uniform not for organizational control but rather as an ego enhancement device by the wearer. These two uses tend to accompany each other under normal conditions; it is only when they fall into sharp opposition that the distinction between them becomes apparent.

INSTITUTIONAL FACTORS IN CONTROL

Thus far, uniforms have been examined as a tool of control vis-a-vis the outside world with the uniformed organization viewed as a single monolithic institution. But no organization is a monolith, and this raises the problem of the dynamics of the uniform when internal differences are considered. The question requires a further examination of how the uniform segregates members from nonmembers and integrates uniform wearers into a cohesive unit. These processes, when applied internally, lead to new formal and informal groupings and often to unofficial forms of symbols which may later be recognized and legitimated. Segregation, followed by later reintegration, begins a set of processes consisting of the creation of new areas within which norms apply and the designation of new audiences with which uniform wearers communicate.

Internal Segregation and Reintegration

An organization beyond a given size must be subdivided into smaller units for administrative purposes. Students of administration have determined that the optimal span of command, the maximum number of units that can be controlled by an administrator, is about six to eight (Graicunas 1937, 183; Gulick 1937, 7–9). Given the concept of optimal size, a wide range of interesting consequences follow. With internal subdivision, the door is opened to centrifugal forces within the organization, since allegiance may become attached not to the parent body but rather to one of its components with which it is easier to identify. A recent chairman of the joint chiefs of staff has decried the parochial affiliations of service heads to their respective services rather than to the defense establishment as a whole. Special ties or affinities may arise between some units and enmity between others. Shaka, the charismatic founding father of the Zulu nation, discovered that his troops were much more likely to be enthusiastic about their units, the impi, than the larger political unit of the clan (Morris, Donald 1965, 50–52). As a result, he was obliged to garrison some units in widely separated kraals to avoid clashes.

One strategem to counteract the tendency toward centrifugal loyalties among smaller units is the adoption of a common uniform or insignia to minimize the importance of subdivisions. The United States Marine Corps maintains that the entire organization is an elite unit and therefore there is no need to demarcate special groups by adopting unit insignia which would detract from loyalty to the corps as a whole (Donovan 1967, 206). But the corps has vacillated between permitting unit patches when it expands during war and abolishing them after the postwar contractions. On an even broader scale, the Canadian Forces have adopted a common uniform for all three services for reasons of efficiency and cost and have apparently achieved, as a consequence, a greater common loyalty (Hellyer 1966, esp. 27).[8]

Another approach is to accept and encourage loyalty to subunits as a means of promoting esprit de corps. Admiral Heywood, a recent chief of naval operations, has considered the use of ships' insignia to instill "Pride and Professionalism" even at the risk of barroom brawls among ships' crews. A similar effort by the United States Army to heighten morale in the post-Vietnam era includes awarding unit patches very early in training; new shoulder insignia for rank, branch, and unit; and wearing berets of various colors to differentiate units (Ludvigsen 1978; NYT 6 Sept. 1980). Attempts to instill unit pride must necessarily include coordination at levels above the unit to counteract the disintegrative tendencies promoted by unit pride.

Part of the effort to encourage unit pride is through the recognition of elites within the organization. However, this runs afoul of a tendency, among the members themselves, to proliferate elites within elites. Aran describes the process among Israeli parachutists.

While the number of parachutists constantly grows, there are many attempts, obviously initiated by the jumpers themselves, to oppose this massive trend. One way of doing this is the creation of classes within the broad group of parachutists. . . . At the beginning, everyone who had five jumps was granted the privilege of wearing wings. Those who jumped seven or more times distinguished themselves by wearing red berets. Within this group, those who jumped more than fifty times received a little star attached to their wings. (1974, 149)

A similar pattern was noted among American paratroopers who received official insignia after five, thirty-five, and sixty-five jumps, and an unofficial award after one hundred (Sarkesian 1975, 98).

The formation of elites is a dialectical process, elites attempting to dissociate themselves symbolically from the mass which tries to join them or form their own select groups. This in turn leads to further dissociation symbolically by the established elites (Aran 1974, 149).[9]

The processes of separation and reintegration are displayed in the interaction of officers and enlisted men. The officer must have authority to command his men, but in modern democracies, and given the nature of contemporary warfare, that authority is most easily and efficiently exercised when the men he commands can readily identify with him. Uniforms therefore simultaneously express the separation and integration of hierarchy. Integration may be restored by dressing like enlisted men and adopting their weapons as was done by many generals in World War II who recoiled from the distant "chateau generalship" of their counterparts in World War I (Keegan 1977, 329–30). A similar process may be noted in the common informality of work uniforms in contrast to the ceremonial, status-bestowing formal uniforms. The recent use of command "baseball hats" in the United States Navy for informal duty which suggests teamwork is germane.[10] In the dress of officers, especially those of high rank who have greater leeway, either of the two tendencies may be given primacy—status emphasis and separation, or identification and integration. The flamboyance of Patton or Custer contrasts with the simplicity of Eisenhower or Grant. Flamboyance makes a distant hero of the leader, while simplicity emphasizes unity with his men.

Symbols of Rank

Uniforms indicate and accentuate differences in rank in the hierarchical structure of organizations. In military organizations, this function of uniforms emanated from the social distinctions of civilian life and is explicitly acknowledged in the United States Navy's history of its uniforms (USN 1981, app.2). The disparity between officer and enlisted man is expressed in a metaphor which compares the contemporary officer to a business executive, his nineteenth-century predecessor to a gentleman, and the enlisted man to a worker.

> The enlisted man's uniform was developed largely as a product of his surroundings, both geographically and technically. Unlike the officer's uniform which began as a reflection of his social status and evolved into one reflecting his environment, his garb reflected practicality and was devoid of superfluity. (ibid., p.2)
>
> From its inception, the United States Navy utilized as officers men who were generally a product of a higher social order. By becoming a naval officer, a man merely transferred the condition [sic] aspects of his background into a different profession. He would not forsake his code of conduct, educational level, mannerisms or least of all his dress by adopting a new means of livelihood. Thus the earliest officer uniforms identified the wearer as a gentleman of the maritime profession. His clothes closely paralleled the cut of civilian garments with color and accoutrements representing his nautical affiliation. (ibid., p.8)
>
> The Navy officers' dress [after World War I] had clearly left the trappings of the early 19th century "gentlemen" and its uniforms now reflected the civilian fashions for business managers. (ibid., p.12)

As this suggests, the uniform was related to class differences in origins and functions of officers and enlisted men.

In Medieval and Renaissance navies, the officers were military men in armor who fought the ships and were usually ignorant of seamanship while the enlisted men and warrant officers actually sailed them (Jarrett 1960, 6–8, 16). In the later sailing navy, the enlisted men performed the manual tasks while officers, by this time more knowledgeable of the sea, directed them. To the extent that uniforms were used, those of officers were more ornate (Jarrett 1960, 124; NHD 1966, pls. 1802, 1812). With the advent of modern machine technology, officers engaged in more active and dirty work, although with some resistance to becoming "chauffeurs", and had to operate in dirtier quarters. Accordingly, officers' uniforms have become more practical, less ornate, and perhaps closer to that of enlisted men (Jarrett 1960, 124; USN 1981, app.2 p.12).

The traditional bell-bottom uniform for enlisted men in the United States Navy was replaced by jacket-and-trousers uniforms similar to those of officers and chief petty officers in the early 1970's. The change was instituted in part by the desire of Admiral Zumwalt, then Chief of Naval Operations, to lessen the distinction between ranks as part of the post-Vietnam reforms (NT 15 Aug. 1977). A reversion to more traditional modes of organization in the United States Navy in the early 1980's included the restoration of the bell-bottoms and revocation of some of the earlier liberal policies. According to the new naval policies, uniforms should reflect "the separate responsibility levels [of officers and enlisted men]. . . . the officer's and senior petty officer's service uniform parallels civilian executive's attire" (NT 10 July 1978). This traditional outlook was shared by many of the enlisted men who, according to several polls, favored the return to the more distinctive bell-bottoms.[11]

Internal Community

The divisive influence of rank is counteracted, in part, by the integrating effects of an internal community created by the segregation of uniform wearers from the outside world. This segregation has very often established an internal democracy in which rank is of diminished importance, especially in elite units. Among parachutists, officers, even those of high rank, will line up with enlisted men to draw parachutes and share equally the possibility of receiving an improperly packed parachute (Just 1972, 136, 140–41). The comradeship within such units supersedes differences in rank; officers and enlisted men feel closer to each other than to corresponding ranks in other groups. Consequently, enlisted men of elite units often obey only their own officers and not outsiders (Sarkesian 1975, 97).

The uniform promotes democracy in civilian schools and military academies by eliminating the social class differences of the outer world (Coser 1962, 44; Gillis 1981, 169–70; Musgrove 1965, 159–60; Young & Willmott 1962, 175–77). The obverse side of the coin is that the school facilitates the erection of barriers between wearers and outsiders. The Prussian Education Ministry of the early 1920's deliberately used sartorial symbols to segregate students from working-class youth. In addition political insignia were banned and school caps substituted for them (Gillis 1981, 164). In these cases, the uniform serves an honorific function and elevates wearers above their peers.

The importation of the Japanese economic miracle into the United States and England included the use of uniforms by both executives and workers in a Honda plant in the United States and a Sony factory in England. Differences in rank were obscured and disputes with unions emerged over the ban on union insignia. Thus one set of insignia was used to suppress others.[12]

Varying degrees of equality often exist in an all-officer situation. To encourage the aristocratic nature of his officer corps and to emphasize their social equality regardless of position, Frederick the Great prevented his officers from wearing any badges of rank (Kitchen 1975, 16). In a similar fashion, the French army commanders during the Seven Years' War were simply *primes inter pares* (Kennett 1967, 35). In aristocratic British regiments, personal relationships among officers, regardless of rank, are emphasized more than protocol or rank (Perrott 1968, 144–45).

Apart from these instances, clearly defined indications of rank within the officers corps denote function, unit, and status within the organization. These insignia are both signals and symbols and their attainment, along with their accompanying rights and benefits, constitutes a goal. They thereby serve as incentive for the individual officer and as control by leaders.

CONTROL THROUGH THE TOLERATION OF DEVIATION

Part of the arsenal of techniques available to uniformed organizations is that of changing from the toleration of deviance to the insistence upon "going by the book''. This device is made possible by the existence of precise uniform regulations. Switching to a strict adherence to norms then heralds a new order and new organizational policies.

Even in the Israeli Army, which is stereotyped as casually dressed, casualness is partly a matter of official tolerance and can be rescinded to inaugurate change. In 1967 the dress codes were tightened in army units to indicate to reservists that troops were now on a wartime basis and that action was impending (Dayan 1967, 10). Military police were imported into the staging area, jails were set up, and other actions were taken. As a result of the 1973 war, Israeli soldiers were ordered to get hair cuts and to spruce up in order to tighten discipline (NYT 22 June 1975). Menachim Begin was known for his wearing of a tie and jacket amid the conventional informality of Israeli politicians. When he became Prime Minister another order was issued to tighten uniform discipline (NYT 10 Feb. 1979). Still, the Israeli Army remains more casual in dress than others; officers, for example, have no formal uniforms and dress only in field khaki.

WITNESSING AND ORGANIZATIONAL CONTROL

Though uniforms are an important means of control, their use may paradoxically boomerang after the wearer has already learned the skills of his job and has internalized the norms of his organization. If the wearer sees the uniform solely as a means of control, he may well feel that his skills and inner discipline are sufficient and therefore resent external controls as coercive, petty, and wasteful of time and effort. The controversy between the advocates of voluntarism (the reliance upon internal discipline), and of witnessing (the reliance upon external controls through observability) affords a test case of the functions of the uniform and the role of visibility within an organization.[13]

The issue is clearly raised in a recent controversy in the United States Navy over the restoration of traditional uniform norms which had been relaxed during the Vietnam era. A tightening of rules and a restoration of traditional standards, described as a ''Pride and Professionalism'' program, began in the early 1980's and included, besides a reversal of previous reforms, a return to the use of uniforms instead of civilian clothes by officers assigned to Washington, D.C. and the restoration of rank differences between enlisted men and petty officers (NT 23 Feb. 1981). The changes were part of a renewed emphasis upon tradition, formality, appearance, and the professional execution of ceremony (ibid.). In advocating the change, the Commandant of the Marine Corps decried the lack of ''uniformity'' and opposed options in uniforms which should be considered traditional and an unchanging reference point in a constantly changing world (NT 30 July 1979; 9 Nov. 1981). Needless to say, other military services exhibited the same tendencies. The return to tradition may be partially ascribed to President Reagan's desire to see more uniforms in Washington (NT 30 Mar. 1981).

The response by service personnel reflects the debate between internal and external discipline as forms of control by an organization. While deploring the

excesses of the 1970's, a lieutenant commander stationed at the Pentagon criticized the obligatory wearing of uniforms.

> But this pride thing is supposed to come from within, not mandated from without. . . .
> I agree enthusiastically with the entire concept of P & P [Pride and Professionalism]. . . .
> But making the wearing of the uniform mandatory in Washington five days a week seems
> niggling and somehow contrary to the spirit of personal probity and accountability that
> P & P seems designed to foster. . . . Wouldn't it be nice to see more uniforms and know
> that every man and woman wearing them did so because they wanted to? . . . Some of
> your proud professionals out there want a day or two, once in a while, when they can just
> *think* blue and gold, not be told to wear it. (NT 6 Apr. 1981)

A retired officer cites the instance of Israel whose egalitarian forces have
become a stock argument for the advocates of voluntarism. "Its Army and Navy
win with success we should envy. But all officers and men call each other by first
names, uniforms are casual and, in general, most elements of our 'Pride and
Professionalism' not only are repugnant but not even thought necessary" (NT 24
Aug. 1981).

These defenders of voluntarism assume a highly socialized membership whose
normative commitment is unproblematic. Uniforms remain essential, however,
where not everyone has learned the essential norms and skills. The Israeli Army
is a case in point. While the infantry and parachute troops manifest
egalitarianism and informality in uniforms and interaction, the armored corps, in
sharp contrast, wears regulation uniforms and undergoes strict discipline (Luttwak & Horowitz 1975, 190–91). Internal discipline, a heritage of the kibbutz
movement and of its military offspring, the Palmach, can still be relied upon to
provide the motivation for the infantry and parachute troops. These branches
understand their tasks and know how their contributions fit into the overall
scheme of things; they can therefore perform their duties on their own. Internal
discipline is, however, insufficent for newly arrived immigrants and certainly
does not furnish the background for understanding tank technology among armored personnel (Etzioni 1959–60). The solution, therefore, is to have armored
soldiers, who have limited insight into their tasks, follow detailed working
procedures, even if they are not fully understood, and adhere to a formal clothing
and disciplinary procedure.[14]

Protestors against the strict uniform discipline embodied in the Pride and
Professionalism program are saying in effect that they possess sufficient internal
discipline and insight to warrant freedom from external enforcement. Indeed,
one contributor makes the intriguing point that the use of uniforms may be the
result rather than the cause of discipline, that the uniform is worn out of a feeling
of pride and loyalty which may even encompass a uniformed service's irra-
tionality. This outlook transforms a job into a calling. "The Navy is a way of
life, not just a job. It is a way of life that demands the most a person has to give.
Long hours, hard work, boredom, and, at times, doing something that you do not
like" (NT 21 Sept. 1981).

MASSING: THE UNIFORMED GROUP SUI GENERIS

Thus far, I have examined the uniform within the context of interaction between a small number of uniform wearers and outsiders. When the context is altered and the uniformed appear in large groups, when we see the uniform en masse rather than seriatim, then drastic changes occur both in social relationships and in the symbolism of the uniform.

Perhaps the greatest change is in the relationship of uniform wearers to their group. As detached individuals, they are representatives of their organization whose existence is implicit behind the uniform and is one of the reasons for the very use of the uniform. In a massed formation, individuals no longer function as representatives but instead are submerged components of the organization. The structure of a massed group is explicitly stated. We are now aware of the relationship between the police officer and his platoon and no longer need to question the legitimacy of the detached representative and his right to act on behalf of the group. In a group formation, the uniform is not necessary as a certificate of legitimacy for any individual.

The question of legitimacy persists but now on a group level. We no longer inquire into the legitimacy of the relationship between individuals and their organization but rather into the links between their organization and other groups or the entire society. Our concern is now with the right of a massed uniformed group to parade, demonstrate, or perform whatever function they purport to possess. The right of official groups, those supporting the state or manifesting its power, is less likely to be disputed, except in instances of mass misbehavior such as brutality, drunkenness, or rioting. The illegitimate massing and the use of "illegitimate uniforms" by unofficial groups such as political extremists are much more likely to be contested.

The individual spectator is even less likely to dispute a massed group than a uniformed individual. At the group level, the image of massed power replaces the legitimacy of a representative as an issue for the spectator. The individual onlooker was helpless in the face of the Nazi juggernaut in street or massed rallies. For a group, then, the uniform operates, not as the badge of certification of group membership, but instead as an indication of the common purpose and organization of a group. The impact of the uniform in the massing phenomenon rests in a new set of mechanisms embodied in the power that uniformed assemblages generate.

The group's power may be presented for others to witness by the use of clothing, not necessarily a uniform, or by participating in a mass assemblage. The participants themselves are witnesses to their collective presence, unity, and power. They draw their individual strength from the mass strength they suggest by their collective presence. In the mass context, symbols indicate the mobilization of individuals on behalf of a common belief, an ideological body count. Any sort of common emblem will serve. For instance, a militant Puerto Rican group fashioned a "uniform" out of commonly available and inexpensive items consisting of white pants, black shirts, and black berets.[15] None of these items worn alone or by only one individual would occasion comment. Worn as an ensemble by many, they create a symbolic sleight of hand and become transformed into powerful political symbols. The display of standardized and uniform symbols suggests to the observer not only the power of numbers, but also the disciplined and coordinated adherence to a cause. The group has become organized and exhibits disciplined power that differs sharply from the raw anarchy of a crowd. The Nazis may have made the most scientific use of the mass assembly of uniformed personnel in their parades, rallies, and demonstrations. The Russian May Day parades in Red Square may outshine all others in the use of numbers to suggest brute power.

Witnessing has many forms. In court trials, it indicates support for one side or the other by ethnic groups in distinctive dress or by racial minorities (NYT 10 Dec. 1979; 28 Feb. 1980; 29 Feb. 1980). A trial lawyer described the intimidating effect of an obvious bloc of ethnic or racial individuals upon counsel and witnesses who felt threatened by their sheer presence (Halbert 1978). Gang members have appeared in court wearing group colors to show solidarity with members on trial (NYT 7 Sept. 1979). Here it is the spectators who wear the distinctive symbols while the key actors are in ordinary dress.

Group witnessing may occur implicitly without the intent of the participants. An aspirant to the Roman Catholic priesthood was greatly moved by the sight of a mass of Jews in prayer shawls which indicated the equality of all in a similar religious status (Palliere 1928, 20–22).

Uniforms in massed formations emphasize the loss of individuality and dehumanize their wearers. When thousands are alike, no one individual seems to matter. In some formations, individuals are aligned by size which heightens the impression of a single important status to which all belong. The extreme is reached in formations such as West Point parades where cadets are arranged in line by height, giving the spectator the impression of a line of uniformly tall cadets.

NOTES

1. My discussion is similar to Hughes on master statuses (1945).

2. The spread of this uniform may indicate the great drive to establish legitimacy by borrowing established symbols. Of course, the police may also be motivated by the loss of status.

3. A striking example of the ludic element was the recent attempt to play with sex statuses by the adoption of unisex dress. With widespread use, the dress lost its ludic quality and became a new group norm, illustrating the dialectical interplay between norms and the ludic element.

4. The categorization of membership by sartorial signs operates in society as a whole through stratification, the designation of minorities and of pariah statuses. See chapter two. When sartorial signs fail, other symbolic systems come into play. Indian untouchables are recognized by speech and deportment as well as dress (WSJ 24 Oct. 1977).

5. See chapter seven.

6. For a similar and earlier distinction, see Simmel on the function of fashion in uniting and separating groups (1957, esp. 544–47).

7. See Gouldner for a discussion of self-esteem and self-regard, and for the distinction between consensual and conflictual validation of the sense of identity (1970, 221–22).

8. The Canadian Minister of National Defence announced his intention in 1984 of reverting to distinctive uniforms for each of the armed services (Nanaimo Free Press 21 Sept. 1984; Winnepeg Free Press 15 Nov. 1984).

9. Officers who have risen from the ranks face discrimination from officers entering through other channels. The former have on occasion preferred to drop their commissions and revert to their original enlisted status (Warren 1946). See chapter six for a contrasting situation.

10. The New York City Police Department has adopted the baseball cap for optional patrol duty because it is cheaper, more comfortable, and was already in use by emergency and other units. It cannot be used by officers or on parade duty (WSJ 13 Aug. 1984).

11. Public participation in the drive to restore bell-bottoms is described in chapter seven.

12. See chapter nine.

13. These issues also relate to the centuries-old religious controversy between those who would display their religious beliefs and those who would keep them private. See chapter three. The controversy is further rooted in the difference between the requirements of functional rationality which is more likely to entail visibility and substantial rationality which centers on internal discipline (Mannheim 1940, 51–54).

14. The Nahal, a youth farming corps of the Palmach, had problems in the postindependence military establishment. Impelled by a desire to preserve their democratic tradition of self-discipline and individualism, they rejected formal, imposed discipline by refusing to stand at attention or salute officers after the inauguration of permanent ranks and insignia, polish boots, or wear shirttails inside their trousers (Schiff 1974, 90).

15. IRA members were convicted in 1974 for wearing dark glasses in defiance of a British law prohibiting the wearing of uniforms for political reasons (Ewing 1975, 107). They are also described as wearing black trousers and shirts (NYT 30 Nov. 1974). The colored shirts of extremist movements between World Wars I and II must not be overlooked (Klein 1940).

6

Nonconformity: The Actual Uses of the Uniform

In this chapter, I shall pose a deceptively simple question, "Never mind regulations, what uniforms did they actually wear?" The query raises the issue and meaning of deviancy from uniform codes. As a mode of communication, nonconformity in uniforms informs us about the other group affiliations and values of the individual and about the reactions of the uniformed group. Furthermore, examination of nonconformity aids in the definition of the circumstances, rare, as we shall see, when total conformity is possible. Finally, nonconformity leads to changes in the norms as innovations work their way up the bureaucratic ladder and are accepted.

The study of nonconformity will include the internal and external causes of under and overconformity, and the physical constraints upon adherence to sartorial norms.

NONCONFORMITY—AN OVERVIEW

Actual use of the uniform may vary greatly from the stipulated norms. The contrast between the Army of the Potomac and Sherman's army in the Victory Parade of May 22–23, 1865 in Washington illustrates the disparity in conformity on a ceremonial occasion when one might have expected a greater degree of formality and conformity.

The contrast in the two armies was a most ludicrous one. As I have already stated, our officers had shown much anxiety to have us present a very soldierly appearance as we marched in review, and, much to our disgust, had insisted upon our drawing new caps and wearing white gloves, but Sherman's men went to the other extreme. One would have supposed, as he observed them, that they were making their renowned march through Georgia, instead of marching in review through the streets of Washington. . . . There were evidently no attempts to keep their lines closed up and well-dressed as they advanced, but each man marched to suit his own convenience. Their uniforms were a cross between the regulation blue and the Southern gray. The men were sunburned, while their hair and beards were uncut and uncombed; they were clad in blue, gray, black and brown; huge slouched hats, black and gray, adorned their heads; their boots were covered with the mud they had brought up from Georgia; their guns were of all designs. . . . (Gerrish 1882, 298–99)

These impressions seem to challenge our previous analysis of the uniform. How can the use of uniforms be described as a system of normatively prescribed communication if its norms are not adhered to? "Talking" to one another verbally, sartorially, or by any other system is difficult if the rules of "grammar" are ignored. On the other hand, using spoken language as an analogy, need we adhere precisely to norms to be understood? Dialects and ungrammatical statements, within limits, are understood with varying degrees of difficulty. Deviations from the norm may themselves carry messages of regional residence, class membership, or educational background of the speakers. Similarly, sloppiness, or deviation from the uniform norms, may not prevent us from recognizing the wearer's organizational affiliation. Instead, sloppiness may also describe behavior in a role and self-definition. The lowered morale of New York City police officers was indicated by their poor grooming (NYT 6 Nov. 1976).[1] To revert to the example of Sherman's troops, their appearance stems from an old tradition of the nonconformity of such military elites as the riflemen of the American Revolution and contemporary special forces.

The norms for uniforms are more precise and demanding than those of ordinary dress. Though we are expected to live up to the norms of fashion, perfect adherence would be disastrous because we are also expected to instill a personal touch. No such deviation is anticipated from the ideal norms governing uniforms. We are thus dealing with a paradox, deviation from norms in an area where it is not institutionally provided for, which can be best understood by an examination of the wearer's status position.

The requirements of a status are often only partially accepted by all of its participants. Deviations in uniforms are more apparent because of their standardization and therefore readily interpreted as a rejection of norms.

In examining the rejection of group norms through individual deviation from uniform codes, several distinctions are useful. First, the target of rejection must be identified. It may be opposition to the uniform itself, to the uniformed position as the master status, or to the group represented by the uniform. The source of rejection also needs to be specified since the relationship between the uniformed and other groups often causes individuals under cross pressure to reject to some degree the uniformed status or group.

An organization's members may accept their group status but refuse the premise that control is best exercised through uniforms. One objection is that uniforms create obstacles to performance. Contemporary Roman Catholic priests and nuns, and European worker-priests have attempted to alter or even abandon the clerical quasi uniform.[2] The separation of the clergy from the laity, one of the results of the quasi uniform, is felt to be a handicap to the fulfillment of clerical obligations as redefined by some members. They advocate blurring the distinction between clergy and laity as a means of reaching the unchurched masses. Redefinition of the clerical status, which entails an altered relationship to superiors and the public, is manifested partly by changes in the language of dress.

Another objection to uniforms is their denial of individuality or the uniqueness of a special status. Police officers may want to escape from the "bag", or uniform, to attain the greater autonomy of nonuniformed status. Similarly, in World War II, many irregular units were manned by those who liked military life but not the standardization imposed by the rigid uniform regulations of conventional forces. Elites within larger uniformed groups attempt to distinguish themselves from the run-of-the-mill member by unofficial changes in the uniform, the twenty-mission crushed hat of American pilots. "Pink" trousers of overseas officers in World War I originally served the same purpose. The relevant reference group in such cases is not the entire organization nor the governing body, but rather a segment deemed superior because of experience, expertise, or mode of selection.

Discontent may be expressed, not with the uniformed status itself, but with its position as a master status. For instance, soldiers in occupying armies may discard their uniforms in off-duty hours, often against regulations, to establish closer relationships with the civilian population. Thus, while control of the uniformed status by the institution may be completely acceptable, there is often a resistance to total control.

Finally, the rejection of the uniform may represent opposition to the group itself. The altered uniform is worn, in this instance, to express opposition to the group short of leaving or destroying it. In Vietnam uniforms were drastically modified by love beads and peace slogans (NYT 28 Aug. 1970). Like the worker-priests, the protesting soldier still retains some ties to the organization but, unlike the worker-priests, he doubts the basic purpose or legitimacy of the group.

What causes rejection of the uniform? One source is conflict between two organizations, each with its distinctive set of symbols, vying for control over the master status. Another is the attempt of a group to preserve its monopoly over symbols and status in the face of attempts at control by an intervening group. Such instances include disputes over occupational dress codes (companies versus unions), the National Guard versus government employees unions, and school dress codes versus individual rights. Where the dress mandated by the organization consists of uniforms, conflicts over dress become conflicts over uniforms.[3]

Professionals may be subject to the conflicting demands of their organizations

and professional associations. To resist complete control by the uniformed services, British and Commonwealth military chaplains retained symbols of their
profession even while on active duty. "Unlike the practice in the American armed
forces, RAF chaplains wear the clerical collar as part of their uniform. . . . The
basic regulation identifies the chaplain as a military officer while the collar is a
constant reminder that he is, after all, a clergyman" (Zahn 1969, 100). Similar
efforts to assert the superiority of professional status may be displayed by visiting
doctors who refuse to wear the white coats of staff doctors in hospitals (Coser
1962, 18; Jones, Maxwell, 1953, 52).

Racial and ethnic affiliations may present another source of status reinterpretation. In the United States Army, a recent attempt to incorporate racial symbols
into uniforms was successfully made by black soldiers who received permission
to wear Afro hairstyles while on duty. On the other hand, the United States Air
Force prohibited an orthodox Jewish officer from wearing a yarmulke on duty
(NT 11 June 1984). Efforts by military personnel to use turbans have also met
with failure.

RESISTANCE TO THE WORKPLACE AS A TOTAL INSTITUTION

Recently, some employers have used uniforms to gain greater control over the
organizational status of their employees. In effect, they have attempted to give
the workplace the characteristics of total institutions by excluding from dress any
indications of other status or group affiliation. In the National Guard, civilian
workers have resisted in order to retain the conventional definition of the work
status as only one of a set, a dominant status to be sure but not a monopolistic
one.[4] Resultant legal proceedings provide excellent material for the study of
nonconformity to uniform codes.[5]

The National Guard and Employees Unions

An additional source of friction, aside from the conflict between uniformed
and external organizations, may be the importation of civilian work attitudes into
the uniformed organization. As a result, the uniformed status may be reduced to
a mere occupation comparable to a civilian job. The contrast in work attitudes
has been variously described as that between the occupational and the professional or institutional definitions of work (Janowitz 1977; Moskos 1977).

Nothing highlights the intrusion of occupational attitudes into the domain of
uniforms, and the reaction by employers, as sharply as the recent legal battle,
before labor relations panels, between the National Guard of several states and
exempted technicians. These are individuals who serve in a dual capacity as full
time civilian employees of the National Guard and, since legislation of 1967, as
enlisted men of the Guard. In their military role, they participate in the same
weekend drills and summer training programs as other "weekend warriors".

Since the National Guard requires them to wear uniforms not only for their stint as part-time soldiers but also during their work week, the ensuing conflict between civilian work attitudes and the military attitudes, embodied in uniforms, has led to controversy between the Guard and employees' unions.

The National Guard contends that the use of the uniform, generally fatigues, is essential for technicians at all times to reflect the military nature of the Guard. The National Guard Bureau further argues that the technician not only should be able to perform his daily function but should also be mentally prepared for mobilization and therefore able to go instantly from employee to soldier.[6]

The organizational structure of the National Guard is basically military and the daily work of the National Guard technician is totally involved with the military purpose of the National Guard's preparedness for the contingency of a callup or mobilization. . . . an organization which is military in nature must manifest a military presence and, the requirement to wear the uniform, viewed in "the context of the chosen mode of organization for the National Guard" is the outward reflection of the military nature of the National Guard. (Consol. Dec. 1977, 12–13)

To achieve these ends, the uniform is even more important for technicians than for the regular armed forces since the latter may also rely "upon external standards, rules, and customs" (Nat. Gd. Bur. 1977). The uniform is also important as a means of differentiating between National Guard technicians and other Federal employees (Consol. Dec. 1977).

The hearing officer for the Federal Labor Relations Board concluded that while the uniform would be helpful in reflecting the military nature of the Guard and in increasing readiness for mobilization, it was not essential (ibid., 13–19). More significantly for our purposes,

for the most part National Guard technicians are employed on military installations out of view of the general public or most other Federal Government organizations. Thus, it appears unlikely that members of the general public or even other Federal Government organizations normally have the opportunity to observe National Guard technicians performing technician duties. Moreover, apart from this consideration, the agency does not establish why it is essential to the accomplishment of the National Guard's mission to distinguish National Guard technicians from other Federal civilian employees. (ibid., 14–15)

The position of the National Guard seems to stem from the transference of the military concept of total status control to the civilian job area. Uniforms are desirable not only because of their effect upon job performance, but also for extraneous reasons such as differentiating technicians from other workers and to prepare for mobilization. The Guard's stance results in a drive for a monopolization of the occupational status.

For their part, technicians contend that they are civilian employees in civilian positions during their work week rather than soldiers. Wearing the uniform was contested only in the civilian phase, not during military service. The objections of the technicians to the uniform during the civilian work week consist, first, of the inability to wear clothing on the job that is comfortable and safe. In testimony during a hearing, an Air Force National Guard employee complained of being compelled to wear a hat and a tucked-in fatigue jacket which made hot weather even more onerous; hats had to be worn on flight lines despite the dangers from propellers (Assoc. Civ. Tech. 1972, 23, 31). The conflict between the military uniform code and civilian standards of occupational dress is apparent.

Second, the military uniform subjected wearers to hierarchical supervision that was more rigid than that of civilian industrial bureaucracies. They were obligated to obey all officers whereas, as one technician put it, in comparable civilian jobs only two supervisors, an immediate, and perhaps a final supervisor, would have been heard from (ibid., 40). Hierarchical considerations were a disturbing factor when the employee in his technical capacity evaluated superior officers (Pa. NG 1975, 174–75). The uniform also created problems for enlisted workers who interacted with superior officers as union bargaining agents (ibid.).

Third, the uniform and its master status interfere with the compartmentalization of statuses that usually characterizes the civilian by inhibiting the ability to shuttle between statuses. When the uniform was worn to and from the job, the wearer could not divest himself of his military identification, resulting in harassment and the damning of one off-duty technician as a "Kent State National Guardsman" by passersby (Assoc. Civ. Tech. 1972, 62; Pa. NG 1975, 154–55). The uniform also curtailed the freedom to visit bars and to shop after work (Assoc. Civ. Tech. 1972, 41; Pa. NG 1975, 162–63).

Opposition to Military Hair Codes

Military hair codes also restrict status shuttling and constitute a major source of dissatisfaction. Although at first it might not appear to be part of the uniform, hair has long been subject to military regulation because of its contribution to the appearance of the uniform wearer. Whereas modern hair codes prescribe primarily a neat and soldierly appearance, older codes called for queues and the powdering of hair in the eighteenth century, and for mustaches in many units of the nineteenth and earlier centuries.

Attitudes toward hair in uniformed organizations are shaped by pragmatic considerations of safety, effectiveness and hygiene, associations with political ideology, connotations of masculinity, and, as with all codes, a vehicle for instilling discipline. In this context, my sole concern will be with hair as a deterrent to status segmentation.

Hair, like race and sex, provides a physical sign of status which cannot be as easily changed as uniforms or other types of clothing. Raymond Firth does report, however, that full-time servicemen have resorted to longhaired wigs for off-duty hours, and part-time reservists to shorthaired wigs for their periodic drill (1973, 292).

Many of the cases brought before labor panels involve the problem of hair

codes which render the transition between civilian and military statuses difficult
(Am. Fed. Govt. Emp. 1972; Assoc. Civ. Tech. 1972). The challenge to the
grooming codes is also reflected by the spate of court cases that involve police
and fire departments as well as the armed services (NYT 5 Sept. 1976; 6 Apr.
1976; WSJ 25 Feb. 1975b).

Besides the difficulties in shuttling between statuses, another reason for dislik-
ing hair codes is stated by a New York City fireman. "If you're single and you
cut your hair according to regulations, you have to have a pretty good personality
to get the girl" (NYT 4 Oct. 1980; also NT 14 Nov. 1977). Opposition to hair
codes is therefore particularly great, not surprisingly, among young uniform
wearers.[7]

Short hair also separates servicemen from the civilian population as a whole in
the United States and Europe, whether on duty or on leave (NYT 21 Apr. 1975;
NT 28 Aug. 1978; 4 Dec. 1978). However, some servicemen welcome the
opportunity to separate themselves from civilians. "I cut my hair short and feel
just 'fine' with the status quo. . . . As long as the rules of our 'occupation' and
our 'employers' require hair length to meet certain standards, it is our duty to
comply" (NT 9 Oct. 1978).

As a wry reminder of the importance of the historical context of symbols,
whereas the older generation interprets the recent revival of short hair for males
as a return to the military look, the younger generation sees it as a reflection of
punk and new wave trends in music and also as rebellion against their longhaired
parents (NYT 7 Sept. 1980).

EXTERNAL STRATIFICATION AND UNIFORMS

Class as an Alternative Reference Group

One of the most important reasons for opposition to uniforms has been the
wearer's social standing in society. The traditional aristocratic disdain of uniforms and uniform wearers is symptomatic of the influence of class on attitudes
toward uniforms. Class affiliations act as countervailing forces to the uniformed
organization's pressure to erase all other social statuses of its members and create
a brotherhood with a common organizational status. When external positions
intrude and serve as alternative organizing principles, then clothing no longer
relates solely to the structure of the group but to the outside world as well.

Uniformed organizations in effect mandate status inconsistency in that their
internal statuses need bear no relationship to external positions. Entrants into
service academies are forbidden to discuss their families, or to possess funds
beyond their pay. This inconsistency is possible because of the monastic conditions and the total suppression of evidence of previous statuses. Inconsistencies
become less severe because other statuses become less salient. They can be
eliminated totally only by becoming a one-dimensional individual with only a
uniform status.

Status consistency occurs when organizational dress reflects the external class of the wearer. The academic dress of Oxford and Cambridge reflected, until recently, the social origins of students who were divided into the nobility, sons of the nobility, commoners who paid tuition, and endowed scholars (Cunnington & Lucas 1978, 221–22). In a reflection of the interplay of forces, all students eventually clamored for the academic dress of the endowed scholars because of the latter's superior abilities. For some time in the nineteenth century, after the establishment of nursing schools in the wake of the reforms by Florence Nightingale, middle-class students wore different uniforms from those of the lower class (Ewing 1975, 45–46).

Status consistency is also found in the incorporation of civilian status into military uniforms. The officers of the Royal Navy petitioned the king in 1740 to grant them uniforms as a recognition of their "rightful place in society" rather than as officials in an organization (Lewis, M. 1957, 140). Similarly, midshipmen were given uniforms later in the century to indicate their position as gentlemen (Lewis, M. 1948a, 221). Very frequent references are found in the literature to gentlemen serving in the armies of the American Revolution in a civilian capacity who were clad in clothing similar to that of officers in order to maintain their high civilian status.[8]

In civilian life, English domestics derived their position in the below stairs hierarchy from their masters' status. Among the servants of several families, gathered for example at a country weekend, precedence would be established on the basis of their employers' rank. Whereas the servants of officers in the nineteenth-century British army could sport a black cockade in their hats, the servants of enlisted men, even "Gentlemen who are N.C.O.'s and privates in Volunteer Rifle Corps", could not (Cunnington & Lucas 1967, 380).

These inconsistencies were not always construed as a problem. At Trafalgar, they allowed enlisted men to orient themselves by class distinctions imported from civilian life.

Here could be seen the whole contrast between the ranks of the navy, and the strata of society: the men stripped to the waist, barefooted, with kerchiefs tied around their heads to protect their ears from the blast of the guns—and the officers dapper and elegant in frock-coats with epaulettes, immaculate silk breeches and stockings, and silver-buckled shoes. The contrast itself was reassuring. To the people, the captain was a superior being, whether they liked him or not, a man from a different world: he knew what was happening, he had talked to Nelson; and if he remained as elegant and unperturbed as usual and calmly spoke of a glorious victory, then a glorious victory it would be. (Howarth 1969, 140–41)

Aristocratic Rejection of the Uniform

Aristocratic rejection means that one is "above" the symbolism applicable to inferior organizational statuses and lesser breeds; the rules governing uniforms are not relevant to such aristocrats. Rejection of these symbols places the aristocrat above the organization and denies the latter's claim to priority of status ascription. The rejection need not stem from dislike, rebellion, or *ressentiment* but simply from the denial of the relevance of ordinary symbols to extraordinary individuals. Their claim to membership in superior classes allows for aristocratic dress codes to take priority. An aristocracy may insist upon the primacy of its class membership even while in the armed services, and may show its resistance to institutional control by departure from uniform regulations. The Duke of Cambridge, commander-in-chief during the latter part of the nineteenth century, punished a subaltern by ordering him to wear his uniform in London (Turner, E. 1956, 239).

The Spanish nobles serving in the King's Guard of Noblemen, founded in 1646, would not wear uniforms and were therefore clad in a surcoat bearing the royal arms while on active service (Kannik 1968, 145). Evidently the acceptance of the king's livery was more congenial to aristocratic norms than the prototypical uniform. The French nobility of the eighteenth century often made it a point of honor to defy regulations and not wear cuirasses in battle; this led to unnecessary casualties but, more importantly, maintained their dignity (Kennett 1967, 69–70). Honor, a patrimonial value, lingered within the burgeoning bureaucratic structure.

In the Royal Air Force during World War II, pilots in the Auxiliary Air Force, an upper-class preserve, wore bright scarves with their uniforms and lined their jackets with red silk (Deighton 1979, 52). One ace was convinced that he had failed to get into a prestigious AAF unit because he was not a fox hunter (Johnson 1957, 3).

General James Gavin describes the dress of an elite group of British officers in 1944 when efficiency and morale were at their highest.

The thought crossed my mind that they had better do something about the appearance of the Guards Armored officers before the King arrived. They customarily wore old corduroy trousers and chukka boots. Frequently they wore gay-colored scarves. Vandeleur and all his officers in the Irish Guards always wore bright green scarves. The only items of uniform they wore were a battle jacket and their headgear. However, under their battle jackets many of them wore colorful sweaters that hung six or eight inches below the jackets. . . . one of the senior British officers appeared wearing a robin's-egg-blue sweater. It seemed to extend halfway from his waist to his knees. He was sent back. After the war a British writer observed, "At the time the British Army was at its best, its uniform discipline was at its worst." (1978, 209)

In these British units, another aristocratic tenet was that of the superiority of the gentleman amateur over the professional. As one critic noted, "In the Brigade of Guards the officers are gentlemen, not professionals. And this was even truer fifty years ago" (Green 1976, 203).[9] The superiority of these officers was manifested by their rising above the symbolism of the conventional uniform and wearing uniforms altered under the personal supervision of the regimental adjutant to fit very tightly. The uniform was converted into the dress of a military dandy (ibid.). The same effect of "degrading" the uniform was achieved by wearing civilian clothing on military duty ranging from fur muffs, sneakers, and bags (very wide trousers popular in the 1920's) to hunting clothes. Elsewhere, a British regular officer reports the disdain with which he was received in a Territorial regiment (a volunteer unit) (Ellis 1980, 330–31).

As part of the same aristocratic pattern, technical skills such as artillery, engineering, or armor in modern times were for long periods thought worthy only for officers of bourgeois origins and were barely tolerated in many European armies (Vagts 1959, 52–58, 141).[10] "Skill of an obscure, mathematical, and technological kind threatened to make old-fashioned courage and muscular prowess useless. . . . Nobles and conservatively minded soldiers in general clung energetically to the old-fashioned, muscular definition of battle. Artillerymen with their cold-blooded mathematics seemed subversive of all that made a soldier's life heroic, admirable, worthy" (McNeill 1982, 172).

This manifestation of superiority does not belong only to an outmoded military mentality. Similar instances in civilian life reveal that aristocrats and upper-class individuals may not feel obligated to adhere to conventional class symbols. A footman snubbed an elderly caller without a mustache or smart clothes, signs of upper-class position, only to discover that he had snubbed the Duke of Westminister (Huggett 1977, 45).[11]

OVERCONFORMITY

Overconformity is a form of deviation in that, as in underconformity, the individual departs from the accepted or accustomed range of conformity. In this instance he rises above the norm. Overconformity has several forms and functions. It indicates an individual's strong effort to identify with the organization or to obtain promotion, "brown nosing" in army jargon. It includes the overly conscientious penitent who requires an even higher standard of himself than the church exacts, or the individual who is more royalist than the king. Overconformity may also be deliberately designed to subvert an organization as with "Private Schweik" whose personal rebellion against the Austro-Hungarian army consisted of obeying literally every command of his superiors. Departures from the norm, intended or not, may be disconcerting to authority.

The institutionalization of extreme conformity occurs when an organization sets impossible standards of dress that cannot be met by ordinary procedure. Sillitoe, himself an RAF veteran, describes in his novel, as we have noted, how a soldier serving as battalion marker was carried onto the prescribed spot on the parade ground before a review so that "not a speck of dust or wrinkle would be picked up on boots or trousers or belt or rifle while walking there himself" (1977, 8).

John Masters portrays his striving for ritualistic perfection while a Sandhurst cadet as departing from any possible norm of military efficiency.

I cleaned my rifle with methylated spirits, wax and Silvo, to the point where it shone like the morning; and I loosened the mechanism and fastenings until the slightest movement caused it to give out a loud clank and any attempt to fire it would have caused an explosion. . . . I cleaned the hobnails under my boots. . . . I bought a set of old buttons and a cap badge from a senior; these were probably ten years old, and the design no longer stood out above the smooth surface to catch shadow and old dried polish. (1968, 43)

Vagts defines militarism as the adherence to norms other than those of combat efficiency (1959, 13–14). Overconformity may also indicate adherence to criteria other than military efficiency, for example the perpetuation of symbols. An institution may become a special repository of "pure" symbols; military academies serve that purpose for uniformed services. Their function as repositories may also be explained as planned dilution, in that acolytes are taught the highest possible standards in expectation of a diminution of ideals after graduation. Selection of military academies for this function is partially due to the identification of youth with idealism and hence with the perpetuation of important organizational norms (Davis, K. 1940).

Overconformity can be a species of what Merton calls "ritualism", or the adherence to means—in this instance the perfect uniform as a tool—to the extent of losing sight of the appropriate goal, that of efficiency in combat (1957, 184–87). What assumes primary importance is not the skill of troops but rather the impression they create in the eyes of their superiors, the public, the enemy, and themselves. Examples of the ritualistic emphasis include the Russian Guard which could not be used in combat during the Napoleonic wars lest casualties among these beautifully attired troops displease the Czar; in the period of military dandyism after Napoleon's defeat when war was thought obsolete, British cavalry uniforms were so tight that wearers could not raise their sword arms.

INSTITUTIONAL SOURCES OF DEVIATION

In a previous chapter, I examined the segregation and reintegration of the organizational components as a means of social control. Paradoxically, these same principles of social structure also create deviation from uniform norms. The use of the uniform suppressed individuality by standardizing the occupants of the same status, making them interchangeable, and attempting to create the image of a homogeneous group. This suppression may be rejected by a subgroup that attempts to assert its distinctiveness through its own unauthorized symbolism. These informal, internal differentiations are based upon principles similar to those used by organizations to separate themselves from the rest of society.

Informal Segregation and Integration

Oddly enough, symbols of rank, unit, and specialty, which one might a priori think essential for the performance of a uniformed organization, stem in part from the lower echelon, often for nonrational reasons. The result is a process by which the lower echelon creates symbols which are coopted by the upper echelon and then in turn imposed upon the lower ranks as part of the official norms.

Much of this unofficial differentiation arises from attempts by members of an organization to create finer distinctions in uniform symbols than those intended by officials. One set of symbols, surprising to modern readers accustomed to the precision of bureaucratic statuses, was intended to compensate for the lack of indications of rank and specialty for enlisted navy personnel during the early nineteenth century.[12] In the United States Navy, petty officers had for a long time unofficially embroidered rank and specialty badges on their clothing (NHD 1966, pls. 1830, 1841). Not until 1841 were petty officers officially given a badge which, however, still did not differentiate between rank and specialty (ibid.). Specialty marks were authorized in 1866; petty officers were divided into separate ranks only in 1885 (ibid., pl. 1898; Tily 1964, 94–96, 174–77).

The failure to provide insignia may exemplify a patrimonial outlook in which enlisted personnel constitute a vast, undifferentiated mob. In the Navy of the later eighteenth century, enlisted men were absent from or appear only as stereotypes in officers' narratives (Harrod 1978, 152). Superior officers interacted only with service personnel such as cooks and yeomen; others constituted a uniformed blur.

Another set of unofficial distinctions made by uniform wearers is that of shared and prestigeful experiences which often form the basis of a subculture. These experiences may be based upon a variety of differences, veteran and newcomer, front and rear echelons, field and administration, and the overlapping split between hazardous and safe duty. They may emerge in any uniformed group including police, fire, and sanitation departments as well as the military. The distinctions derive from several sources. The internal segregation may rely upon deviation from uniform norms which may be interpreted as sloppiness or informality. Examined more closely, such deviation has a variety of forms and meanings. It may assume the functionality of the veteran's dress and equipment in contrast to that of the rookie. A Canadian reports the reaction of a newly arrived armored unit to the appearance of his veteran unit in France during World War II.

Resplandissant, in their clean new battledress, black belts, black gaiters, shiny new tanks with some sort of gleaming polish over them, squadron signals and pennants all new and crisp. . . . They looked at us with as much surprise as we at them. Dirty, battle-scarred, tanks patched up, unshaven men, berets in all sorts of colours instead of steel helmets (which were too uncomfortable on the earphones), dirty old coveralls which had seen filth and fighting grime ever since the landing, no insignias of rank on our shoulders . . . these fellows were shocked. (McKee 1964, 275)

In these instances, the uniform operates as a tool whose efficiency has been increased by the test of usage and which then becomes a sign of experience. The veteran may divest himself of all unnecessary items until, to use the Confederate soldier as the extreme example, he "dresses out and out", owning no clothes except those he is wearing and relying for replacement upon captured clothing or items sent from home (McCarthy 1882, 16–28). Uniforms may be augmented with civilian dress as with the troops in the Indian Wars whose uniforms were inadequate (Rickey 1963, 217, 256–57). Eventually, these changes may become signs informally demarcating veteran units.

Unofficial distinctions may arise from the use of the front line groups as reference and adopting their standards of "sloppiness", not as a functional vehicle of dress but rather as a method of thumbing one's nose at authority (Shibutani 1978, 7). Here, sloppiness changes its meaning from an adaptation to a combat situation, where defiance of authority is irrelevant and perhaps absent, to deliberate defiance of superiors.

A corollary set of distinctions emerges when rear echelon personnel exhibit greater adherence to protocol. Front line troops on a Pacific Island during World War II were denied permission, because of improper dress, to visit rear cemeteries where their buddies had just been buried (Manchester 1982, 434). Similarly, Israeli front line officers met with discrimination at the hands of better dressed rear echelon personnel (Dayan 1967, 100). We may hypothesize that these distinctions are not only an adherence to the norms but also a means of establishing the independence of a subunit.

The shared experiences include the recognition of one's unit. The use of shoulder patches to identify units in the American army originated during the Civil War, was resurrected again unofficially after the war, and was later institutionalized and legitimated (Goodman 1954).

Internal segregation is also manifested in the use of distinctive caps by student nurses, in one institution against the opposition of an educator who decried their cost and impracticality (Int. 3). The pride in differentiating caps will also be found among graduate nurses. The distinctive habits of traditionally dressed nuns are zealously retained (Int. 1).

At times, units have unofficially defined themselves as elite groups and have modeled their uniforms after those of the officially designated elite. Unofficial berets have proliferated in the United States Army, maroon for the air borne, olive for Alaskan units, black for armor, and unauthorized black Stetson hats for cavalry (Ludvigsen 1978). The destroyer captains of the Royal Navy in World War I regarded themselves as a dashing elite and followed the sartorial lead of their charismatic hero, Admiral Beatty, by not wearing war service chevrons or wound stripes and not buttoning their jackets completely (Blackman, C. 1971, 108–9).

These patterns may be partially explained as the self-enhancement of the individual through the accentuation of his or her status within the context of the organizational idiom. At the same time, it may also be seen as a pattern of overconformity by the assertion of distinctions finer than those required by the rules.

Modifications or reversals of official insignia represent another mode of unit demarcation and status enhancement. James Jones reports that members of his veteran unit, recuperating in New Zealand in World War II, refused to wear medals or chevrons and attacked replacements in fresh uniforms who often fraudulently wore medals (1976, 137–38). At times, these veterans would wear only the Combat Infantryman's Badge and refuse all others.

A description of the denigration of heroes and medals in the Korean War helps explain the reversal of symbols. A "hero" makes it "necessary for others to follow or at least expose themselves to additional risk" (Little 1967, 203). Furthermore, the medal received for overconforming to the norms was intended to be approved by his peers and act as an inspiration to them (Moskos 1970, 155). The award of medals, however, depended upon the *official* recognition of bravery and such recognition was not always forthcoming due in part, perhaps, to the quota system regulating the distribution of medals (Little 1967, 222). The attitude of the combat soldier toward medals is understandable.

Status enhancement may assume the panache of the swaggering veteran as in the "affected raggedness of the German [seventeenth-century] lansquenets who sometimes wore one leg covered and the other with the garment hanging around the ankle", and of the Stuart pikemen who may have imitated them by wearing two pairs of stockings at a time, the outer set loosely (Carman 1957, 21).

Group Mobility through the Uniform

Mobility in uniformed organizations consisting of a single branch and based entirely upon considerations of merit presents relatively few problems. The officially recognized rise of the individual uniform wearer is indicated by his adoption of the appropriate insignia of higher rank and occasions no special interest at this juncture. When the organization, however, includes more than one branch or when the criteria for initial placement and subsequent promotion are based upon nonbureaucratic considerations such as class, then mobility assumes additional forms. An entire branch of a uniformed organization may attempt to rise through structural change; an individual may strive for mobility through unofficial means. In both instances, uniform symbols may function in an unintended or unofficial manner.

In most, if not all, of the Western navies that date back to sail, the executive officer corps—the combatant branch—long held pride of place over other components. In the Renaissance, the aristocratic executive officers, who did the fighting, held command over the officers, usually of plebian origin, who actually sailed the ships. Later, with the advent of the steam engine, the executive or line officer's superiority to the "plumbers" or "chauffeurs" of the engineering branch was manifested by sharp differences in uniforms. Similar condescension was displayed toward such other branches as pursers, surgeons, and chaplains (Marder 1961, 1:29).

Differences between the several branches were reenforced by the mystique of command which stemmed both from aristocratic birth and the imputed "natural" superiority of the executive or line officer (Herwig 1973, 35, 102–5, 135, 139; Marder 1961, 1:29–31, 46–48). In the Imperial German Navy, the executive officer embodied authority as the direct representative of the Kaiser and therefore could command any engineer, even if the latter had greater seniority and higher rank (Herwig 1973, 49, 69–70, 83, 116). As previously described, similar relationships existed in armies between officers of elite units or of aristocratic birth and those in the middle-class branches of artillery, engineers, and later armor.

Nonexecutive branches attempted to achieve parity with line officers through improvements in pay, privileges, and titles—many branches did not bear line officers' titles but were instead labelled ''surgeon'', ''purser'', or ''engineer''. Symbolically, these efforts at mobility centered on the salient insignia demarcating the several strata. In the Imperial German Navy, engineers strove for equality with the executive branch by obtaining their sash and also made strong efforts to differentiate themselves from the deck officers, a corps of junior officers who were, in turn, attempting to achieve parity with the line officers (Herwig 1973, 134–53). Deck officers, besides other privileges, aspired to the sword, also an earmark of the full-fledged officer. In turn, they separated themselves from the next lower group, the petty officers (ibid., 139).

Similar struggles occurred in other navies, although the symbols differed. In the United States Navy, claims to higher status focused on the color of uniforms (surgeons desired the standard blue instead of their original bottle green), and in the Royal Navy on the colors between stripes for the various branches (Lewis, M. 1948a, 241; Tily 1964, 58, 63).

To place these struggles in perspective, it should be noted that the symbols overlay a variety of differences in privilege encompassing the regulation of marriages, the military and civilian statuses with whom one may associate, and the jobs available after retirement. While appearing to be entirely on the symbolic level, the very minutiae of differentiation among uniforms may make the differences in status privileges all the more apparent and galling. Finally, the same struggle over seemingly minor symbols is mirrored in contemporary life. The key to the executive washroom remains important because it symbolizes a host of rights, privileges, and statuses, and may indicate the supreme achievement of an entire career.

PHYSICAL CONSTRAINTS ON CONFORMITY

Although our primary concern is with clothing as communication, the physical vehicle does influence the degree of adherence to norms. First, insofar as a uniform is not suited to field exigencies, changes may occur. The United States Army, after the Civil War, attempted to accommodate a one hundred degree range of temperature on the frontier with one type of woolen uniform which was too heavy for the desert and too light for the mountains in winter (Utley 1973, 73–77). Since the uniforms were also often of poor quality, they were augmented, as previously noted, with civilian clothing and patched with canvas or flour sacking (Hutchins 1976, 2–21).

Even when of good quality, the design of military uniforms, especially in peacetime when appearance becomes an important criterion, may make them unsuitable for field use. An additional prerequisite to conformity through standardization, that of a technology suited to the provision of adequate numbers of properly dyed and sized uniforms, has also been noted.

The most suitable uniforms cannot be properly maintained without sufficient supplies and replacements. The problem of poor supplies is obvious, but what does require exposition is the very notion of supply which is itself culturally determined. The idea that armies are obligated to furnish all the needs of their members—the contemporary concept of the service as a total, bureaucratic institution—was not always present. Instead, the patrimonial idea often persisted that the soldier was obliged to fend for himself, partially or totally, for weapons, food, and clothing. The probability of achieving uniformity of appearance under these conditions was slight. Indeed, the perfect adherence to uniform norms is attainable only under special circumstances, those of the garrison soldier and others with access to supplies and maintenance facilities.

By the eighteenth century, European armies in garrison had access to assured supplies and maintenance, resulting in "perfectly" and elaborately clad armies, especially at the beginning of a campaign before the inevitable drain on supplies set in. British and German troops were therefore an awe-inspiring sight at the outset of the American Revolution for which they paid a price (Bliven 1964, 40). One is equally impressed by references to heat exhaustion and sun stroke which produced many casualties (Ward 1952, 327, 574, 585, 824). Among the German troops was a dismounted cavalry regiment compelled to tramp through New York and New England forests during the very hot summer of 1777 while wearing heavy leather breeches, high boots, spurs, and trailing long sabers (ibid., 401–2). Having no comparable access to supplies, as is probably true of all revolutionary armies initially, the Americans had to dress themselves; their militia fought in shirt sleeves.

Napoleon's army at the outset of the Russian campaign offers additional insight into the reverse side of sartorial glory. "On 24 June 1812—sunshine and humid heat, a day for sweating wet inside serge and braid, fur and steel and brass—the Grande Armée crossed the Niemen by pontoon bridge and set foot on the soil of Russia" (Barnett 1978, 169).

In sharp contrast, in the less brutalized armies of Wellington especially during the Peninsula campaign, and in the American Civil War, innumerable incidents occurred of troops dressing informally and discarding cumbersome equipment and clothing. Wellington seems to have drawn the line primarily at the use of umbrellas by his officers. Under these physical conditions, it would of course be extremely difficult to maintain strict adherence to uniform regulations.

Aside from the physical difficulties, the organization itself may have problems in maintaining uniform regulations. The history of the Royal Navy during the latter part of the eighteenth century and the early part of the nineteenth is illustrative. At times the norms were not clearly specified; parts of the uniform code were left implicit with a phrase such as "according to civilian specifications". Even when norms of dress were established, communicating them precisely to a widely dispersed force was difficult. Sealed uniform patterns were sent to tailors at Plymouth but these seem to have been insufficient.[13] Finally, nonconformity stemmed from reasons of economy (previously, officers had worn old, comfortable civilian dress), practicality (officers, and later enlisted men, abandoned hats and coats which were useless in high winds), other social distinctions (the warrant officer who wore a cocked hat as an indication of his genteel origins rather than the round hat worn by his peer of lesser origins), and perhaps a generalized reluctance to surrender personal autonomy.

In sum, the perfectly dressed or uniformed unit is more of a rarely obtainable ideal than a realizable fact. Under most circumstances, the soldier is not dressed "uniformly". Adherence to norms requires material resources and socialization into the stipulated bureaucratic role. Functionally, these problems are met by minimal symbols which means that one need not conform to the norms absolutely—itself a relative matter—to achieve recognition as a member of an organization or to communicate.

After the analysis of conformity, one wonders about the insistence upon the rarely attainable perfect uniform. The answer is that even if not adhered to precisely, a norm does limit deviation. More significantly, the perfect uniform as described in regulations communicates a different message from the ordinary one. Just as precise speech may convey not only the same basic message as ordinary usage but also subtle nuances, so may a perfect uniform have additional overtones. Rigorous conformity may communicate any of a wide variety of meanings depending upon the context, such as ceremonial occasions when the group is renewing loyalties to its symbols, the existence of a high degree of discipline or morale (from the command point of view), or closeness to headquarters socially or geographically.

NOTES

1. Sloppiness may indicate not lowered but rather heightened morale as well as adherence to norms differing from official regulations. Terms such as "sloppiness" assume the perspective of the upper echelons of bureaucracy. As industrial sociologists have long informed us, what is poor morale from management's viewpoint may be the esprit d'corps of lower echelon groups in opposition to official policies.

2. See chapter nine on quasi uniforms and their function as barriers between wearer and client.

3. See chapter nine on the conflict between groups over clothing codes.

4. In earlier times, medieval Europe for example, occupational dress had some of the characteristics of the clothing of a total institution in that occupational dress, or parts of it, were worn off the job as identification. Festive clothing, such as that of Welsh fishwives or German miners, consisted of elaborate versions of occupational dress (Davis, B. 1980, 217–18; Oakes & Hill 1970, 202–5; Schramm 1960). Occupational dress became the key

symbol for establishing position. Dress codes for white-collar workers are not recent and were established in the early department stores of the nineteenth century. Attempts to control the entire life of the employee off the job were also widespread.

5. Comparable conflicts occurred in industrial plants such as Honda and Sony. See chapter nine.

6. Historically, the military tends to assimilate civilian employees into its service and place them in uniform. Artillery men, who served the guns, and drovers, who transported them, were once civilians who contracted for a specific campaign.

7. Reservists object the most to the new hair code of the United States Navy because they shuttle between statuses the most (NT 31 Dec. 1984).

8. An example of status inconsistency is the gentleman ranker, of the late nineteenth century British army memorialized by Kipling. They were upper-class members who could not obtain a commission, often through inability to pass the Sandhurst entrance examinations, and enlisted in the army (Turner, E. 1956, 245–46). In one instance, diametrically opposed to the hazing of total institutions (mortification), a gentleman ranker was given a private barracks room to avoid stripping before other enlisted men and accorded personal drill instruction (Goffman 1961, 14–35; Turner, E. 1956, 245).

9. The purported superiority of amateurs over professionals is also evidenced by the attitudes of militia toward regulars in the United States during the nineteenth century (Cunliffe 1973, 19–21, 107–11).

10. Solidarity among technical officers, who were usually middle class, paralleled the aristocratic bias of line officers. The close ties among artillery officers of European nations in eighteenth-century armies cut across national boundaries. They dressed alike in dark blue uniforms and exchanged scientific data and drill manuals (Knoetel & Todd 1954). For additional discussion of the antiscientific and antiprofessional animus of the aristocratic officer, see Huntington 1957, 24–28, 32–44; Kennett 1967, 67–88; Perrott 1968, 145–46.

11. The poor who lived in St. Cross, a very old English charitable organization, were divided by uniform into the noble and the common poor (Cunnington & Lucas 1978, 235–36).

12. These ranks and specialities had existed previously but were devoid of official insignia. In the United States Army, unofficial and unauthorized chevrons were used to indicate branch of service, speciality, and status as volunteer rather than draftee (Emerson, W. 1983, 158, 170, 186–88). In the eighteenth-century British army, clothing warrants often legitimated prior unauthorized clothing modification (McMaster 1979).

13. "Sealed [clothing] patterns" bore admiralty seals to indicate approval.

7

Sartorial Perceptions and Misperceptions

Were the import of the uniform confined to its description of statuses and relationships, important though it is, the uniform would not matter much outside of the organizations employing it. However, much of the significance of the uniform stems from the qualities imputed to it, correctly or not, by both outsiders and wearers to create their pictures of the social world. A similar process takes place in familiar occupational clothing such as the cowboy's. The meaning of clothing is thereby often distorted and subjected to mythmaking or abstraction where the lack of strict congruence between symbol and reality is irrelevant. The result is a sartorial vocabulary of stereotypes, cultural exemplars, and free associations.

I shall examine this vocabulary, the structural factors and processes creating it, and its importance to the public for whom it may become ideology. Finally, two complexes which rely heavily upon these perceptual categories, youth in uniform and the cowboy as symbol, will be analyzed.

SARTORIAL DISTORTIONS

Role Stereotypes

Sartorial stereotypes are created when one role is selected to exemplify an entire role set. The routine of the uniform wearer in the military, for example, includes a wide variety of activities with an appropriate uniform for each (fatigue, leisure, ceremonial, and combat). In the same vein, the duties of any job are telescoped by eliminating behind-the-scenes activity, so that the lawyer is seen only as a practitioner of courtroom histrionics, the physician as an emergency room surgeon, or the police officer as a front line combatant against crime.

This distortion is mirrored in the complaint of the Smithsonian curator who is unable to obtain fatigue uniforms or prosaic implements such as ships' coal shovels for his collection, whereas dress uniforms and glamorous equipment such as swords are readily available (Langley 1980). "It is no accident" that these items are lacking, since it is the ceremonial role, as indicated by formal uniforms, that is usually stressed symbolically. Similarly, the American Indian was often characterized primarily as a warrior and depicted by early photographers as performing mundane daily tasks in ceremonial dress (Scherer 1975, 68–73).

Stereotypes in uniforms are also caused by the homogenization of symbols which uses a single image to describe a range of uniforms and ignores the variation due to chronological change, unit distinctions, or individual nonconformity. The visual depiction of uniforms often relies on artistic ideal types. Using the 1975 issue of United States postage stamps on uniforms of the Revolution as an example, a soldier is depicted in the blue uniform coat with buff facings associated in popular mythology with the Revolutionary Army.[1] In reality, brown was the official color of coats until 1779 (Finke & McBarron 1962). After that, only the Middle Atlantic states in the Continental Army wore blue coats with buff facings. Other states wore white, red, or blue facings.[2] Another stamp in the series portrays a sailor although no uniform was authorized for the navy until 1847; dress before that period consisted of standardized nautical attire.

The United States Postal Service indicates awareness of its poetic license in selectively depicting an idealized uniform. "Shown are typical uniforms of the army, navy, marines, and militia of the Revolutionary War. Not all of America's fighting men wore these uniforms. Because the textile industry could not produce enough cloth, a soldier wore what he had and this often was a deerskin jacket and overalls" (SD 1979, 264). The postal service is also aware of chronological changes and regional differences in facings. The alternative, depicting the actual range of uniforms on stamps, would have been expensive and awkward. I am not belaboring the shortcomings of officialdom, but rather indicating the tendency of visual media to be highly selective and to seize upon idealized types for the portrayal of uniforms. The result is the creation and perpetuation of stereotypes.

The homogenization of symbols also helped create sartorial stereotypes of the American Indian. The dress of the American Indian differed greatly among tribes and cultural areas, yet their variety has been reduced to a few, readily identifiable salient symbols. The feathered war bonnet, the emblem of the Dakota tribes which was reserved for special occasions and then for only a few, now symbolizes all Indians, regardless of tribe. Even contemporary Indians themselves use the bonnet as a universal emblem (Wissler 1945, 157).

Exemplars: The Sartorial Personae of a Culture

Sartorial stereotypes create a vocabulary of exemplars which are abstractions made flesh. Evil, bravery, and patriotism are personified in ideal types made easily recognizable by appropriate, if historically inaccurate, dress. The clothing becomes a symbolic shorthand; any person can express his self-image and beliefs or lay claim to a social position and style of life by borrowing the apparel of the exemplar. The claim may be made as an individual, the hippie who used the Indian headband to denote his commitment to the simple preindustrial values of the past, or as a group, the nineteenth-century militia companies dressed in democratic hunting shirts. The exemplars of a group may change over time; the German youth movement borrowed the apparel of scholars, knights, the military, and the American Indian (Laqueur 1962, 29, 133–43). Deviant figures may also be used; the beatniks of the 1950's and the hippies of the 1960's borrowed the clothing and loose hair of the nineteenth-century Bohemian.

Many of a society's exemplars stem from military or quasi-military sources. The chevalier was an important figure, especially in the antebellum South, with strong links to the cowboy (Cunliffe 1973, 417–23). The cowboy, as we shall see, is a figure of laissez-faire individuality and the last upholder of untrammelled freedom. Other exemplars capture some of the amateur militia spirit of early nineteenth century America. Besides the Rifleman, another yeoman hero is the Minuteman who reflects individualistic tendencies. The Minutemen were of little actual importance in the American Revolution. In Massachusetts, their principal center, they were in existence only from a few days to six months and had little effect upon the war (Ward 1952, 30). The symbol persisted, and its continued presence in advertising and official documents such as World War II Savings Bonds testifies to its hold on the American imagination. The Minuteman's dress symbolizes the American patriot-at-arms always ready to drop his civilian preoccupations and leap to the defense of God and Country.

The exemplar in uniform is drawn from contemporary armies as well, notably in the persona of the modern paratrooper who became a very important symbol in France during the Gaullist era.

The paratrooper was as celebrated a figure as Brigitte Bardot. Like Bardot, he fulfilled escapist fantasies. As the retreat from empire created deep divisions in French politics and society, the paratrooper became as much a political symbol as one of sex, violence, and adventure. Some detected in his image the lineaments of fascism; others the last remnant of virtue in an otherwise decadent society. (Talbott 1976, 69–70)

The paras' uniform, along with their distinctive headgear . . . became as much a staple of political cartooning as the capitalists' top hat, and . . . symbolic of the cause of *Algerie francaise*. . . . For some of the diehard settlers, the leopard uniform became a sort of talisman; they dressed their children in it and took to wearing it themselves on occasions of high seriousness. (ibid., 73)

Exemplars permit a cognitive structuring of the universe. By identifying with them or opposing them, we display our preferences immediately without the need of thought. Jerry Rubin, one of the leaders of the countercultural movement of the 1960's, urged a youthful audience to remove their neckties to indicate instant opposition to parents and the establishment (NYT 29 Nov. 1978). The passage of youthful political radical to adult conformist is denoted by the adoption and later abandonment of jeans, dashikis, beards, and long hair. At the same time, the symbols of protest enabled disapproving authority to exercise its power. The Prussian government of the nineteenth century forbade its mailmen to wear mustaches which symbolized radical beliefs (Mollo, J. 1972, 133). A political rally by Nixon supporters refused entrance to those with granny glasses (NYT 30 Apr. 1975).

The Free Associations of Uniforms

Clothes, particularly uniforms, also have "free associations", to borrow a term of Max Black, which are more diffuse than those derived from exemplars. These associations arise from other sources as well; we project on to them meanings obtained from our stereotypes of their wearers or of the occupations associated with the dress.

For a traditional middle class dominated by the Protestant Ethic, the officer was an idler. In the mid-nineteenth century, his evaluation was shaped in part by the time-honored system of purchasing commissions in Britain, and by the lack of a professional orientation in most nations that stood in sharp contrast to the rationality and bureaucratic ethos of a rising middle class (Harries-Jenkins 1977, 60–66).

Especially in the United States and Britain, this class saw the enlisted soldier as, at best, a necessary evil recruited from the economically unproductive, the very dregs of society (Cunliffe 1973, 101–11, 147–51, 282–86). "To soldier" is defined as "to make a pretense of working while really loafing" (Webster 1984, 1122). For a long time, the soldier was regarded as a misfit who could not survive in the civilian world through honest labor and who sought refuge in the army or, in modern parlance, "found a home in the army". He was irresponsible, part of a "brutal and licentious soldiery", to use a British phrase. Parson Weems felt that casualties among regulars in the Battle of Fallen Timbers in 1794 were no great tragedy since men who could easily get their "half dollar a day at the healthful and glorious labours of the plough" and instead enlisted for only four dollars a month were worthless (Cunliffe 1973, 103). This very alienation from society made the misfit more suited for the military. Before the middle of the nineteenth century a prevalent attitude was "the greater the rascal, the better the soldier" (Anderson 1971, 47).

A drastic change in the military as symbol took place in the mid-nineteenth century. The army was now seen as an organization of rational and sober technicians by an era enamored of technological progress. In the same vein, the contemporary uniform very often has connotations of orderliness, efficiency and precision, probably stemming from its nexus in bureaucratic and technologically oriented organizations. These connotations are especially apparent in scientific or medical uniforms which carry an aura of hygienic coolness and efficiency.

The qualities of selfless service, patriotism, and gallantry stem from another major referent, the nation-state, and adhere to its uniformed forces. In patriotic art, especially of the past, a frequent stereotyped depiction of these attributes takes the form of "heroic death" in which the hero dies calmly, bleeds very modestly or not at all, and is dressed in a neat or at least carefully dishevelled uniform. Death becomes an uplifting and ennobling experience. An engraving of Benjamin West's painting of the death of General Wolfe on the Plains of Abraham, a picture that has appeared in countless American history texts, exemplifies heroic death (LC 1947, pls. 6, 7, 56; Meredith 1955, 42). Wolfe's principal officers, instead of pursuing the foe, take time off from battle to form an awe-stricken group around their dying leader who has incurred bloodless wounds. An indecorous wound in the groin is omitted from the picture.

Uniform wearers may also be seen as oppressors. This adverse view of the state is revealed by the old term "dragooning"—"to subjugate or persecute by harsh use of troops"—a connotation arising from the use of dragoons as police (Webster 1984, 380). The modern counterpart is the accusation of fascism against troops engaged in warfare against guerrillas or in contact with a civilian population. Liebknecht described the uniform as a device to delude poor peasant boys into opposing their own class interests (1917, 65–69).

Another set of characteristics, not associated with the primary functions of the uniform, is the erotic. On a less explicit level, these connotations have long been used in a genteel fashion. In the past, women served as worshipful audiences in ceremonies such as reviews, presentation of colors, and farewell observances (Cunliffe 1973, 403–4, 419). More explicitly, uniforms have enhanced the sexual attractiveness of their wearers, both to heterosexual and homosexual observers. During World War I, even the quasi-military uniforms of elevator operators and mailmen shared in the increase of pederasty (Fussell 1977, 279). Finally, uniforms have been used as fetishes, even in the absence of their owners (Kern 1975, 200).

The sexual connotations of uniforms stem, first, from the function of violence as an aphrodisiac for some (Fussell 1977, 270–72). Again, uniforms tend to accentuate height and breadth of shoulders and thereby increase sexual attractiveness. This is reinforced by a popular stereotype of the handsome soldier as romantic and daring.

That we are dealing with the uniform on a connotative level is made evident by the frequent disparity between the uniform as a symbol revered from afar and the less lofty attitudes toward specific wearers. Whereas ceremonial parades and the changing of the guard are admired in Britain, in former years soldiers have often been barred from public accommodations, transportation, theaters, and the front pews of churches (Harries-Jenkins 1977, 5). Similar discrimination has been

been meted out to officers. American servicemen have fared no better. James Jones, in his semi-autobiographical novel, *From Here to Eternity*, describes the cynical response of servicemen to their greatly increased popularity among civilians on December 8, 1941. In an almost identical episode, soldiers were given luxurious railroad accommodations on their way to battle during the Indian Wars in sharp contrast to miserable facilities on their return (Rickey 1963, 45–46, 240).

SOCIAL SOURCES OF MISPERCEPTION

Historical Reconstruction

History is reconstructed when the remembered past never was, when the past is nothing more than the present stereotype of bygone eras. In examining historical misconceptions, the purpose is not to debunk but to understand the process of falsification and the present functions of symbols derived from a nonexistent past. The legends of General Custer and the rifleman furnish excellent examples.

General Custer has been depicted extensively in films, paintings, and books. In one film version, all the troops die at the feet of the last survivor, General Custer, wearing "new and barely wrinkled uniforms" (Taft 1953, 331). In the many paintings of the battle, members of the Seventh Cavalry are portrayed in full dress blue uniforms, or at least in regulation blue trousers and dark blue army shirts, sometimes even with shoulder knots and brass shoulder scales, fighting to the last with sabers (ibid. 132–41).

Reality was far different. The clothing issued to enlisted men at the time by a parsimonious government was neither durable nor adapted to the climate, being too hot for summer and not warm enough for winter (Hutchins 1976, 3–4). Uniforms were therefore supplemented by civilian dress and also frequently patched; when regulation blouses (jackets) were worn, they were of four different models. In hot weather, which included the day of the battle, blouses were discarded and only shirts were worn (ibid., 5; Stewart 1955, 485). The colors of the regulation shirts were gray, white, and blue; the frequently used civilian shirts were checkered. Owing to the disgust with the defective service hat which lost its shape when wet, civilian hats—broad brimmed, white, brown, or black—were used (Hutchins 1976, 6). Officers' uniforms were similarly varied and nonregulation. They ranged from undress uniforms to the buckskins of civilian plainsmen with all sorts of mixtures in between (ibid., 13; Taft 1953, 132). Since sabers were nuisances, they were ordered left behind and were not used in the battle (Hutchins 1976, 29; Stewart 1955, 485).

Another reconstruction of the past originated with the rifle which became the key symbol for two contrasting complexes of cultural values, elite and democratic, in the late eighteenth and nineteenth centuries. As is true of many new weapons, the rifle was part of the mystique of elite units in European and American armies. These stressed individual fitness and initiative, and performed a role comparable to that of modern commandoes or rangers (Barnes 1951, 66–69; Bryant 1972, 21–29; Young, P. 1967, 106, 124–25). The uniform of rifle units in all armies was usually the dark green associated with foresters and hunters from medieval days (Knoetel et al. 1974, 64). Though the rifleman's uniform is reputed to have served as camouflage, it "was a green so dark as to be almost black and not at all inconspicuous in open country" (Laver 1948, 21). Green came to represent military daring and toughness, and it is used today for those associations by organizations like the Green Berets to enhance their self-image and claims to esteem. Not only is green symbolic of a complex of associations, but the designation of the color itself has become a symbol rather than a description of reality.

In a display of military metaphor, British rifle regiments were dressed as hussars, still in green. Originally Hungarian, the dashing hussar uniform became widespread among European light cavalry units. Since the riflemen compared themselves to light cavalry in function and in the connotations of gallantry and status, they adopted the hussar uniform. Some practices of the ordinary British infantry of the line, a slower marching pace or the use of colors, were rejected (Barnes 1951, 68–69; Masters 1968, 94–96). Although these differences were originally functional—riflemen had to march more quickly in order to strike out ahead of the main body and could not carry colors since they never formed a line—they persisted long after all military units had been armed with the rifle and "rifleman" had become honorific. The symbolism of the elite rifle unit spread to the public and became part of the nomenclature of volunteer units. The volunteer movement in England during the later, militaristic stage of the Victorian era assumed the title "rifle" and was duly commemorated by Tennyson (Newsome 1961, 237).

A second symbolic complex, this time democratic, centered around the American rifleman and his hunting shirt (McBarron & Elting 1979). The rifle was a frontiersman's weapon practically unknown in New England, and at no time did it displace the musket as the primary infantry weapon in either army (Mollo, J. 1975, 58; Ward 1952, 106–7). The hunting shirt, derived from the frock of European workers, became very popular during the Revolution because it was practical, comfortable, and inexpensive (McBarron & Elting 1979). Washington emphasized its propaganda potential; if it became standard dress, the British would be misled into believing all Americans were expert riflemen (Bliven 1964, 62; CMH 1976). Although his plan could not be carried out—the usual lack of funds—nevertheless the shirt became an important service dress (Mollo, J. 1975, 57–58). British and Tories also used rifles or hunting shirts.

The hunting shirt subsequently spread to other parts of society and formed an important part of popular mythology after the Revolution. In the first part of the nineteenth century, during the heyday of American voluntary militia, the hunting shirt often became the uniform of working class or ethnic units because of its inexpensiveness and democratic connotations (Todd 1976). It was also popular with members of the Republican Party, who were more likely to draw support from lower income groups, and correspondingly out of favor with the Federalists (McBarron & Todd 1954). ''The dress of the American rifleman: 'Hunting shirt & leggins, picturesque costume of the Woodsmen,' was once called 'the veritable *Emblem of the Revolution*' '' (ibid., 12).

Uniforms marked other distinctions within the voluntary militia of the early and mid-nineteenth century. Wealthy groups were more likely to wear elaborate uniforms and join the cavalry and horse artillery; middle income groups preferred the artillery and other units (Cunliffe 1973, 218–20; McBarron et al. 1977a; Todd 1976). Ethnic groups such as the Irish, Germans, Italians, Scots, Jews, and French maintained their own units, often with distinctive national uniforms (Ahrenholz et al. 1979; Brown, A.S. 1952; Cunliffe 1973, 223–26). Several were established with the express purpose of freeing their respective homelands from foreign rule (Cunliffe 1973, 94).

These ethnic groups were targets of xenophobic opposition aroused by a combination of anti-Catholicism and antiurbanism (especially toward groups associated with the frequently unruly volunteer fire departments) (ibid., 227–30). The nativist opposition in the militia appropriated a greatly distorted version of the Continental Army uniform.

However, the reality of the Continental Army uniform differs greatly from its later ideological employment. In 1860, Thompson Westcott, who wrote one of the earliest accurate accounts of Revolutionary uniforms, described the misapprehensions prevalent in the nineteenth century and undoubtedly still widespread today.

In this country there seem to be very erroneous ideas of the colors and materials of the uniforms of the Continental troops during the Revolutionary War. The popular notion is that the regular colors were blue and buff. Such undoubtedly were the colors of the commander-in-chief and his staff; but the rank and file rarely wore these colors. The prevailing uniforms were brown, mixed with red or white; and green with like trimmings. We have in our Atlantic cities, certain companies of volunteers called ''Continental companies'' which, through ignorance on this subject, have adopted uniforms such as the private soldiers of the Revolutionary War could never have worn: and indeed, in these modern companies, each member appears with blue and buff coats, buff breeches, and usually, top boots, cocked hats, and ruffled shirts, such as Washington and the major generals usually wore upon grand parade days. (Elting 1960, 2)[3]

Symbols did not occur at random but were borrowed from the qualities imputed to the particular uniform, democratic independence for riflemen in hunting shirts, loyalty and patriotism for the Continental uniform, dash and prestige for the cavalry of the wealthy. These distinctions were not unique to the United States. Similar instances could be found in the identification of the country gentry with the British yeomanry—voluntary cavalry—or the bourgeoisie with the French National Guard. In all instances, the identification had political overtones.

The distinctions express more than vanity or status enhancement. The nineteenth-century militia was analogous to modern social clubs and fraternal or voluntary organizations. It operated, depending upon the social level, as a center for engaging in business or politics, reminiscing about the old country, and "socializing". (Craighead 1963, 73; Cunliffe 1973, 230–35). Some of these functions are still filled, although in a greatly reduced fashion, by modern elite militia units.

Thus there existed in greatly distorted and simplified fashion, a system of sartorial codes derived from the uniforms and popular mythology of the Revolution. The system has provided a basis for the belief in the "natural" affinity between Americans and the bearing of arms, which has led in the past to the credo that the United States is a nation ready to spring to arms overnight. This view is of course combined with the myth of the Minuteman whose importance has been exaggerated but who nevertheless still has a central place in American mythology. The code also serves a function for the public, apart from any thought of the military, by forming part of our vocabulary of stereotypes which can be used to conceptualize the world.

Historical reconstruction does not necessarily create sartorial illiteracy, because the public can still identify the inauthentically dressed individual of the past. An acute student of theatrical costume described the historical inaccuracies of stage dress as having become a convention, varying with the era and the accepted depiction of the clothing of a given period (Hollander 1980, 237–310). Within a given convention, the viewer relies upon certain salient symbols. "So long as Queen Elizabeth's courtiers wear ruffs, it doesn't matter what else they wear" (ibid., 300). The actual prior existence of these symbols is irrelevant; the "Juliet cap" worn in *Romeo and Juliet* was devised by Theda Bara in 1916 (ibid., 305–7). The symbols create their own reality.

What is true of theatrical costumes is also true of uniforms. Portraits of Washington depict him, and others of the same era, in the fall down collar which was not introduced until the French Revolution some fifteen years later (Brown, A.S. 1974, vi). The anachronism is of no importance except to the historian. We recognize the picture as an "authentic" portrait of Washington by the salient symbols; the historical inaccuracy of the collar style is irrelevant to its symbolic function.

Misplaced Referents of the Uniform

The culture and historical experiences of a society and its components are primary sources of structured misreadings of dress. The medieval world viewed ancient Rome as a kindred society with the Roman soldier cast in the role of knight. As a result, lawyers could claim that Roman military law legitimated their definition of chivalry as a Christian profession (Keen 1965, 56–58). How culturally derived categories of perception and thought distort the meaning of dress is the problem to which we now turn.

At any given time in a society's history, there is a tendency to perceive and understand its own past in contemporary terms, a failure of historical imagination. For example, our contemporary experience with military organizations and uniforms leads us to believe that the present hierarchical military structure with its uniforms that clearly distinguish among ranks was always present. But an American tradition, dating back to Revolutionary times when hierarchical organization was equated with monarchy, consists of a notable reluctance to establish a permanent hierarchy at the upper ranks. There were no permanent officers above the rank of captain in the Navy before the Civil War, and no permanent full generals and lieutenant generals in the Army until World War II.[4] Ad hoc provisions were made for wartime heroes such as Washington, Grant, and Pershing.

At the root of our misunderstanding is the assumption that the military in the past was completely bureaucratized and, therefore, we can read historical military dress in modern terms. In reality, contemporary rationalized military service evolved from patrimonial types of social organization; military dress before the modern era represented not a uniform but a livery—clothing that symbolizes a personal tie to an individual leader rather than membership in an impersonal organization. Acceptance of the change depended upon the society and class. As previously noted, members of the Spanish King's Guard of Noblemen defined the uniform as demeaning and rejected it in favor of a form of livery denoting personal service to the king. The King's livery was acceptable to an aristocracy that had preserved a sense of honor rooted in feudal values. In contrast, the police in mid-nineteenth century New York at first refused to wear any uniforms precisely because they defined them as livery which symbolized degrading domestic service (Richardson 1970, 48, 65). Police uniforms in Boston during the same period met with derision from the public as the livery of popinjays (Lane, Roger 1967, 105).

We project our image of a modern, separate uniformed organization into the past when, in actuality, military organizations were of an entirely different character. In a society where the bearing of arms is the perquisite of an elite or of males in general and does not constitute a specialized occupation or profession, the military does not exist as a separate group. Part of the difficulty in the professionalization of officers in the last two centuries has been the acceptance of the status as an achieved, professional one rather than one that is ascribed on the basis of birth into the upper classes. In the older context, martial symbols do not indicate membership in a military organization but rather membership in the appropriate class or gender. As we shall see, a wellborn two-year-old boy is painted wearing a sword, not because of his military affiliations, but to describe his gender and status.

Uniforms of older periods may be misperceived as indicating military rank when in actuality they reflected social status. The amount of gold lace (braid) worn by British generals in 1688 depended mainly upon their affluence as there were no dress regulations. They probably wore more lace than regimental officers since they possessed greater power and wealth (Barnes 1951, 51). To infer rank from the amount of lace on their uniforms is the error of a later bureau-cratized outlook which is accustomed to a precise system of graduated ranks with exact insignia for each.[5] Where indications of rank were essential, as in battle, generals carried batons (ibid.).

If contemporary values and assumptions lead to a misreading of the past, they can also lead to a misreading of the present. We are frequently misled by the assumption of bureaucratic rationality and read uniforms as conforming to an ideal type based solely on official regulations and ignore the possibility of per-sonal whim and chance.

At the first mass celebrated by a newly ordained priest, and witnessed by me, about a dozen other celebrant priests were dressed in the same basic vestments which, however, bore differing embroidered insignia. The marked variation created some discussion among congregants who finally concluded that they represented membership in various clerical orders. A subsequent conversation with some of the participating clergy revealed a very different story. The vest-ments had accumulated in the parish over time and had been borrowed by the celebrants for the occasion. Variation in insignia was due simply to differences in the esthetic outlook of the original owners, did not pertain to any organizational differences, and had been previously unnoticed by congregants since the vest-ments had not been all displayed at once. At the service, the congregants viewed the vestments from their accustomed perspective, the bureaucratic outlook. "Uniform" clothing indicated membership in an organization, variation in that "uniform" must have been organizationally sanctioned and therefore indicated membership in a specific component of the organization.

The reader of all but the most recent and sophisticated account of military uniforms must be prepared to encounter edifying references to the values incor-porated in them. The British redcoat and the Prussian bluecoat are often in-terpreted in terms of the virtues inherent in these colors rather than in the ready availability of madder and indigo. One is reminded of the outlook of old primers which seek a similar symbolism in all items of God's creation. This outlook does not allow for idiosyncracy, whim, or fashion. If a uniform has some distinctive feature unascribable to symbolism, why then it must inevitably serve some practical function. The flared bell-bottoms of naval uniforms, for example, are variously explained as derived from the need for easy removal in case of emer-gency, or their ready conversion into flotation devices. In reality, bell-bottoms originated as an imitation of civilian pantaloons popular at the time of the establishment of naval dress (USN 1981, app.2 p.3). Fashion does influence the military as seen in the spread of the spiked helmet, Zouave dress, French kepi, and hussar uniform. In the conventional outlook, fashion cannot be used, howev-er, as an interpretation of national symbols. Instead there must be an explanation based upon some underlying rational purpose.

Contemporary assumptions and beliefs lead us to interpret uniforms, es-pecially ceremonial ones, as wholly symbolic and never as merely signals or occupational tools. The three white tapes universally found on the collars of the naval uniforms of enlisted men are very frequently interpreted as commemorating Nelson's victories, and the black scarf on the same uniform as mourning his death. Actually, both items preceded Nelson. The scarf had the utilitarian function of protecting clothing from the seaman's greasy or tarred queue while the tapes are of unknown origin (ibid.). The guard and hilt of the West Point cadet officer's sword form a cross, creating the myth that they were modeled after those of the Crusaders. In reality, they were probably derived from the Army Finance Department's pattern (Todd 1955, 40).

Uniforms and "Uniformity"

The confusion among "uniforms", "uniformity" and "military dress" is the root of much of the misreading of sartorial signs. Though the identification of military dress with uniforms is justified in the present, that association is neither inevitable nor eternal. Military dress has taken many forms over the years, each one indicative of a distinctive organizational structure and reflecting its own set of assumptions.

Military clothing may simply be a form of working clothes, rough clothing for a rugged job. In sixteenth and seventeenth century England, clothing worn by soldiers consisted of tougher civilian dress such as leather (Barnes 1951, 42; Gessler & Schneider 1952, 3334). Militia and regular army units in colonial and early nineteenth-century America used similar clothing (Ainome & Ainome 1976; Chapman & Parker 1974; Sowers & Kimmel 1979). Mercenaries of earlier centuries provided their own clothing as might a worker in other occupations (Atkinson 1910–11, 582; Gessler & Schneider 1952, 3334). Conversely, sixteenth-century military clothing was ornate civilian clothing for English officers and the cavalry, both usually wealthier groups, to indicate their social standing (Carman 1957, 19). A similar pattern for naval officers corresponded with the difference in working conditions between them and sailors until the technological revolution of the nineteenth century led to somber and identical dress for both castes (USN 1981, app.2 pp.9–10).

Military clothing may be a form of standardized clothing, nonuniform occupational clothing which follows a common pattern, the pervasive use of coveralls by automobile mechanics for example. Though recognized as a standard form of dress, it does not have the same meaning as contemporary uniforms. This was the type of nautical clothing followed in the eighteenth century when it became economical to issue clothing in bulk. Clothes were issued from the slop chest but they were not prescribed uniforms in the modern sense. Uniform regulations for enlisted seamen, as noted earlier, were not promulgated until 1841 in the United States Navy and 1857 in the Royal Navy.

Just as organizational clothing has not always consisted of uniforms, so has the uniformity of clothing not always indicated membership in an organization. Much of the confusion in reading uniforms is the result of the conflation of "uniform" with "uniformity", and it is necessary to disentangle one from the other.

Uniformity, as distinguished from a uniform, may arise through a variety of circumstances, serve many functions, have a wide array of connotations, and not necessarily denote membership in a formal organization. The similarity of dress may stem from common exigencies of work. The commonality of dress arises in this instance through the normative control in the subculture of an occupation and in its work requirements. These dress requirements change with the definition of the admissible risks in a work situation. The safety norms may change drastically over the years from those of medieval seamen who worked nude, to the Georgian seamen who had no waterproof clothing, to the modern sailor who has foul weather gear. Commonality of dress occurs in other nonoccupational areas, such as youth subcultures and fashionable elites.

Other exigencies may create similarity of dress within a group. Uniformity may not have any significance as a symbol or sign but stem instead from a narrow range of options of dress forced upon the wearer by the limited material base of an economy and technology.

Uniformity of appearance may be honorific as in wedding processions. They may be in part stigmatic, for the wearers at least, as in the obligatory appearance at funerals of the illustrious by the inmates of orphan asylums and poor houses in early Victorian England.

Finally, groups other than the state may be represented by common clothing, such as corporations and private individuals. In earlier Western society, uniformity of dress constituted livery and indicated an entirely different set of relationships based upon personal ties to a powerful patron. In still other periods and other societies, uniformity of dress designated membership in a broad social category such as social class.

From a sociological perspective the uniform is a learned category which is acquired only through socialization, exists and has meaning only within certain social contexts. The uniform is an artificial construct insofar as one of its characteristics, uniformity, is a matter of definition and learned perception rather than immediately apparent fact. We are taught to look for uniformity in the clothing of a group such as the military and police and to overlook differences; homogeneity is relative and may occur only in the eyes of the beholder. Total uniformity is impossible; uniformity as a similarity of dress is less than absolute.

Our previous discussion of minimal symbols indicates that we perceive wearers of a wide range of dress as being in uniform. Indeed, it is only in the modern era when it has become economically and technologically feasible to provide all items of dress that an approach to total uniformity becomes possible. In earlier centuries, only part of the outfit, usually the coat, was provided; other parts and even equipment had to be provided by the wearer himself. In other instances, even items provided by a central agency might vary greatly in color, resulting in a great heterogeneity in appearance. Yet would we not see members of these organizations as being "uniformed" despite heterogeneity and reliance upon civilian attire?

Even when an entire outfit is provided, there may be patterned variations indicating differences in organization and rank which we have learned to subordinate perceptually to a basic similarity. As seen earlier, although there were actually three varieties of ''redcoats'' in the British army, all were seen as part of the same organization.

THE UNIFORM AS IDEOLOGY

Both uniformed organizations and the public view the uniform as ideology, the former to proffer a desired image to outsiders, the latter to retain cherished emotive symbols. Both, therefore, attempt to control or manipulate the uniform.

The ideological function of the uniform is reflected in the type of uniform presented to outsiders. All uniforms do not have equal symbolic value for the public. In some, the wearer is more likely to be on stage or a witness to important values; in others, the wearer may work unseen by the public. These roles may be at odds with each other in symbolism. Janowitz distinguishes between the working uniform (fatigues) and ceremonial uniforms (1960, 230). The former, analogous to civilian working clothes, are the mirror of the internal workings of the organization and unsuited for public scrutiny. There may even be dismay at the public display of these symbols. Uniformed services usually forbid the wearing of work uniforms in public. A retired naval warrant officer commented on the appearance of sailors from a vessel undergoing repair.

The sailors from these ships are seen every day in the general public going to and from the ships to their homes or wherever wearing dungarees, foul weather jackets, flight jackets, blue working caps, hardhats, no hats, etc., and in very many cases the clothing is absolutely filthy. They look worse than skid row bums. And this includes whitehats, chiefs, and officers.

The Navy in general and myself in particular have every right to be ashamed to have them represent the Navy. (NT 5 Jun. 1978)

Uniformed organizations, aware of the cost of uniforms, often display a utilitarian outlook as well. The frequently voiced contrast between a conservative, traditional uniformed group lagging behind a progressive, modernizing public is often mythical. On the contrary, at times the changes proposed by a group in the appearance it presents to the world may be resisted by the public which has a stake in the old manner of dress.

The huge symbolic investment of the public in uniforms is illustrated by the reaction to attempts by the United States, British, and West German navies to change their regulation dress.[6] The ''jolly tar'', marked primarily by the universal bell-bottoms and jumpers, has long been a stock figure in Western myth.[7] The popularity of these symbols was reenforced by their introduction as children's wear in 1846—in keeping with the pattern of drafting the young as symbol bearers—when it was inflicted upon young ''Bertie'', the future King Edward VII (Ewing 1977, 87–90). The style, suitably adapted to different national uniforms, then spread almost worldwide.

The sailor, however, is not only an exemplar but also an integral part of a functioning contemporary organization. The personae of the sailor, a member of a uniformed service and a symbol bearer for the public, clashed with each other after World War II when the three navies proposed the substitution of conventional coats and trousers for the traditional attire. Since officers and chief petty officers had worn conventional uniforms, the abolition of bells and jumpers meant the substitution of a single uniform for all ranks.

When the change was finally made in the United States Navy in 1973, after a quarter century of discussion, many reasons were given (NT 31 Jan. 1977; USN 1981, app.2 p.8). The changes attempted to revitalize the service after the Vietnam era, and to adjust to the countercultural movement by removing "Mickey Mouse" restrictions governing dress (Zumwalt 1976, 182–96). The reforms blurred differences between sailors and civilians; the traditional uniform would no longer accentuate the distinction between the two statuses.

In the West German Navy, the traditional uniform was abolished in 1977 and a coat-and-trouser uniform substituted (Katz 1978; Preuschoft 1978). The new uniform would be modern, practical, comfortable, and less expensive for the navy. Moreover, a survey had shown that the change was favored by most enlisted men. Although the Royal Navy had contemplated change and had polled the attitudes of its personnel, it was decided, in the absence of overwhelming opposition to the traditional uniform, not to perform drastic changes but to make some minor modifications (Dickens 1977, 2, 10).

Within a short time the changes had to be rescinded by both the United States and West German Navies. In West Germany, the about-face was attributed to pressure mounted by the press and former naval personnel, largely officers, who opposed the loss of traditional symbols. They wanted to remain in step with other navies (the United States Navy had announced its intention to revert to bells), and disliked the loss of the old distinction between sailors and civilians which they felt might lead to sailors being mistaken for bus drivers (Preuschoft 1978). The public reaction seemed to have altered the attitudes of current naval personnel who now also opposed the new uniform.

In 1976, after the inauguration of the new uniform in the United States Navy, surveys of enlisted men indicated that from 77% to 90% of the five lowest grades favored a restoration of the traditional bells (Res. Cons. 1980, sec.1 p.1). Bells and jumpers were reinstituted beginning in 1978. A later poll in 1979 of men in the fifth grade revealed that 85% of enlisted men felt that the "Cracker Jack" uniform is what a sailor *should* look like, while 68% felt that the new uniform is what he should *not* look like (ibid., sec.3 pp.1–2).[8] As in the West German Navy, many of those polled stated that the coat-and-trouser uniform led to wearers being mistaken for other services or uniformed civilians, thereby losing their distinctive identity. Letters to the *Navy Times,* the unofficial service newspaper, over a period of years voiced the same objection (24 Oct. 1977; 23 Jan. 1978; 30 Apr. 1979; 6 Aug. 1979). Recruiting personnel reported the popularity of bells among recruits (NT 23 Jan. 1978; 5 Mar. 1979).

While there is no available data to suggest a public campaign in the United States comparable to that mounted in West Germany for the restoration of the traditional uniform, survey reports indicated a civilian preference for bells (NT 31 Jan. 1977; 5 June 1978).

YOUTH IN UNIFORM

There is, in modern times at least, an association between youth and the wearing of uniforms, and for good reason. The young are still in the preparatory stages of life; they are still in the process of socialization and training for specific skills and roles. In many educational contexts, the uniform is an important mechanism, and it is to an examination of these functions of the uniform that we now turn.

The Uniform as Institutional Device for Socialization

In some instances, the uniforms worn by the young have little relation to socialization. In the first half of the nineteenth century, youth served in the regular military services of the United States and in volunteer militias and fire companies, in the latter as both members and hangers-on (Cunliffe 1973, 89–90, 234–35; Kett 1977, 38–39). These groups are not socialization agencies of the young; they merely fill the military and other needs of the adult world. This may also be true of the local militias in today's Beirut which are "filled with teen-agers—school dropouts who swagger and strut about heavily armed and wearing a hodgepodge of uniforms. 'In a normal society you compete in studies and athletics. . . . Here we have a chance for them to play the hero of a Western movie' " (NYT 26 May 1981). In these instances, the uniform is not a metaphor for the young but a device of social control as for any adult organization.

In another pattern, the young are enrolled in uniformed groups under the aegis of adults as a means of inservice socialization which fits the young into future uniformed roles as nurses, police officers, and soldiers. The young are socialized either by "training uniforms"—those of student nurses or West Point cadets—which differ entirely from that of the parent body, or "continuous uniforms" which resemble the dress of adult members with differentiating insignia. Training or discontinuous uniforms isolate the young and facilitate their designation as symbol bearers. They enable the growth of sentimental symbols attached to the "Army gray" of West Point cadets or the "candy stripes" of student nurses, both among members of the organization and outsiders.[9] The same symbolism may not adhere to continuous uniforms which are more likely to be used in brief courses. Practicality sets boundaries; uniforms cannot be provided for a short period. The symbolism of continuous uniforms is that of pragmatism rather than sentimentality.

As a device for institutional socialization, the uniform operates, first, as a ritualistic instrument which emphasizes the means instead of the content of socialization.[10] The essential purpose of West Point's "Beast Barracks Summer", the initial socialization period for entering cadets, is to instill "reflexive obedience to established authority" (Ellis & Moore 1974, 91). Any training whether it be teaching "how to do Sanskrit or how to brush their teeth" would serve as well as the uniform, for it is not the content that matters but rather learning "to subordinate their personal hopes, aspirations, desires, whatever, to the group" (ibid.). The uniform is superior to ordinary clothing for this purpose because of its greater precision and ease of observing adherence to norms.

The uniform permits the wearer to adopt the stratagem of outward conformity to the dictates of the role instead of the internalization of its norms. One may adhere in a ritualistic manner to official dress regulations and yet not fully conform to other norms. Oleson and Whitaker contrast the novice nun who learns her role through internal conviction and motivation, and the military recruit who conforms only outwardly (1968, 66). Although the dichotomy is not necessarily mutually exclusive and both processes may occur in the same organization, the uniform does facilitate the possibility of outward conformity only.

The uniform also influences the wearer's role set. Outsiders legitimate the wearer's self-image by interaction. Patients, for example, may accept the ministrations of student nurses and thereby define the students as worthy practitioners (ibid., 271–72). Even in the absence of immediate clients, as in the instance of West Pointers, the uniform wearer is automatically designated a representative of the organization who is called upon by civilians to interpret and, in the Vietnam era, to defend it.

The uniformed instructor within the role set becomes an extremely effective model in that his master status as a professional is heavily reenforced by the uniform and consequently bolsters his subsidiary status as educator. As previously mentioned, a West Point instructor is heeded not so much because of his scholarly abilities but rather because his uniform and medals designate him as a combat veteran and therefore a model for his profession to be respected and emulated (Ellis & Moore 1974, 112, 132–33).

General Socialization—The Uniform as Metaphor

The uniform was described as a means of institutional socialization and control by an organization to fulfill its functions. The uniform, however, also serves as an important device of general socialization to prepare the young for their future social positions as adults rather than fit them into specific occupational or professional niches. After all, organizations such as the Boy Scouts use uniforms, not because of any urgent need for institutional control over members as in correctional institutions or mental hospitals, but instead as part of a complex of socializing devices. Uniforms, both military and nonmilitary, also implement general socialization into adulthood without any intent to prepare the young for future uniformed roles, a function we shall now examine.

In this form of socialization, the uniform becomes a metaphor, primarily military although not exclusively so, for the recruitment of the young into society. The clothing models the relationship between socializer and the young in a hierarchical manner and describes the appropriate channels of learning such as drill, outdoor activities, and life boating.[11]

The perceived need for the metaphor became apparent during the latter part of the nineteenth century in Great Britain, the United States, and elsewhere. Around this time, a multitude of uniformed and nonuniformed youth movements were established, impelled by the discovery, or invention, of adolescence—a status between childhood and adulthood and seemingly free from the institutionalized constraints of either. These new, interstitial cohorts had outgrown the childhood controls of family and school and were not yet subject to those of adulthood. New youth groups arose to meet institutional lacunae (Gillis 1981, 144; Springhall 1977, 15). Founders of the Jewish Lads' Brigades wanted to "keep boys out of mischief after they had left Board School, and before they were old enough to join the Jewish Working Men's Club or the newly emerging Jewish Boys' Club" (Springhall 1977, 42). The Catholic Boys' Brigades were intended to safeguard "their faith and morals after they had left school and before they could be reached by either the Society of St. Vincent de Paul or the Catholic Young Men's Society" (ibid., 43–44). American movements such as the Christian Endeavor and the Student Volunteer Movement also used the uniform metaphor (Kett 1977, 196–97).

The dreaded "mischief" or "lapses from faith and morals" included adolescent sexuality which was greatly feared by middle-class youth leaders. Youth groups constituted part of a regimen which included strenuous exercise, sports, diet, and other measures intended to sublimate, or divert, youthful sex drives (ibid., 164–65, 193, 208).

The metaphor had class as well as sexual undertones. Middle-class adults, who were the mainsprings of the youth movement, established uniformed organizations not only to counteract the apparent anomie of working-class youth but also to commit them to patriotism and to suppress working-class militancy (Springhall 1977, 14–15). The basic clash and mutual distrust of styles of life— the contrast between working-class spontaneity and middle-class self-control— were also factors. Predictably, the instillation of middle-class values succeeded primarily among the lower middle class and the mobile sons of skilled workers rather than the working class at large (Springhall, 1971, 138–40).

Turning to the dynamics of the metaphor, it enabled adults to locate socially adolescents who were no longer a free-floating conglomerate but a tangible, organized, and recognizable entity. London youth in the mid-nineteenth century were organized into brigades of shoe blacks, pavement sweepers, and rag collectors (Anderson 1971, 69). A wide range of religious groups in Great Britain— Anglicans, Presbyterians, Roman Catholics, and Jews—used the metaphor. As previously noted, the range of uniform metaphors was not restricted to the military but has included lifesaving, woodsmanship and outdoor survival, and seamanship.

The metaphor was less essential for adolescents of other classes. In Britain at least, the public school served as the agency for socializing middle- and upper-class youth. Indeed, the uniformed youth movement has been described as a channel for spreading public school values among the working class (Springhall 1977, 40, 53, 123–24). As for the upper classes, the military in Britain and on the continent has long been regarded as the natural preserve of the aristocracy for whom the military is not a metaphor but rather part of their way of life. Young British aristocrats and gentry used the army frequently in the nineteenth and earlier centuries as a period of socialization (Harries-Jenkins 1977, 29).

The uniform metaphor was applicable to the young only as the result of a revolution in symbols which involved a reevaluation of the military and its dress. The animus against the military had to be overcome, and it was. Attitudes toward the military changed in the middle of the nineteenth century because of the religious discovery of soldiers during the Crimean and American Civil Wars, especially by evangelical sects. The heathen constituency of missionaries was discovered within the gates of the city. The religious needs of troops had been previously met by the army but in a cold and perfunctory manner. Now they were adopted by the civilian population as "our suffering heroes" and "the peoples' army" (Anderson 1971, 46; also Kett 1977, 196). The reevaluation was aided by the advent of "muscular Christianity", the reconciliation of religion with a vigorous life of achievement and action rather than contemplation, which found the role of the soldier much more congenial than that of the intellectual recluse (Newsome 1961, 195–239). The resemblance to the myth of the cowboy is apparent; Theodore Roosevelt provides an excellent example.

The symbolic context within which society operated had changed. The military became an increasingly popular metaphor (Anderson 1971). As an indication of acceptance, clergy and lay practitioners would almost automatically exhort their audiences to armed mortal combat although they faltered in their description of the foe (Kett 1977, 197). The metaphor was a double one; religious groups defined their own activities in military terms and in turn imposed a religious-military version upon the young.

The use of the uniform may not be pure metaphor if military authorities or youth leaders attempt to convert these movements into military auxiliaries. After all, it does make sense from a practical standpoint to regard an organized, drilled, and uniformed group of adolescents as a partially trained reserve.[12] Indeed, some would deny the possibility of any use of uniformed youth groups entirely as a metaphor (Springhall 1971).

While not denying hidden motives and militaristic tendencies, nevertheless antimilitaristic countertrends are also manifested in youth movements which accept uniforms but reject military affiliations. Whereas the British War Office, before World War I, attempted to incorporate uniformed youth groups into its training and reserve components and succeeded with the Church Boys' Brigade, the Boys' Brigade resisted, despite the blandishments of financial and other aid (ibid., 140–48). Schismatic scouting and youth groups arose to protest what was perceived as the underlying militaristic tendencies of the parent organization of Scouts (ibid., 138–40).

A contemporary account of a private military group for boys in New York City, the Knickerbocker Greys, similarly stressed its nonmilitary ideology. "The Greys is essentially *not* a military experience. It uses military trappings to teach the rudiments of playing a responsible role in a democracy." The spokesman goes on to say that, "you know that what this really is is a tunnel leading into the old boy network" (NYT 10 Sept. 1979).

THE COWBOY—ANATOMY OF AN IDEOLOGICAL SYMBOL

Military dress is influenced not only by public involvement in its symbolism, as we have seen, but also by institutional requirements. Other occupations also furnish important symbols to a society but are not subject as much to the needs of a contemporary institution.

The clothing of the working cowboy of 1880 served the same functions as any occupational dress; it was simultaneously a vehicle or tool, a sign, and also an item subject to economic constraints. It had to fill the needs of the cowboy as a worker, and a poorly paid one at that. His clothing allowed the cowboy to perform his job and, at least as important, express his status and differentiate it from bull-whackers (wagon train drivers), wranglers (horse tenders), farmers, soldiers (from whom they obtained some of their clothing), and sheepmen (Rickey 1976, 10–11). In 1980 there were still cowboys extant, albeit subsumed under the Census category of "agricultural worker", but now the cowboy is also the hero of an American myth.

The cowboy is "pure" symbol, an exemplar of the values we use to depict the world. His clothes become symbols not of an actual occupation but rather of a Manichean struggle between white hats and black hats. He rides trails not to bring cattle to market, but rather to tame the West and to conquer nature out of a spirit of adventure. "The cowboy hero endures *because* he is in large measure divorced from history, *because* his heroism derives from altogether different sources. . . . The significance of his myth—and the reason why it is so vigorously defended by the cowboy establishment—is that it suggests to Americans what they might have been and what they might yet become" (Savage 1979, 38).[13]

And Americans would have it no other way even though reality strongly contradicts the myth. As agricultural workers, Blacks, Mexicans, Jews, and other minorities were represented in their ranks; they were dominated by large scale organizations; they were organized briefly by the Knights of Labor and participated in a strike that failed (Hine 1973, 130–35). The contemporary cowboy who sees his job as simply a way of making a living, as work and not a calling, is disqualified from the role of symbol bearer. Rather, we would have him as someone for whom the occupation is a total way of life. Whenever occupational roles are given mythical proportions, there is the tendency to agree with the admiral who deplored young men who join the Navy, not for patriotism but for practical, economic reasons. The reduction of these pursuits to the category of ordinary motivation and purpose robs them of some of their symbolic functions for the culture. The relevance of the contrast between the real and mythical pursuits lies in the contrast between the criteria for a pursuit as a working occupation and as a symbol for the culture. While the wearers of symbolic dress often evaluate it themselves in terms of utility and economy—the requirements of a profession or occupation—outsiders are more likely to view the dress as a symbol of patriotism or adventure. A complicating element is that the status occupant himself may incorporate the symbolic views of his status derived from the outer world.

As we shall see, sartorial symbols are used to different degrees of intensity or realism by various subcultures. The corresponding differences in criteria governing the use of symbols vary from the exigencies of an occupation to pure fantasy.

The Differential Use of the Cowboy as Symbol

Differences in the use of historical symbols is nowhere better seen than with the cowboy and those who borrow his dress. At the center of the subculture of the cowboy—from which other subcultures radiate—there is an admixture of myth and existential reality. The demands posited by peers and the job situation mingle with the myth and expectations of the public which are reflected back to and absorbed by the contemporary cowhand. Unlike other heroic figures such as the knight, minuteman, rifleman, or continental soldier, the cowboy exists in the present and is thus subject to two conflicting sets of demands, those stemming from his work and those from the imitation of art by life.

The clothing of the older generation of cowboys, especially in the 1880's before the advent of inexpensive new clothing on the frontier, was ill-fitting, patched and second hand (Rickey 1976, 8–52; Savage 1979, 53, 64–65).[14] Whatever other purpose they may have served, all elements of apparel such as boots, hats, bandanas, and chaps also had a utilitarian function (Rickey 1976, 8– 52; Univ. of Wyoming).

Occupational clothing is never determined only by the demands of the job itself but also very frequently by the need to place the wearer socially. As previously mentioned, cowhands made an effort to differentiate themselves from similar statuses. Cowboys displayed regional differences in styles of dress until the 1920's when the homogenizing influence of films and mail order catalogues created a universal style (Brownlow 1978, 296).

The impact of externally derived images is seen in an account of a contemporary cowboy who dresses in black, not for the original reason mentioned by cowboys of hiding dirt but because it is the color worn by film cowboys (Kramer 1980, 31; Rickey 1976, 27). This cowboy also uses film heroes as his role model rather than his own father or grandfather, both of whom were cowhands. Another cowboy does wear simple, practical clothes but adopts the Hollywood actors' mode of creasing his hat (NYT 4 July 1981).

At the same time, real cowboys try to distinguish themselves from the simulated variety by preventing outsiders from borrowing western symbols. Long haired strangers who attempted to buy cowboy hats during the counterculture era of the 1970's were assaulted by cowboys (Kramer 1980, 41). But the confusion between the real and the mythical persists. In one incident, women preferred the pseudocowboy to the real one because the former dressed more like a cowboy (NYT 4 July 1981).

In the next concentric circle of subcultures, that of the rodeo, the contrast between fact and fiction becomes more apparent and we see a gradual transition between the cowboy as worker and as myth. Originally started in the nineteenth century as a virtuoso display of skills by cowboys, rodeos have by now assumed a life of their own. Their performers often do not come from the ranks of actual cowboys but follow a separate career line starting in elementary school and progressing through high school and college in a manner parallel to the development of professional football players (O'Neill 1979; Savage 1979, 125–28). The skills emphasized in the rodeo have been described as not being useful to the working cowboy, for example bulldogging (Savage 1979, 124). If used, these skills are certainly not employed with the same frequency in ordinary life, just as the police do not engage in daily gun battles. The more frequently used, but less heroic skills, such as carpentry, applied veterinary medicine, or the castration of young bulls are ignored in rodeos. These mundane skills would detract from the image of the cowboy as a heroic, mythical figure.

Other, still more peripheral, subcultures and groups also use the cowboy as symbol. Organized costumed groups which simulate the life-style of cowboys and related figures such as the Indian and frontier soldier have proliferated even abroad in West Germany and in Communist nations such as Rumania and East Germany (NYT 8 Aug. 1977; Time 18 June 1979; WSJ 13 Nov. 1981). Many of these groups insist upon absolute accuracy, hence the ironical reluctance of non-Communist groups to admit to membership Americans because they are less likely to know the minutiae of the Wild West. Even more ironical, the accuracy is self-defeating and unobtainable because it does not allow for even the minor deviations from clothing norms that so frequently occur.

The cult of the urban cowboy was the center of a youth subculture focussed on the riding of a mechanical bull and also included "socializing" and sexual encounters.[15] The sharp distinction between the requirements of the cowboy as worker and as symbol for the outer world becomes very clear.[16] The simulated cowboy wears clothes suggestive of the real cowboy which, however, would be utterly unsuited to the actual work situation. He wears a shirt of Western cut, to be sure, but with short sleeves which would be disastrous in cactus country under a harsh desert sun.

Another group employing the symbol of the cowboy and his clothes is the long distance truck driver who identifies with the cowboy's supposed qualities of laissez-faire individuality and machoism (NYT 26 June 1981; Savage 1979, 49). A prevalent joke is that the difference between the cowboy and the trucker is the latter's greater use of cowboy boots, another instance of the imposter being more royal than the king (Savage 1979, 49).[17]

Functions of the Cowboy as Symbol

The cowboy symbolizes a preindustrial American past, mythical in large part, that offers a refuge to those dissatisfied with the routinization of industrial society. The cowboy is above all a rugged, laissez-faire individualist who survives through his own efforts and courage.[18] Hence, his appeal to the long distance trucker, who is also a free-moving, autonomous entrepreneur. Similarly, the cowboy is described, with doubtful accuracy, as a small businessman-rancher. Accordingly, a contemporary cowboy, working for wages, was encouraged by the myth in his improbable dream of becoming a rancher (Kramer 1980, 114–15).

A related component of the cowboy myth is that of the mobile and active individual.Neither the cowboy nor the trucker are tied down to a desk job or factory bench but are free to roam the trails or highways—a theme emphasized in Western novels and films. They are actively engaged in "doing something", in man's work rather than the meaningless routine of office or factory. Part of this component is that of the cowboy or trucker as an errant chevalier who performs good deeds in his travel in the fashion of "Shane" or by aiding stranded motorists.[19]

For the public at large, the cowboy is a patriot who can solve problems in an active manner. The national frustration over the Iranian hostage situation several years ago was in part alleviated by the irrelevant campaign to wear yellow ribbons which did not resolve the issue but provided some catharsis. A cowboy, in popular mythology, could well have blasted his way into Iran and freed the hostages (NYT 8 June 1980).

Cowboy dress enables assimilation not only into the subcultures previously mentioned but also into the regional ones of the West and Southwest. Newcomers to the sun belt can identify immediately, at least on a superficial level, with the outlook of the area by the adoption of popularized versions of cowboy boots and Stetson hats (NYT 3 May 1980).

Finally, as the bearer of a moral code, the cowboy stands in a special relationship to the young like the knight for Victorian England (Girouard 1981). The code, for which the mythical cowboy is socializing agent, is for the most part a blend of the previously discussed symbols and the standard platitudes of society. Films and television have established conventions in keeping with this function, such as always depicting the cowboy as clean shaven and wearing his proverbial white hat.[20]

NOTES

1. Raymond Firth describes the importance of flags, emblems, postage stamps, seals, and coins as national symbols, labeling them "an exercise in practical Durkheimianism" (1973, 341–42). The slogan, "In God We Trust" was originally put on American coins during the Civil War only after a heated debate echoing the dispute between overt witnessing versus internal adherence to beliefs.

2. Uniforms of the 1779 pattern were not issued until the Yorktown campaign in 1781, almost at the close of the war (CMH 1976).

3. Illustrating a lack of uniformity, Revolutionary War units also wore yellow or black hunting shirts and black, gray, white, yellow, undyed, and even red coats (Elting 1960; Mollo, J. 1975, 156–211). Trousers similarly varied in color.

4. Subterfuges and euphemisms were used, such as "senior captain" and "flag officer", to meet the need for higher naval officers (Tily 1964, 24–25, 47, 52, 58). Since elaborate uniforms also smacked of monarchy, the officers' uniforms in the Continental Navy during the Revolution were very plain until officers protested and designed more ornate dress patterned after the British (USN 1981, app.2 p.8). The Soviet Union abolished army ranks and uniforms indicative of the old regime after the revolution and designated all officers "commanders" (e.g. "division commander") (Mollo, A. 1977, 53–57). Midway through World War II, Tsarist ranks and uniforms were restored to define the struggle as patriotic.

5. The perception of a bureaucratized military structure with a continuum of ranks is modern. Until the end of the eighteenth century, only two commissioned combatant officers, captain and lieutenant, existed in the United States Navy instead of the current six (excluding flag officers) (NHD 1966, pl. 1797). A third in Britain was the equivalent of commander (Lewis, M. 1948a, 192–224). Turning to structure, the divisional system was introduced into the Royal Navy about 1775 (Lloyd 1970, 234). In the earlier Georgian navy, the division of the crew into only two watches resulted in an "indiscriminate mass of humanity, individually indistinguishable to the average lieutenant" (ibid.).

6. According to a French naval attaché, proposed changes in bell-bottoms never gained substantial support in the French Navy (Menettrier 1978). He also notes that French sailors feel that women in France and abroad have a special liking for their uniform. Canada introduced a common uniform for all services in the late 1960's which will shortly be abandoned in favor of separate dress for each (Hellyer 1966; Morrison 1971).

7. The sailor was regarded as industrious and likable and much less of a threat than his military counterpart.

8. "Cracker Jack", the boy in bell-bottoms used as a logo for a brand of candied popcorn since 1919, illustrates the diffusion of symbols between the military and civilians (NT 31 Jan. 1977).

9. A United States postage stamp of 1961 commemorates the nursing profession with a student nurse in striped uniform lighting a candle.

10. Reliance upon the uniform for institutional socialization varies with the use of the total institution as a model. At one extreme, the organization may rely heavily upon the total institution, attempt to instill traditional values, and use the uniform as a device. The U.S. Air Force Aviation Cadet Pre-Flight Training School, no longer in existence, stressed heroic qualities in future officers and employed the uniform in the manner

described in this section (Wamsley 1972). Similarly, traditional hospitals and some conventional diploma schools inculcated the traditional image of the nurse as a subservient auxiliary and relied upon rigid dress codes (Oleson & Whitaker 1968, 111–12). In contrast, a contemporary Air Force training organization, the Officers Training School, which instills managerial qualities in its students, does not rely greatly upon the uniform as a training device (Wamsley 1972). The University of California nursing school which views the nurse as a professional similarly emphasizes dress codes much less than the nursing schools previously mentioned (Oleson & Whitaker 1968, 111–12). In this section, the emphasis will be upon traditional uniformed organizations.

11. That the uniform is a metaphor for general and not institutional socialization is indicated by the discontinuity between present uniforms and activities and future adult roles projected for the adolescent. One may see, or think he does, the importance of close order drill for a future soldier, but what is its relevance for the embryonic physician? Recognition of the discontinuity compels a rationalization ranging from a well thought-out ideology to a casual association of symbols (Kett 1977, 196–97; Springhall 1971). Ideology stresses the relationship to military preparedness; casual association describes the acquisition of abstract virtues such as discipline, self-reliance, and punctuality.

12. The leaders and founders of the youth brigades adopted the military role based upon the linear tactics of earlier centuries in which the soldier was subject to rigid control, moved in precise formation, and harshly disciplined. When the military metaphor is adopted, the linear role is the one usually conceived of, in varying degrees, as the appropriate model for indoctrination and control. To some extent, the model is adopted in any school where students, uniformed or not, are taught to keep in line and march in step. At an extreme, it becomes robotic control which ignores the existence of other military roles. Skirmishers, scouts, or rangers rely more heavily upon individual initiative and are therefore less likely to be employed by those seeking strict control. The latter model was used by Baden-Powell whose early Boy Scout handbook was drawn from his previous military manual on scouting (Springhall 1977, 55–61). Not surprisingly, the Boy Scouts in Britain retained their popularity after the decline of the rigidly controlled Boys' Brigades after World War I.

13. In reality, the early cowboy was not highly regarded and "cowboy" was a term of opprobrium during the American Revolution. In the West of the 1880's, he had an unsavory reputation. His image was laundered and he received the initial impetus toward heroic stature through the efforts of William Cody ("Buffalo Bill") and his "Wild West Show", and dime novelists (Savage 1979, 109–10). The cowboy is one of a constellation of personae of the Old West which includes sheriffs, outlaws, Indians, and frontiersmen.

14. The clothing of contemporary cowboys is still simple and cheap (NYT 4 July 1981; WSJ 10 June 1981).

15. This paragraph uses the following references: Latham 1978; NYT 10 June 1977; 8 Oct. 1980; 27 Dec. 1981; Slesin 1978; WSJ 9 Oct. 1980; 10 Nov. 1980; 7 May 1982.

16. The change in the role of pain for the cult is significant. One would assume that originally the primary purpose of riding a bronco or bull would be to tame him—although we must not fall into a utilitarian trap and overlook the auxiliary function of proving masculinity. In the cult of the mechanical bull, however, the primary purpose becomes not that of taming a machine but of proving one's ability to endure pain. Masculinity cannot be tested since "cowgirls" also participate and at times surpass the men. The performance has become ritualistic in that former means are now goals; pain is not the by-product of taming a wild animal, but has itself become the end.

17. Players of popular music or country and western, and homosexuals or gay machos, also rely upon cowboy dress (Savage 1979, 80–84, 104–5).

18. In the nineteenth century the early proponents of the cowboy canon, Remington, Wister, and others were strong advocates of Social Darwinism, racial superiority, and were opponents of the newer wave of immigration (Gerster & Cords 1977, 173–75; Hine 1973, 138).

19. To introduce a few notes of reality, not all cowboys were good shots (Rickey 1976, 64). Furthermore, the frequent interchangeability between the roles of peace officer and outlaw casts doubts upon their actual function in the past as upholders of morality (Snell 1980).

20. Canadians have protested the spread of the legend of the Western sheriff to their culture through films and television which has resulted in the depiction of the nineteenth-century Canadian Mounty as merely a Northern counterpart of the American sheriff (Preston 1978, 63). This is another example of the homogenization of symbols and exemplars.

PART THREE
NONUNIFORMS

8

Nonbureaucratic Dress: Knights to Guerrillas

The modern uniform is closely linked to the central structural tendency of our age—an increasingly pervasive bureaucratization. The intent of this chapter is to determine how departures from contemporary bureaucratic structures are reflected by nonbureaucratic dress.

Prebureaucratic feudal and patrimonial structures provide a test for the results of substituting personal ties for bureaucratic relationships based upon rationality and impersonal loyalty to a formal organization. The postbureaucratic structure of recent guerrilla movements, and significantly their establishment opponents, reflect a situation where indications of organizational affiliation are shunned. In this instance, wearing a uniform to demarcate boundaries between members and nonmembers of a group is highly disadvantageous. More importantly, the autonomy of decentralized units may be preferable to a rigid bureaucratic structure.

Within these two contexts, I shall concentrate upon those sartorial signs which designate key relationships and their attached norms and values. My focus will be upon military dress since the abundance of data allows us to trace the parallel changes of structure and clothing in detail.

FEUDAL LIVERY AND PATRIMONIAL WHIM

Feudalism and Bastard Feudalism

The distant ancestor of the modern officer is the feudal knight and, as feudalism is succeeded by bastard feudalism and later by patrimonial structures, the knight and his dress change too. These stages are reflected in the changing loyalties of the officer and his predecessors from the feudal era to the present when the modern state claims a monopoly of the instruments of violence.

The medieval knight was a lifelong member of a Christian profession who derived his rights from membership in a knightly estate rather than a military organization (Keen 1965, 56). In contrast, his modern counterpart, the military officer, is a member of a bureaucratized profession whose status derives from belonging to an organization and lapses upon leaving it (Huntington 1957, 14–17).[1]

The norms governing the knight were those binding upon his estate rather than a particular army to which he belonged. It was this obligation that, as we have seen, led Henry V to execute a French knight who had violated the norms even though the knight's action had benefited the king (Keen 1965, 46). The historical distance we have come since then is measured by our reaction of incredulity to the British Air Minister who refused to order the bombing of a German target in 1939 because it was private property (Deighton 1979, 56).

Knightly insignia indicated the position of the combatant as an individual rather than a member of a military organization. Or, if he were not of sufficient stature, his insignia was indicative of his obligations toward a more powerful individual and not a group. Heraldry proclaimed the individual and not a military organization.[2] The captured knight had a private and contractual obligation to his captor that had priority over obligations to his liege. When he was paroled to raise his ransom, insignia of his captor would be worn to reflect his changed status and to serve as passport or safeguard (Keen 1965, 110–11).

"The medieval system of values placed obedience to the public authority and devotion to the common goal below individual loyalty—whether feudal, between the lord and his man, or contractual, between the lord and his retainer" (Stone, L. 1967, 199). The concomitant value for the nobleman was personal honor which led in combat to the ideal of the individual champion skilled in arms (Bendix 1960, 363). The chief combatant was not a modern bureaucratic officer, but rather an individual hero.

The importance of honor is reflected in the reciprocal ties between opponents where honor was achieved by defeating a powerful foe in personal combat. High-ranking knights fighting in the mines under the walls of besieged cities, a very difficult form of warfare, sometimes knighted common-born foes in order to enhance their own honor (Keen 1965, 48–49). Honor even superseded tactical considerations. Several days before Agincourt, Henry V erroneously bypassed the village at which he had intended to spend the night but could not retrace his steps since he had ordered knights not to retreat while armored for battle and he himself was in panoply (Huizinga 1954, 98–99). Adherence to the chivalric code of honor, stress upon the knight as hero, and emphasis upon individuality obviously made it difficult to implement any complex tactical plan.

Not only was personal insignia a means of asserting individual identity and gaining honor, but conversely, it was also a means of enforcing the chivalric code by degrading the knight who dishonored the terms of the parole granted by his captor. Dishonor was inflicted by dragging the offender's insignia through the dirt, or hanging them backwards (Keen 1965, 54–55).

In later medieval England, the military exigencies of the Hundred Years War created a revival of feudalism—bastard feudalism—in which an even greater stress was placed upon personal honor (Lewis, N. 1968, 200). Whereas loyalty to a lord during feudalism might be based upon hereditary ties and therefore not entirely voluntary, in the later period lord and retainer personally and freely selected each other and frequently sealed the arrangement contractually (ibid., 209). Additionally, the retainer was fed or paid rather than tenured, thereby remaining permanently dependent upon his lord (ibid., 208; McFarlane 1973, 105–6).

The key relationship was that of superior and inferior, of landed magnate and his dependents who comprised three concentric circles (Lewis, N. 1968, 201). A core group of household servants was augmented by a larger group of lifetime retainers with written contracts and finally by those who merely accepted the lord's fees to render him service (ibid.). In none of these groups was service to the lord construed as menial in the modern sense.[3] Each group contained a wide range of strata including gentry, knights, and those with independent means (McFarlane 1973, 105; Stone, L. 1967, 208).[4] Service was an assertion of personal affiliation with an individual. Although in this instance our interest lies in hierarchical loyalties or affiliations, personal loyalty could also extend to equals, even foes. For example, "brothers-in-arms", even though they were on opposite sides, had special obligations toward each other (Keen 1965, 48–49).

The function of the personal affiliation changed. At first, household armed servants and the armed retinue were primarily an instrument of power, militarily as a source of fighting men for the magnates' own use and as a force supplied to the king upon demand; politically as a means of overawing juries, defying courts of justice, influencing Parliament, and even rebelling against the king (McFarlane 1973, 114–16; Stone, L. 1967, 202, 225–31). Later in more settled times, the display function of the retinue increased in importance (Girouard 1978, 20). The vicarious consumption by dependents indicates not only differences in status and wealth, but also in the possession of power.

The relationships within a patrimonial organization had an economic as well as a power and status tinge. In the era of bastard feudalism, the magnate not only benefited by the power accruing from his retinue, but also profited financially from the ransoms collected by the retainers he contracted to the crown (Lewis, N. 1968, 203–4).

The advantage of the affiliation for the retinued retainer was the identification with a great patron in a ruthless struggle for power. Even men of substance, landowners, justices of the peace, and members of parliament were included in the retinue (Stone, L. 1967, 208). At the lower end of the social scale, strolling players sought the protection of the lord against vagrancy laws (ibid., 210).

These ties between magnate and dependents were expressed by livery which indicated personal ties to individuals and not membership in impersonal groups as with modern uniforms. "The livery or badge of a powerful man was a sign of privilege not servitude. It showed that its wearer belonged to the exploiting rather than the exploited classes" (Girouard 1978, 16). Often the retainers wore livery when carrying out their own business as an added advantage. The lord's emblem was at times even reproduced in stone on the facade of the retainer's home (Stone, L. 1967, 208).

Retainers were obligated to serve the lord in all circumstances, and the same livery was worn in peace and war. Troops furnished to the king remained the magnate's personal retainers (ibid., 203–6). The units permanently attached to the king, for example the Yeomen of the Guard established by Henry VII, were retainers of the king functioning as a powerful magnate; the dress of the Yeomen was therefore royal livery rather than a military uniform (Laver 1951, 126). Captains of royal ships appearing at the court of Elizabeth I wore her livery in accordance with their status as personal retainers rather than members of a military organization (Jarrett 1960, 16).

Livery, then, indicated a particularistic and patrimonial relationship to a chief, rather than to an impersonal and permanent organization. Military and nonmilitary service, combatant and civil servant, were not distinguished from one another as they are today.[5] One is the retainer of Earl Grey under all circumstances and wears his livery whether serving him on his estate, as part of his armed entourage while he is traveling, or while serving under him or his surrogate in time of war. The totality of the relationship is indicated by the original definition of livery as the complete support received from one's patron including food as well as clothing (Laver 1951, 126; Unwin 1938, 189).

The Patrimonial Army

Under the Tudors and Stuarts, and for some time thereafter, the proprietary army unit, raised and managed by the colonel as its owner and subcontractor for the crown, was an important component of the British, French, and other armies. The private character of the organization perpetuated the personal ties of the bastard feudal period and was reflected in dress. These ties received additional emphasis from the ad hoc nature of the units which were raised for specific campaigns and then dissolved.[6]

The colonels selected the dress for their respective regiments well into the eighteenth century, very often basing them upon family colors or armorial bearings. After the initial period of the English Civil War, when armies "dressed according to men's stations in life" and wore civilian clothing, regimental dress of both sides ranged over the spectrum and included green, yellow, blue, white, buff, and red (Barnes 1951, 42). Later, Cromwell's New Model Army instituted red dress as standard attire.

Indications of personal affiliations disappeared only with the advent of the modern, government controlled army. In France the control of officers over uniforms ended toward the close of the eighteenth century when regiments became permanent organizations of the state, rather than ad hoc proprietary groups disbanded at the cessation of hostilities, and officers became full-fledged state servants (Barnett 1970, 227).

Military dress in the patrimonial era was often of poor quality due to the position of colonels. The patrimonial colonel as contractor profited from the size of his unit, being paid by the crown so much per head. The colonel benefited by procuring clothing for his men as cheaply as possible, leading to skimping on the quality of cloth and dyes. The parsimonious attitude toward military clothing stands in strong contrast to the simultaneous use of ornate dress for military musicians and the later use of livery for servants. In these forms of vicarious consumption, a cheeseparing attitude would have subverted the entire function of ostentatious display.

The realization of a major function of modern uniforms, identification of the enemy, could not be attained by the accepted vagaries of dress in premodern armies. Instead, temporary field signs, adopted for the day of battle, differentiated friend from foe. These included handkerchiefs, scarves (or *not* wearing scarves), rear shirt tails worn outside trousers (an added inducement not to turn one's back on the enemy), and leaves (Carman 1957, 25–26; Gessler & Schneider 1952, 3334). At the Battle of Marston Moor in the English Civil War, a Parliamentarian leader, Sir Thomas Fairfax, saved himself by removing the white handkerchief from his hat, the sign for the day, and riding undetected through enemy ranks (Firth, C. 1962, 232).[7]

The absence of field signs and standardized uniforms often led to disaster. The similarity of the Hessians' blue and red coats to those of Delaware troops led to confusion by the British and the capture of some of their troops during the Battle of Long Island (Ward 1952, 224–25). As late as the beginning of the Civil War, each side fired on its own men due to the lack of a single distinctive dress for either army (Cunliffe 1973, 11–12).

In proprietary units, the importance of the personal nature of the tie to the colonel was often indicated by the designation of a unit with the colonel's name rather than by a number or other impersonal label. When the unit changed commanders the name of the regiment became that of the new colonel. In a revealing instance of the personal relationship, the Earl of Chesterfield dressed his regiment in uniforms with black facings upon the death of his mother (Carman 1957, 34).

The personal position of the colonel was paramount and reflected in other forms of symbolism. Whereas the size of modern military units is based on criteria derived from military doctrine, the size of companies of the English army was often determined by the rank of the commanding officer.[8] The difference in size reflected not only differences in status, but also profitability since the income of the proprietors of the regiment depended upon the number of men serving under them.[9]

In a modern bureaucracy, the hierarchy indicated by distinctions in uniform is internal to the organization and is based upon the need for specifying chains of command. Distinctions originating outside the organization are irrelevant and to be ignored or eradicated. Within patrimonial armies, on the other hand, status distinctions were based not only on rank but also on membership in civilian elites. As previously described, in the British Army of 1688, due to the absence of dress regulations—a significant omission—the amount of gold braid worn by officers depended mainly upon their affluence. The establishment of rank markings in the American Army in 1775 was partly the result of Washington's annoyance with the "leveling influence" among New England troops. Officers in these units, often elected by their men in collegial fashion, fraternized with enlisted men to the extent of serving as their barbers and cobblers—to the dismay of troops from less egalitarian colonies (Finke 1956; Ward 1952, 103–4).

What is true of the army is also true of the navy but with some structural differences. Almost immediately upon the use of sailing vessels as warships, a distinction arose between those who sailed them and those who fought in them.[10] In part, this was due to the source of combat vessels. Until the advent of the big gun ship under Henry VIII, merchant ships, both King's and commoners', were drafted into naval service and temporarily converted into warships armed with small guns (Lewis, M. 1948b, 25; Preston et al. 1956, 123–24).

The drafting of ships was reflected in personnel. The original crew was retained to sail the ship and was augmented by a force of soldiers who embarked to fight. The latter were commanded by gentlemen officers who knew little of the sea; the crew was commanded by civilian officers who ran the ship under the supervision of the military. Although both groups were later amalgamated into permanent crews, a remnant of the old distinction remained in the Royal Navy and other navies. Bos'ns and masters, descendants of the sailors, were treated as permanent appurtenances of the ship and assigned rank by Navy Board warrants—the same procedure used for ordering ship's equipment and supplies. Commissioned officers, descendants of the fighting men, were commissioned directly by the monarch and, until the middle of the nineteenth century in the Royal Navy, assigned to ships on an ad hoc, cruise-by-cruise basis—a reflection of a patrimonial outlook.[11]

The difference between the patrimonial and modern naval officer is reflected in the parallel distinction between post and rank (Lewis, M. 1948a, 60–78). In the former, the officer was appointed to a specific position aboard a designated vessel (third lieutenant of HMS John Doe) for the duration of the ship's commission. His commission would be renewed for each position with intervals, lengthy at times, of unemployment. Between cruises, he received half-pay as a form of retainer. His status could rise or fall, depending upon the posting he was able to achieve. Rank, on the other hand, designates a position within a permanent, full-time career in a service, regardless of specific posting. Defining officers in terms of rank rather than post is indispensable for the attainment of the modern bureaucratic structure. One of the reformers instrumental in the transition from post to rank was the indefatigable Pepys.

Naval clothing reflected these changes. The naval uniform was not introduced into the Royal Navy until 1748 and then probably at the request of officers who wanted to differentiate themselves from their military counterparts rather than for purposes of internal control (May 1966, 3–4). The original function of naval uniforms, then, seems to have been the certification of status based upon civilian society rather than the meeting of organizational requirements. The distinction between commissioned and warrant officers remains; the latter did not receive uniforms until 1787 which, in the Royal Navy and later in the United States Navy, carefully differentiated between the two strata (ibid., 4–5; Tily 1964, 92–94).

The inauguration of officers' uniforms did not mean immediate adoption by all. Reluctance to adopt a dress code which required the abandonment of the distinctions of civilian status may have delayed change. Because of his higher civilian origins, a purser wore a cocked hat rather than the top hat of the boatswain even though both were of similar rank (Masefield 1937, 107). The problem of costs, especially for those risen from the ranks, impeded change. Even those from the lower middle class who were accustomed to wearing comfortable civilian clothes while in service found the expense burdensome (Jarrett 1960, 47, 108; Manders & Snook 1965). Permission was subsequently granted to wear out older uniforms before newer models were purchased.

Within any patrimonial organization, the arbitrary will of the leader has leeway for display. For the navy, the free display of patrimonial privilege was manifested in the use of personal insignia by members of the crew under an officer's direct command. The naval captain or admiral regarded his boat crew as a personal retinue to be clad as he saw fit and whose clothing reflected this personal tie. Early nineteenth century ships' captains in the Royal Navy placed their personal insignia on their gig crews and admirals on their barge crews (Dickens 1977, 7,14). A famous example is that of the captain of HMS Harlequin who of course dressed his crew in harlequin clothing (ibid., 7). Another captain's boat crew had highlanders' clothing. Still others wore the personal colors or armorial bearings of their commander.

The recruitment of officers indicates the strength of patrimonial ties, especially in the Royal Navy from the days before Elizabeth I until about 1794. In this period many aspirants entered the service as "captain's servants", a patronage position couched in terms of personal retinue and subject to free selection by the captain (Lewis, M. 1948a, 78–86).[12]

Whereas personal relationships within contemporary organizations are not usually reflected in the formal structure, within a patrimonial organization they *are* the structure and are signaled by dress.

GUERRILLA DRESS: THE MILITARY NONUNIFORM

If the lack of uniforms is highly correlated with feudal and patrimonial social structures, as my analysis indicates, what are we to make of the lack of uniforms among some military forces in this era of the centralized and bureaucratized state? Here, of course, I am pointing to the seeming anomaly of guerrilla and even regular units not wearing uniforms. We may discern three major reasons for this situation: first, irregular dress is related to a frequent inability of newly raised military units to obtain regulation uniforms; second, a lack of uniforms may be more beneficial than their use to such groups; and, finally, regular units behind enemy lines may find it advantageous to abandon their regulation uniforms.

In the first type of irregular military dress, new units aspire to uniforms because of their adoption of the conventional military as a metaphor. Older generations of guerrillas, say roughly those between the two World Wars, saw themselves as a makeshift for conventional military organizations and activities. Even the Russian and Chinese Red Armies evaluated the conventional military more highly, a surprising outlook given their reliance upon partisans (Kossoy 1976, 56–58).

The new units cannot however immediately achieve conventional uniforms for financial reasons or the need for concealment. Successful guerrilla movements go through several stages, in the last of which the combatants, on the verge of success, "go public" and don uniforms—emerging from the military closet as it were. The IRA prematurely surfaced and donned uniforms during the Easter Uprising of 1916 (Cross 1975, 86). A loophole in British law which permitted militia units to be raised under the authorization of local magistrates allowed the Irish to organize uniformed units of Irish Volunteers and of the Irish Citizens Army before the uprising. These groups could not afford uniforms for all their members who consequently often resorted to minimal symbols—slouch hats, bandoliers, colored armbands, and ties—to suggest the presence of a uniform.[13]

After the failure of the attack on the Dublin Post Office in 1916, the use of uniforms apparently lapsed until the final successful stage. In the interim underground period, the only occasion for the wearing of uniforms seems to have been members' funerals (O'Malley 1937, 20, 38). In the last stage, when they emerged from underground but still had shortages, the old minimal symbols remained in use (Holt 1961, photo 39).

Other approximations of a uniform by the IRA included the trench coat which had the further advantage of being used by both civilians and the British, creating additional anonymity and concealment. Indeed, it has been used by other urban guerrillas from "Dublin to the Mediterranean", not to mention its subsequent career as a badge of the foreign correspondent and a fashionable item for the romantically inclined public (Hobshawn 1969, 97).

The guerrillas' desire to discard civilian dress and don conventional uniforms is related to the problem of legitimacy. The self-image of guerrilla forces is that of a government-in-exile or part of such a government, and to legitimate such claims they are quick to appropriate and use the symbols of the organized, modern state. And one of the prime symbols of that state is a standing, modern army.

A uniform also secures the rights of legitimate belligerents under international law. Use of civilian dress by guerrillas has caused severe reprisals by uniformed regular forces, often as the result of a feeling of revulsion over the employment of "unfair" tactics (Laqueur 1975, 373). Whether or not the protection of international law is always desired by guerrillas is another matter which entails the discussion later of the second pattern of guerrilla dress.

The uniform is also a form of psychological reenforcement through symbols, and the best example is a pattern of seemingly foolhardy episodes in the Irish uprising of 1916, the French Resistance of the 1940's, and in Northern Ireland in the 1970's. In all of these conflicts, the occasion for the wearing of uniforms by guerrillas, even in the face of extreme danger, was the funeral of comrades. During World War II, the French Maquis seized control of a town from the Germans for the day to commemorate the dead of all wars on Armistice Day of 1943 (Ehrlich 1966, 148–50). During the 1970's and 80's, the IRA engaged in funeral processions like the ones staged after the Easter uprising in 1916. "All of them [funerals of hunger strikers in Ulster prisons] were accompanied by paramilitary displays—shots fired over the coffin and slow marches by masked men in uniforms" (NYT 16 Oct. 1981). To use a much abused term correctly, these are truly "symbolic" actions. They had no practical or military results but served other, perhaps equally significant, ends. One function of all funeral rites is to reenforce the solidarity of the mourning group in the face of a loss. Military funerals with their reliance upon the uniform as a symbol of nationhood and the military metaphor as a symbol of unity draw the civilian spectator into the overall ceremony by public parades. Not only do funerals shore up the solidarity of the guerrillas but they also turn the fallen into comrades and, importantly, heroic members of the nation. Thus the funeral may forge another link between a society and rebellious groups within it.

The military metaphor is based on the acceptance of the belief that war is solely the business of regular armed forces with the civilian population restricted to the role of passive spectator, in short conventional warfare (Best 1980, 112–27, 190–200). However, even when this definition is rejected and the populace is urged to take up arms, civilian militias or *levées en masse* may still abide by the codes of war and don some minimal symbols. In the 1916 attack on the Dublin Post Office, while some of the participants wore uniforms, most were dressed in Sunday suits or work clothing crossed by bandoliers with yellow armbands on their left sleeves (Coffey 1969, 4). The participants seemed eager to proclaim their affiliations sartorially rather than hide their identities.

When adherence to the codes of war is completely abandoned and no attempt is made to achieve even the semblance of uniforms, then the second pattern of guerrilla dress is apparent, that of deliberate deviation. Any established symbolic pattern creates the possibility of communication by departure from it. Once group norms have been established and defined by clothing and other symbolic systems, then the erasure of these boundaries may become a stratagem of war—the Maoist dictum of "fish swimming in the sea". An irregular military group removes the boundaries between it and civilians, largely by wearing civilian clothes rather than military uniforms, to gain the advantages of concealment.

This tactic, like much of modern guerrilla warfare, is the result of the intentional contravention of the differences between civilians and combatants which are spelled out by the Hague and Geneva treaties. These pacts specify, among other items, that combatants wear a "distinctive emblem recognizable at a distance" and not conceal arms (Miller, R. 1975, 29–30).[14]

Guerrillas in this second pattern use the metaphor of the revolutionary movement rather than that of the conventional army. Thus, guerrilla dress after World War II very often consisted of jeans or combat fatigues not only for economy but also because they suggest, along with beards, the militant left made popular by Castro and others (NYT 23 Jan. 1976). In the same vein, successful Rhodesian rebel leaders returned home in fatigues, shined shoes, and the caps of USSR generals (NYT 27 Dec. 1979). Other instances of the guerrilla use of fatigues and jeans are reported from such diverse locales as Angola, Lebanon, and El Salvador (NYT 24 Mar. 1981; Time 18 June 1979).

Regular or simulated uniforms are avoided as a matter of principle or ideology. The new mode of dress has been created by a change in the metaphor and concomitant system of symbols. A parallel change in organization was noted in the IRA which, organized in brigades from 1916 to 1922 in keeping with conventional military practice, changed to small cells of four or five men "in keeping with European terrorist tradition" (NYT 25 Sept. 1979).

The choice of a metaphor is not a matter of caprice but is related to the values and circumstances of the group. Thus, partisans often wore civilian dress in World War II to avoid cruel treatment upon capture (although Tito's guerrillas did wear a distinctive uniform) (Draper 1971, 203). Captured IRA members in Ulster prisons in the early 1980's used hunger strikes to obtain symbols of legitimation—the right to wear uniforms and organize themselves as soldiers— in short, the status of prisoners-of-war (NYT 20 May 1981).

Finally a contrast between the use of uniforms by the Boers and British in the Boer War points up the existential base of symbolism. Because of frontier exigencies, the Boers did not think in terms of professional soldiering since all adult males were soldier-farmers, somewhat analogous to American colonists. They used ordinary clothing while in the field and provided their own weapons, equipment, and horses. Organization and discipline were similarly informal (Morris, Donald 1965, 300–301). On the other hand, since European colonists saw war as a separate institution in the control of the military, service at the outbreak of war required the formation of colonists into regiments, the enforcement of discipline, and of course military uniforms. Because they scorned the professional military, however, the European colonists opted primarily for volunteer units (ibid.). Subsequent attempts by the Boers to use captured British uniforms led to reprisals on the grounds of violation of the rules of war.

The final use of "nonuniforms" characterizes those detached groups of regulars who have long engaged in special warfare behind enemy lines and, as part of their counterinsurgency tactics, deliberately avoid the use of uniforms (Laqueur 1975). The British Special Air Service Regiment (SAS) is one such organization which also is organized in modules of four men like the cellular structure of terrorist groups (Geraghty 1982, 2–4, 122, 139, 168). The use of uniforms has now come full circle. Standardized or occupational military attire was replaced by uniforms to indicate the compartmentalization of warfare; now modern warfare's destruction of the barrier between civilian and military has been accompanied by the abandonment of uniforms.[15]

NOTES

1. Huntington contrasts the customary sociological analysis of the military as a bureaucracy with his own approach toward officers as a profession in which he sees bureaucracy as a secondary characteristic (1957, 469). For this study, however, an emphasis upon bureaucracy which stresses clothing as a means of social control is more suitable.

2. Feudal heraldry consisted of signals which identified the knight and his personal following. Later national armies wore royal insignia, such as coats of arms on their caps, as symbols to remind the wearer of his proper loyalties (Mollo, J. 1972, 30).

3. An attitudinal change took place in the eighteenth century when livery was redefined as a badge of servility (Stone, L. 1967, 214).

4. The personal quality of the relationship between superior and inferior is reflected in the difference between medieval and contemporary attitudes toward inferiors in one's household. "Family" at this period included both servants and kin; by the nineteenth century, the term included only wife and children (Girouard 1978, 10). A general's entourage during the American Revolution was designated his family (Ward 1952, 4).

5. The split between military and civil dress did not occur until the seventeenth century (Laver 1951, 126).

6. Allegiance to an impersonal organization would seem to be facilitated by awareness of its longevity. The longer a unit is in existence the stronger may be the ties among its members and hence there may be a shift of allegiance to the group qua group rather than to its leader.

7. Flags, another symbolic system, served as unit identification and rallying point and also reflected the internal structure of military units. Down to the early eighteenth century, British units carried flags for each officer from colonel to captain, in addition to the king's colors. The officer's own armorial colors, crest, or coat of arms were very often used on unit standards, grenadier caps, and other parts of the uniform until the regulations of 1751 (Barnes 1951, 73, 100–101; Firth, C. 1962, 45). The traditional Bourbon flag—the fleur-de-lis—was not adopted by units of the royal French army until 1789, at the very last moment as it were (Leliepvre & Elting 1974).

8. In the armies raised during the Civil War, of the ten companies in a foot regiment, the colonel's company consisted of 200 men, the lieutenant-colonel's of 160, the major's of 140, and the remaining seven, usually commanded by captains, of 100 each (Firth, C. 1962, 43).

9. The nonrationality of the prebureaucratic army is further evidenced by the striving for special privileges. During the Seven Years' War, preferential treatment in the French army included differences in pay for the common soldier, seniority as the basis for assigning the positions of units in combat and on the march, and the right of elite units to select the other units with whom they would march and to refuse to accept staff orders (Kennett 1967, 36–38). Enlisted men in the French and British Guards ranked with

lieutenants in other units (Barnes 1951, 144; Kannik 1968, 169). Though the drive for special privileges undoubtedly exists in modern bureaucracies, it is not a basis for institutional structure and operation. The claim to special privilege in modern armies is usually based on a rationale of efficiency and need rather than seniority or honor.

10. I am referring to the sailing ship designed for navigation in the Atlantic in contrast with Mediterranean craft which evolved earlier into specialized combat or cargo vessels.

11. The preceding paragraph is based upon Michael Lewis (1948a, 17–51).

12. A significant class distinction was the right of a knighted captain to appoint twice as many servants as a commoner-captain, partly as additional remuneration (Lewis, M. 1948a, 78–79). Owing to the need for special training, as well as the desire to climb the promotion ladder quickly, officer aspirants were recruited as young as twelve. This patrimonial system of recruitment is a form of apprenticeship rooted in a familial relationship with a parental surrogate and applicable to all social classes.

13. This discussion of the IRA is based upon: Coffey (1969); Holt (1961); Neeson (1966); O'Malley (1937); Younger (1968).

14. A commentary on the growth of "liberation movements" and guerrillas occurs in the 1972 changes in these treaties which specified that either the emblem or the open bearing of arms was acceptable as a criterion of a lawful combatant (Kossoy 1976, 152).

15. Information on organizations such as the SAS is understandably difficult to obtain but they exist in several military services. These organizations are to be differentiated from those regular units which operate behind enemy lines but wear identifiable uniforms in accordance with international protocol and are therefore protected by the rules of war (Baxter 1951; Draper 1971; Paddock 1982, 27–28).

9

Occupational Clothing

A type of dress often confused with uniforms is that of occupational clothing—the white dress of nurses and domestics, the coveralls of automobile mechanics and repairmen, and the gray flannel suits of Madison Avenue. Yet these are not true uniforms since they lack precision and legitimating insignia. Nor are they ordinary dress since they always denote activity that is distinct from leisure or domestic routines and sometimes indicate an organizational affiliation.

This chapter defines occupational clothing, establishes a typology, and compares the modes of interaction enabled by uniforms and quasi uniforms—a form of occupational clothing.

AN OVER-VIEW

A Typology

Occupational clothing is any dress that indicates participation in a specific type or general category of jobs. The clothing may consist of an elaborate outfit as in the dress of astronauts or commercial pilots, or of a single item such as a hansom driver's top hat in New York City's Central Park.

The several types of occupational dress form a continuum of precision in the employment of sartorial signs. The most precise is quasi uniforms which approach uniforms in that they describe an organization and suppress individuality but lack the cachet of legitimacy conferred by a government. Clothing in this category includes that of nurses, nuns, merchant marine officers, and air line personnel. This analysis will concentrate primarily upon quasi uniforms.

A great deal of occupational dress is standardized clothing, previously discussed, which is a pattern of dress arising among members of an occupation, or family of occupations, partly because they share similar social and physical conditions. This includes mechanics' coveralls, the wet-weather dress of seamen, the working clothing of cowboys, and the clothing of chefs and bakers.[1] Standardized clothing differs from quasi uniforms in that the former denotes membership in a diffuse, unorganized group and the latter in a specific organization.

Career apparel, "business clothes for white collar workers", is an adaptation of sports or informal clothing, often designer made, for corporate use (NYT 28 Feb. 1971). Companies furnish clothing similar in color, fabric, or style to white-collar employees, especially those in contact with the public. Unlike uniforms or quasi uniforms, it consists of various items which may be "mixed and matched" by the wearer, thereby preserving freedom of choice. Career apparel can be recognized as such only when worn by a number of individuals within a specific location.[2] The clothing combines visibility and identification with an organization without resorting to quasi uniforms or dress codes. Most significantly for this study, it prevents competition through clothing among white-collar employees and thereby helps to eliminate clothing manipulation for the purpose of mobility within an organization.

Dress codes are the most unstructured form of occupational clothing. Generally, they consist of setting limits on the styles of ordinary or conventional clothing that may be worn at a place of business (Prentice-Hall 1976). As of 1978, some New York department stores required male employees in contact with the public to wear conservative business suits or coordinated sports jackets and slacks (Altman 1977, 1978; Macy's 1973). The incidence and type of code varies with the region, the period, the establishment, and whether or not the employee is in contact with the public (Margetts 1978; Myerscough 1978; Prentice-Hall 1976).[3]

Occupational Clothing and the Utilitarian Fallacy

Before occupational clothing can be studied as a system of signs, the utilitarian fallacy must be examined. This approach sees occupational dress primarily as a physical vehicle which enables wearers to perform their duties in locations ranging from the sea to the moon and from hospitals to mines. Such clothing serves as a tool because of its carrying capacity for hammers or railroad time tables or the protection it affords against weather, the near vacuum of space, or infection.

While the utilitarian aspect of occupational clothing is undeniably of great importance, nevertheless it is only one of many functions served by such clothing. Alternatively, occupational clothing may be rooted in an ethos which stresses the importance of visibility for internal organizational surveillance. Visible dress may also facilitate interaction with customer or client first by advertising the presence of the worker and then by placing interaction on the desired level of intimacy. Finally, occupational clothing may assert superior status vis-a-vis colleagues.

The utilitarian function, itself, is the product of an occupational ethos which places a high value upon work and the relationship between the worker and clients rather than other considerations such as social position. As we shall see later, nurses with this outlook view their uniforms primarily as a practical device to enable them to work with patients comfortably and efficiently. If need be, nursing garb may be discarded in favor of ordinary dress if the latter proves more practical. This "practical" outlook was made possible only by the decline of earlier alternative approaches to nurses' quasi uniforms, as in England, which stressed their ability to differentiate between nurses of lower and middle class origins (Ewing 1975, 45–46).

In a form of reverse symbolism, utilitarian or protective clothing may be discarded to demonstrate fearlessness (the worker who scorns safety regulations as unmasculine), or virtuosity (the typesetter who worked in street clothes without soiling them to demonstrate his skill) (Cunnington & Lucas 1967, 391–92; Int. 15). Discarding protective clothing becomes institutionalized to describe superior and administrative ranks. Aprons decrease in size as British nurses rise in rank and disappear in the top echelon (Cunnington & Lucas 1967, 321, 390).

The Contexts of Occupational Clothing

Examination of the societal conditions necessary for occupational clothing upsets many prevalent assumptions. No matter how patently useful, we cannot take its existence for granted. First, the economic resources and value priorities of a society or of an occupational group must allow for special occupational clothing in addition to ordinary dress. German vitriol miners of the eighteenth century could not afford special protective clothing against the corrosive effects of the ore and therefore worked nude (Schramm 1960, 4). The British Parliamentary Papers of 1842 are replete with examples of nudity among miners of the period, presumably due to their poverty or the penuriousness of their employers (Cunnington & Lucas 1967, 69). Even in the twentieth century, some English miners work in the nude, although it is not clear whether it is out of choice or necessity (Sigal 1961, 155–59, 167).

Distinctive occupational dress also rests upon the assumption that wearers will downplay personal taste and their positions in life, such as class, gender, or religion and instead use clothes that emphasize occupation. Nowhere is the resistance to this ordering of priorities demonstrated more clearly than in the attitudes of medieval master craftsmen.

Some of the reasons for this insistence on [medieval artisans] carrying on their trade in ordinary civilian garb no doubt were as follows: Guild members lived almost exclusively in towns where the ever-present example of their fellow-citizens was too much for them not to want to emulate it at all times. Besides, a master craftsman was a person of some consequence. . . . Accordingly, social rank was emphasized by fashionable dress.

Quite possibly, the traditional practice by which artisans worked in full sight of passers-by may have contributed to their sumptuousness of dress. Until the eighteenth century, most workshops were situated on the ground floor and had a large open window giving on the street, enabling customers and passers-by to look in. A plain work dress would have attracted undue attention and might have detracted from the master's prestige (Schramm 1960, 8).

In modern times, British bargemen on the Thames, bicycle repairmen, and utility servicemen work in street clothes—not discards but ordinary clothing complete with jacket and tie—which stress status rather than occupation (Bailey 1975; NYT 28 Mar. 1976).

The most important societal condition for occupational clothing is the separation of work and domestic routines which is reflected in the different location of home and the work place and in sartorial signs.[4] We read a complete outfit of occupational clothing as indicating that the worker is on duty and not subject to domestic and other nonoccupational demands. Where no sharp distinction is made between work and domestic life, then occupational clothing may not develop. The farmer does not use occupational clothing if he wears identical garb for working the fields and for free time. Instead, he may wear dress distinctive of a region or an estate (in the stratificatory sense), both of which may be folk rather than occupational clothing.

The function of occupational clothing depends upon the societal context. In a society where illiteracy is prevalent, occupational clothing may act as credentials for prospective employers in lieu of "previous advertisement or correspondence" (Cunnington & Lucas 1967, 376–77). At the English statute fairs from the fourteenth into the twentieth centuries, the equivalent of the modern hiring hall, occupational dress greatly facilitated the process of hiring by indicating occupations. Female domestics seeking jobs appeared in their appropriate aprons, cooks in colored aprons, nursery maids in white linen, and chamber maids in lawn or cambric (Hecht 1950, 28–29).

Placement through occupational dress is of extreme importance in the anonymous and bewildering urban context. In response to the threatening aspect of the city a variety of occupations assume a protective function. The red cap or railroad porter broadens the interpretation of his job beyond the manifest or ostensible function of carrying luggage to include the additional, and more important, duty of providing an introduction to the city. The porter does not see himself as a menial but as a provider of personal services, a source of information, and a trusted confidant in the urban jungle.

They can spot you in a crowd, they don't have to feel around if you not in these clothes— now they know you are a red cap. Every time they see you in that uniform, they going to come to you and ask the questions. . . . Eighty-five percent of the public knows the red cap as we are the first one to greet him and the last to say goodbye to him in the station, and I have a lot of old people come here and say, my son say get a red cap, don't trust no one but a red cap, and they will take care of you, which we do. (Int. 12)

Similarly, the quasi uniforms of other urban occupations signal places of refuge or advertise community services. Doormen in New York City have assumed, or have had thrust upon them, the additional function of guardians of sanctuaries in the Hobbesian streets of the city. Children traveling to and from school have been urged to notice the apartment buildings along their route which have uniformed doormen who may serve as protectors in time of danger (NYT 23 July 1976). Public health nurses are frequently accosted in the streets by residents of poor neighborhoods seeking information on medical centers, asking for medical aid or even drugs (Int. 7).

The prevalent type of organizational structure also determines the use of occupational clothing. This type of dress assumes a distinctive form when an organization attempts to maintain total control over its members by a repertoire of uniforms, each for a different occasion including work and leisure. Nuns in one traditional order wore "total uniforms" or organizational clothing in all aspects of their lives (Int. 1). Sunday worship demanded their best habits; older, worn habits were relegated to daily use. Similar efforts to provide for all aspects of a nurse's life, particularly in England, have been noted. In these instances, dress had the primary function of distinguishing between members and outsiders and, secondarily, of demarcating work from other activities.

The Locus of Occupational Clothing

The locus, or the immediate environment within which one works, greatly influences interaction and the use of sartorial signs. It may consist of the client's own "turf" as with the insurance salesman visiting a ghetto who faced the dilemma of either dressing to meet local standards and promoting rapport with clients or abiding by his own standards. " 'I don't go in there with a fancy briefcase. . . . I work out of my pocket and they like that. And I don't go in there in an insurance salesman's suit. I go there in a pink suit, something that gets their attention' " (WSJ 17 July 1978). The locus may be the client's home as with the patient visited by the public health nurse whose uniform emphasizes the nonsocial quality of her visit (Int. 4).

The locus provides corroborating or complementary symbols to compensate for a lack of precision in occupational clothing. A white jacket worn in a hospital has very different connotations from one in a beauty parlor. On the other hand, there is little doubt about the reading of police attire in any locale, one of the advantages of the legitimated uniform of a public bureaucracy. The location within the working arena identifies the man in shirtsleeves behind the desk in a second floor office of a New York City precinct house as a detective, or the woman in ordinary dress behind the bank counter as a teller. Familiarity with locale also allows complementary systems, carriage and gait, to operate.[5]

Differentiation of the locus into back and front regions divides the people with whom the worker interacts, and prescribes the appropriate dress (Goffman 1959, 22–30, 106–40). The printer wearing work clothes in the back region of the shop puts on his jacket to enter the customer's room in the front region (Jaffe). Ship's personnel dress more formally in areas frequented by passengers unless thay are aboard freighters where the interaction is more informal (Int. 14).

When the quasi uniform is a wardrobe the type to be worn varies between front and back stage. The operating room of a hospital, the ship's engine room, and the galley are more likely to call for utilitarian rather than organizational quasi uniforms—working clothes rather than those displaying position within the organization. These are relative terms since even in a ship's galley there are overt status distinctions depending upon the nationality of the ship.[6] Manipulation consists of transferring quasi uniforms from back stage to front stage locations; young interns wore their blood-stained uniforms off-duty in contrast to the morgue attendant who did not. For the latter, bloodied dress indicated low level duties rather than professional responsibilities and hence a loss of status (Sudnow 1967, 55).

Where back and front stage areas intertwine, and the imposter may mingle with the legitimate role occupant, dirty occupational clothing may act as signs of authenticity to differentiate the two. The cowboy looks for the strategically located dirt spot on the brim of the Stetson hat to distinguish the professional from the would-be cowhand (NYT 23 Feb. 1973). Since the working cowboy always puts his hat on in the same way, the dirt spot will be sharply defined and localized; the amateur's will be diffused.

On the other hand, within a restricted area where outsiders or amateurs do not appear, dirt may denote inefficiency. A ship's steward labeled a cook who *began* work with a dirty apron, or who dirtied the rest of his clothing during his shift, as an inefficient worker (Int. 14). Finally, there is the tale of the bravura performance of the typesetter who would appear on the job in street clothes and whose sole concession to the dirt of the shop consisted of rolling up his sleeves. At the close of the day, he would roll down his sleeves and leave the job, immaculately dressed (Int. 15).

The locus influences the range of signs used by an organization. A circumscribed or delimited locale provides a framework within which to recognize diversity of symbols. The hospital setting permits a wider range of uniforms to be included in the category of medical personnel whereas, outside the hospital, the similarity between these uniforms might not be recognized and the commonality of the subcategories might be overlooked. An enclosed or protective locus may also permit a greater variety of clothing. For one nurse, a pants suit would be suitable for hospital use but provocative and less practical for streetwear (Int. 6).

The locus also has a temporal dimension as seen in the contrast between the relaxed informality of the midnight watch aboard a tanker and the tense formality of the captain's first visit to the bridge in the morning (Mostert 1975, 129).[7]

The routines of any occupation vary with the rhythms of the day, week, or year and with the irregular patterns of special events (Strauss, A. 1962). Temporal cycles are indicated and facilitated by the use of occupational clothing. The night watch of a supertanker was informal and accompanied by relaxed discipline and sloppy uniforms (Mostert 1975, 123–30). Brokers working in the stock exchange over the weekend dressed in sports clothes and were accompanied by their families (NYT 9 Feb. 1976). Special events include organizational rites of passage such as retirement, recruitment, promotion, and degradation. The symbolizing of these events may range from elaborate dress to the simple gesture of a New York City sanitation foreman putting on a clean shirt, attaching his badge, and calling his workers together to announce firings for budgetary reasons (NYT 19 July 1975).

Manipulation Versus Control

Occupational clothing may be used as a manipulative device by wearers and as a means of control by their superiors. For wearers, clothing may be utilized in impression management to create a desired image for the initial job interview and then for mobility within an organization. Manipulation is much more likely to be used by middle-class employees who define work as a career which one actively selects and pursues throughout life (Ginzberg et al. 1961; Schneider & Dornbusch 1953). The working class, on the other hand, is more apt to view occupational dress from a utilitarian or economic perspective (Form & Stone 1955).[8]

Manipulation also occurs in interaction with clients. A worker may dress up to meet a customer, for example the printer who puts on a jacket to enter the front region to talk to a customer. Or, he may "dress down", as in the instance of the country store owner who conformed to his customers' style of dress, or the successful door-to-door encyclopedia salesman who dressed in shorts and a paint-spotted sweatshirt (Buller 1975; Trillin 1969).

The contrary trend which curbs the manipulative tendency of the individual stems from the wearer's superior who controls workers' dress to insure internal conformity and, externally, to regulate the worker's role as an organizational representative vis-a-vis the client or public.

QUASI UNIFORMS

Control

Quasi uniforms are associated with nongovernmental organizations, usually private bureaucracies, including hospitals, airlines, merchant ships, railroads, and religious orders. Such dress reflects a mode of control which differs from that of public bureaucracies in several ways.

First, the private organization shares control over its staff with external professional associations which serve as reference groups for the staff. Quasi uniforms, when worn, are evaluated not solely by organizational utility but also by professional standards set by the associations.

Japanese factories in the United States and Great Britain have attempted to achieve control over a nonprofessional staff of workers by converting the work place into a community in which no other organization or social affiliation may even be indicated, let alone have any influence. Honda attempted to convert a quasi uniform into a total uniform by eliminating symbols of other organizations, particularly those of unions (Honda 1981). A Honda plant in the United States supplied personnel of all ranks with a white occupational uniform bearing the company insignia which was to be worn at all times during the workday, whether in the working area, offices, cafeteria, or other facilities.[9] When the rule forbidding the wearing of any emblem other than that of Honda was applied to union hats and pins, the resultant union protest led to NLRB proceedings (Honda 1981).

Honda tried to promote internal egalitarianism by eliminating all insignia of company rank (Shiffer 1982; WSJ 12 Dec. 1980). Nonsartorial symbols of equality included a common cafeteria and locker room for all ranks, and the absence of reserved spaces for vehicles (Honda 1981). In a hearing before the NLRB, the plant manager of Honda explained that the rules were intended

to help create team work; show and maintain the Honda quality image and cleanliness of the work area; [for] use as a company identity; and to prohibit wearing anything that might cause damage to the product or parts. Further, visitors to the plant such as distributors, customers and local people, could observe employees wearing uniforms which would help present a good quality image to them. (ibid., 4)

The NLRB found that union emblems did not scratch or otherwise damage products under manufacture, nor were they visible to customers or the public, nor did they weaken the team concept (ibid.). Honda was therefore ordered to allow the wearing of union insignia by employees.

Simply to say that Honda exhibited an antiunion animus is insufficient explanation. We may surmise that Honda's efforts stem in part from a desire for complete control over the occupational status to implement its patrimonial conception of the proper structure of the workplace.[10]

A second social characteristic shaping the quasi uniform is the existence of multiple private organizations, in contrast to the monopoly of the military establishment within a nation, which weakens the control of any given organization over its staff who may find alternative sources of employment. The modern military officer, on the other hand, pursues his profession only within the confines of a single public bureaucracy; he is a "bureaucratic professional" (Huntington 1957, 14–17). He has no external professional reference groups; employment in identical alternative organizations within the nation is not available.[11] Furthermore, the private organization does not usually have the same legal protection for its insignia as a government agency and runs a greater risk of imposters and of dilution of its emblems.

Finally, modern private bureaucracies usually do not have the same control over off-the-job activities as uniformed military organizations, especially in times of war. The more an organization approaches a total institution, the easier it is to make membership in it a total status. Such a status differs from a master status in that the latter may be displaced by other statuses at times as in the instance of the off-duty policeman in street clothes or the peacetime soldier on weekend pass in "civvies". In monastic orders or wartime armies, however, membership status becomes total and the uniform is worn constantly. Until Vatican Council II, nuns of one order were not permitted to leave their rooms with any part of their habits missing (Int. 1). Control was extended to all hours of the day; even in their sleep they were required to wear a white veil.

The Role Set of Quasi-Uniform Wearers

The quasi uniform facilitates social interaction by introducing wearers to clients, bolstering their authority, and giving assurance of the wearers' competence. The quasi uniform also serves the needs of the organization by enabling outsiders to enforce group norms and permitting supervision by superiors and peers. In addition, it may enable wearers to proclaim their status, assert their affiliation with peers, and their separation from similar groups. These functions emerge clearly through an examination of the operations of the quasi uniform in each component of the wearer's role set. The definition of the norms appropriate to the role set differs sharply between bureaucratically and professionally oriented wearers of quasi uniforms, the former stressing obligations to the organization and the latter obligations toward an outside group or set of norms. The variation in norms is manifested throughout the role set.

Quasi uniforms operate within the wearer's role set by raising or lowering barriers and by separation and reintegration among actors. Within this role set, as with uniforms, quasi uniforms cannot be understood simply as a one-to-one relationship between wearer and viewer. Instead, others form a background against which the pair operates and include extraorganizational reference groups such as professional associations.

The client is the specific individual for whom professionals or semiprofessionals perform a service and with whom they interact. The relationship may be fleeting as between the ticket seller and purchaser or last for many years as between the nurse and chronic patient.

The general public are outsiders who are enlisted as members of the wearer's role set by the existence of a quasi uniform. As we shall see, the presence of such clothing enables them to react to the wearer as the occupant of a given status and not simply as an anonymous individual.

Superiors of the wearer, where they exist, stand in a dual relationship—as supervisors who utilize the increased visibility and control conferred by the clothing and as regulators who grant the use of organizational dress.

Reference groups outside the organization may comprise peers of a sister organization (another corporation, nursing school, or order of nuns) or a professional body whose norms may implement or conflict with those of one's own organization. Closeness to others is reflected by occupational dress. At times a nurse may stress her commonality with peers by her quasi uniform. At other times, caps or pins indicate her membership in a specific organization and her separation from peers in other hospitals or nursing schools.

Interaction within a role set always carries undertones of the "invisible others" present alongside the immediate actors. Outside of the organization, invisible others include professional associations, unions which intervene in the matter of dress codes imposed upon government or private employees, courts which rule on the rights of employees to reject codes and employers to impose them, and interest groups upholding the right of students and teachers to political symbols such as long hair or arm bands.

The role set is visualized primarily from the viewpoint of the quasi-uniform wearer. A description of interaction may also be drawn from other role perspectives. To the patient in a hospital anyone in white is a nurse and available for patient care. The distinction between wearer and superior or peer vanishes and all are subsumed under the amorphous category of "nurse". In extreme instances, nurses may be combined with police and watchmen in an even broader category of detested "authority". This section is written from the perspective of the wearer. Subsequently, the differential perception of symbols among members of the role set will be analyzed.

Since wearers interact with a variety of others, their clothing becomes a complicated communication channel bearing many simultaneous messages, like a modern telephone cable, to individuals in their role sets. Complications ensue. First the quasi uniform is not read in the same manner by all but is interpreted in various ways, depending upon individual needs, by each of the others. The patient who is hospitalized for a short-term physical ailment is more likely to be ignorant of the niceties of rank and function among medical personnel and to demand attention from any passing uniform. One nurse describes the patient who sees a bewildering array of uniformed personnel passing before his door, none of whom respond, or is even capable of doing so, to his call (Int. 2). Obviously, uniform wearers, their peers and superiors, are cognizant of status differences among them and will extend aid if it falls within their purview. Acuity of perception accompanies experience and the chronically ill patient, physically or mentally, learns to interpret medical dress in detail (Ints. 5, 6).

The desperate and "illiterate" viewer—the helpless passenger in a terminal—may read any uniform or quasi uniform as a source of help. Even an unusually or vividly colored jacket may be interpreted as a uniform. In the 1960's, many bus passengers such as the elderly were fearful of flying. A Los Angeles bus official of the period reports that he was frequently approached for information by these passengers who seemed to be reassured by his conservative business suit in contrast to the casual dress of others in the terminal (Int. 16).[12] Lacking such cues, the passenger may be driven to read alternative symbolic systems, such as carriage or gait, in an effort to find assistance. The resort to alternative symbolic systems is found even among experienced personnel such as a nurse who cites her ability to differentiate among medical students, interns, and residents, all in white jackets, by their behavior (Bradshaw & Cheng 1963, 363). Ironically, one purpose of uniform clothing among doctors and students is precisely to conceal the differences among them (Coser 1962, 44).

Additional problems may arise through the ordering of priorities of relationships within the role set, for example the relationship to clients and superiors. One may adhere to organizational procedure at the expense of the client or provide service to the client at the risk of violating the rules set forth by one's superior. A controversy in a Social Security Administration office arose over the removal of neckties by employment counselors, in violation of the dress code, in order to make their working-class clients feel more at ease (SSA 1975). Apparently, neckties had inhibitory middle-class connotations for the unemployed.

The Wearer

Wearers' self-images are shaped by the acceptance of occupational norms which define the occupational status as the dominant one, at least while they are at work. The use of the quasi uniform emphasizes the dominance of the occupational status and the organizational definition of appropriate behavior. In a quasi uniform one does not function merely as a public health nurse but as the designated representative of the Smith Nursing Association.

Wearers may reject the work status as the dominant one, thereby rendering the quasi uniform ineffective as a means of control. The use of the quasi uniform, like the military uniform, is often handicapped by wearers' individuality. Their personal beliefs or priorities on the ordering of statuses may prevent them from accepting the quasi-uniformed status as the master status or from using the quasi uniform if their work status conflicts with other statuses. Wearers cannot, or will not, permit the master status to become dominant, at least not to the extent desired by the organization.

Workers may express their individuality by allowing statuses other than the master one to enter into the interaction. For the wearer of the quasi uniform, the mandates of the master status can often be best carried out through the use of ordinary clothing rather than quasi uniforms. Workers define their role as autonomous representatives of their groups who have leeway in interpreting their duties. Their task may be rendered easier by allowing their other statuses to resonate, much as one musical note is enriched by the vibration of others. A public health nurse strongly advocates the use of street clothing because the patients "would see me more as an individual person helping them personally, giving of myself and not as an agency to them" (Int. 7).

Similarly, a nun lauded the freedom she felt after abandoning her habit for conventional dress, the freedom to interact with others as an individual rather than a group representative.

I felt much freer [in street clothes] in relating with people because I felt they were responding just to me and they didn't have any preconceived notions of what I should be or what they had to talk to me about, you know, like "watch your language", and that type of thing. I was talking to two of the squatters the other day and one of the men was speaking very beautifully and spontaneously about their whole experience, using good everyday language, and the woman who was there said to him very quickly in Spanish, "Watch your language, she is a lady from the church." I know that much Spanish. So, he began to apologize and I said, "Forget it. You know, you are not saying anything that I haven't heard before or am not used to hearing". (Int. 1)

In sharp contrast, a nun from another order interprets her role as that of a nonautonomous group representative whose individuality is severely circumscribed and whose position is clearly indicated by her habit.

It never bothered me to follow the [dress] regulations because I felt these were made for everyone and if we wanted to do our own "thing" this was not the time nor place. . . .
. . . When Sisters all wore a religious habit they told something to everyone they met or came in contact with them, just by their exterior appearance. They were a visible sign that they belonged to the Church. . . . I have heard on many occasions the Sisters feel they could get closer to the people in the ghettos and other low economic areas if they dress just in secular clothes and I don't really agree with this. . . .
. . . You know I always feel very strongly when some of the Sisters say we shouldn't want to be dressed to be recognized as different. Well what about the policemen, firemen, men in the service, policewomen, etc. who wear a special and distinct uniform to identify themselves? . . . These people dress for their job while on duty, yet we Sisters have a lifetime job and if a Sister feels she does not want to be identified with her Community or as being a Religious, I feel she should evaluate her attitude and the motivation of her work. (Sister C. 1973)

Opposition to the uniform is accentuated by a role definition which stresses the relationship to the client as basic to the role set of the professional. The best judge of performance in this relationship is the practitioner herself, guided by the internalized professional code and using the profession as a reference group. This definition of the practitioner's role also describes the degree of acceptance of a position as organizational representative, relationship to superiors, and, ultimately, attitudes toward the quasi uniform. The quasi uniform is indicative of external surveillance and of organizational monitoring of professional behavior, the antithesis of the role definition which emphasizes the competence of the autonomous professional. The presence of the organization, as indicated by the quasi uniform, is a third party to the interaction which may at times interfere with client relationships.

Professionalism operates as a rationale for the practitioners' behavior by enabling them to transcend the norms of a specific organization and turn to the directives of an external, professional reference group. The outward orientation is based on the belief that one is actually carrying out the organization's mission but in a superior fashion by ignoring inappropriate directives. The professional outlook provides a justification for opposing the organization, not in its purpose but in its means.

The conflict between the professional role described above and the bureaucratic role in which the actor functions as a nonautonomous representative of the organization does not occur at random. Instead, it is more likely in a field such as nursing which is subject to strong cross pressures. On the one hand, professionalism is encouraged, as will be seen later, by the growing redefinition of the nurse's occupational role as one requiring rapport with the patient. In opposition, a bureaucratic role is fostered by the organizational need of the hospital to control a large patient population with an invariably small staff.

Differences in role interpretation are reflected in the functions ascribed to the quasi uniform. The professional is likely to regard it as a barrier between herself and the patient and as a denial of her self-image as an independent professional. The quasi uniform may also be valued as a utilitarian device which protects against contagion, makes the performance of chores more comfortable, and reduces the cost of working clothes. One nurse views the use of ordinary clothing on the job as a welcome professional challenge which requires her to rely upon her expertise rather than prestige of the group to do her job. She defines the quasi uniform as a "cop-out", as nursing without fully and truly giving of oneself (Int. 6; Brown, E. 1966, 196–97; Jakubovskis 1968). The bureaucratically oriented nurse, on the other hand, is more likely to stress the organizational function of the uniform.

The Wearer-Client Relationship

The importance of this relationship is twofold for the wearer of occupational clothing, especially the quasi uniform. The quasi uniform enables the wearer to be identified by and to interact with the client. Additionally, the client is vital for the wearer's self-image which is based upon the client's reaction. During socialization into her role, a student nurse learns the norms of her position and acquires a self-image by testing the new role on patients, partially through quasi uniforms (Oleson & Whitaker 1968, 271–73). She accepts herself as a nurse because patients do so.

Role Ideologies. As previously described, use of the quasi uniform and uniform is based upon a bureaucratic ideology which stresses external identification of status and accountability through observability. A quasi-uniform wearer is a group representative who is engaged primarily in carrying out the directives of an organization; the relationship with the client is shaped by the relationship toward one's superiors. The opposing role ideology of professionalism states that a worker may better interact with a client as a professional practitioner rather than as group representative. In the professional approach, the best guide to interaction with a client is the informed opinion of an autonomous expert on the scene who may be a better judge of the situation than a remote superior. The professional relies upon an alternative reference group and set of norms—professional peers and standards—which may supersede immediate superiors.

The contrast between the two role ideologies is particularly apparent in nursing which is redefining itself as a health profession with a claim to autonomy and expertise equal to that of any other. The movement toward professional status is reflected in general nursing by the change from the original emphasis upon bedside care to technical and administrative competence. The claim of professionalism is strongly reenforced in psychiatric nursing by its technical requirements of skills in interpersonal relationships and nonroutinized behavior with the patient. For the competent discharge of her duties, the psychiatric nurse must operate as a professional who initiates at least some decisions dealing with the patient rather than serving as a bureaucratic representative.

Public health nurses also emphasize greatly the nonroutine nature of their job and claim the need to exercise their own judgement. One practitioner prefers her speciality which confers autonomy unlike rigid hospitals where

you come in the morning to report, you are assigned cases, you read cases and in the afternoon you do your charting or what have you. . . . the care is not really individualized the way it should be. Because it is the same cardiacs, it's the same blood pressure, the same medication, the same diet. You know it is just a monotonous sort of thing as far as I am concerned. But, out here, I get diabetics, cardiacs. I get mothers with babies, I get all kinds of people in all kinds of homes. It is very different, you have variety, flexibility to do things the way you want to. (Int. 4)

The use of the quasi uniform implicitly denies the claim to professional status because it suggests both nonprofessional routinized behavior and the need for continuing the external control that began with professional socialization. Obviously, differences will always exist in the mastery of and degree of comfort in a professional role.

With the adoption of a professional role ideology, the quasi uniform may now operate primarily as a means of role identification to the wearer herself. The nurse's cap and pin become a personal reminder of her position and past achievement. Similarly, a nun indicates that the only reminder of her professional role is a ring engraved with a cross (Int. 1). The habit is no longer necessary; indeed it is regarded as a crutch necessary only for those without the inner resources to perform independently. No longer is there a need to render the wearer highly visible to external monitors of her performance. Indeed, this function of the uniform is resented as casting aspersions upon her ability to operate as an autonomous professional.

For the professionally oriented nurse, the functions of the quasi uniform may be examined from a rational perspective. It may be discarded in favor of street dress or made the subject of radical innovation should that prove advantageous. It may also serve as a utilitarian device to ward against contagion, protect one's personal clothing, or shield against danger. It may be accepted as a social tool when the practitioner desires the impersonality of an organizational representative.

The Quasi Uniform in Interaction. After the initial placement and identification, the quasi uniform separates actors into their respective statuses. Such dress is useful not only in setting the stage but also throughout the interaction where it forms a running commentary on conversation.

Separation from the client is appropriate when there is no need for individual rapport and the service can be provided by anyone in a quasi uniform. The intrusion of other statuses or personalities is detrimental if the client wants only segmental interaction. A nurse's training in viewing patients as entire individuals is of little use when they want to be treated only for their ailments and resent probing into their lives (Int. 2).

Group boundaries may be expanded or contracted to include or exclude others for a variety of reasons. Medical students are dressed in white jackets to assimilate them into the community of physicians (Coser 1962, 44). Similarly, the researcher may be assimilated into the same community by virtue of the same jacket (ibid., xxi, xxxi; Mumford 1970, 9).

These devices may be used by the group because of its control of the format of the quasi uniform and its distribution. By so doing, the group attempts to structure the perception of the outsider-onlooker. The perception of the group affiliation instituted by the quasi uniform is also incorporated into their self-perception by the wearers themselves. In a revealing anecdote, a psychologist said that when he addressed a priest in lay clothes at a convention as "Father", the priest blushed and touched his neck. Upon later questioning, the priest admitted that he had involuntarily put his hand to his neck to feel for his Roman collar (Cohen).

The demarcation of group affiliation and status may sometimes be evaluated as highly functional by those committed to the professional role ideology. The quasi uniform converts the home into an outpatient clinic wherein a visitor is not regarded as a friend but as a professional who has arrived for a specific purpose. This definition of the situation is especially important for the public health nurses interviewed in this study because their patients were very often lonely individuals with few contacts other than the nurses. A public health nurse discusses the influence of the quasi uniform upon her housebound patients. "Right away they [the patients] are able to see I am a nurse, I'm not a friend, this is not a social visit; it's a sort of a formal visit. If I walk in in my street clothes then I imagine they would see me in a different light perhaps" (Int. 4).

The quasi uniform serves a very useful function by establishing the wearer's right to a given status without her need to prove herself. "If you just walk in in dungarees, they look at you and say, do you know what you are doing? Are you really a nurse? . . . But with a uniform, it does reassure them that you are a nurse, you must know what you are doing" (Int. 6).

Quasi uniforms are advisable for evening shifts so that the awakening patient immediately knows where he is and is not confused (Jakubovskis 1968). Furthermore, quasi uniforms reassure patients and their relatives that proper care is being provided by professionals (Brown & Goldstein 1968; Ints. 2, 3, 6; Jakubovskis 1968).

Finally, the quasi uniform reenforces nurses in difficult situations such as persuading recalcitrant patients to take medication or escorting psychiatric patients off the ward (Brown & Goldstein 1968; Int. 3). It also helps minimize the sexual factor in interaction with male patients (Ints. 4, 6; Oleson & Whitaker 1968, 63, 240).

On the other hand, drawing boundaries between patient and practitioner may be regarded as inappropriate for a professional role ideology. The quasi uniform may become a barrier to interaction with the patient and a means of avoiding getting close to a patient as described by a nurse.

If you have a terminal patient and you get close to them and they die, that can be very upsetting. Or have a psychiatric patient turn on you and physically attack you, that is upsetting. But [if] you are behind your uniform and do not get to know these people, then you do not have to worry about being hurt. . . . It's just like when I was a student, some of the older nurses would stay in the office and never come out to the ward. They were hiding in the office, yet they were there. Some nurses do it behind the uniform (Int. 6).

In another type of interaction, a session of family court closed to the public, the difference between the adversaries and the judge was decreased by the latter's use of ordinary dress. Furthermore, participants were not differentiated by elevation as in ordinary courtrooms; all sat around the same table.[13] An Australian judge also omitted judicial robes to decrease the tension of divorce proceedings (NYT 7 May 1977).

The process is the same in all of the previous instances, the manipulation of the barriers between professional and client by use or nonuse of the quasi uniform. The difference lies in the evaluation of the desirability of barriers for a given relationship.

The quasi uniform may be vital for some service occupations. For the red cap, far from interfering with his client relationship, the quasi uniform makes it possible by certifying his respectability and competence. Without his traditional quasi uniform, the red cap would not be deemed capable or trustworthy enough to give this information; he would lose all the advantages of his visibility as a *red* cap and the heritage of prior generations of red caps. Though the quasi uniform makes some service positions possible, under conditions of urban doubt and anonymity, it may not be sufficient to legitimate the wearer and may require supplemental confirmation. A public health nurse combines the quasi uniform with a preliminary telephone call to insure her reception by the client since the legitimacy of the quasi uniform has been diluted by imposters in various parts of the city (Int. 7).

The Wearer and the General Public

The closer occupational clothing approaches a quasi uniform, the greater the interaction of the wearer with the general public. Whereas a professor in a large city becomes anonymous as soon as he leaves the campus, or at times the class room, the quasi uniform of others signals to everyone their occupation or organizational affiliation. Everyone whom quasi-uniform wearers meet in the course of the day becomes a member of their role set which enlarges to include the entire population. In a sense, the entire network of city streets becomes their front region.

The relationship of the general public with quasi-uniform wearers takes several forms. The general public may interact with wearers in their occupational capacity and become self-selected clients. Public health nurses are asked for medical advice by strangers on the street; others see them as a source of drugs. Uniformed doormen are viewed as citadels of safety in a hostile environment. Nuns are stopped in the street and asked to pray for the stranger. A quasi uniform may vouch for the wearer beyond his area of competence; the use of firemen for delivering children, a duty far beyond their original function, is an example. Quasi-uniform wearers become a public resource whom anyone may freely call upon, even in remotely related capacities, without any introduction.

The transformation of a quasi-uniform wearer into a member of a general service occupation for the public may be accompanied by a change in symbols. Blue, for example, has become a generalized category for all helping professions, placing police, public health nurses, and others into a vast amorphous and vaguely governmental group.

As with uniforms, the general public plays a second and perhaps more important part in the role set of the quasi-uniform wearer, that of reenforcing the norms relevant to the wearer (Joseph & Alex 1972). At times, the relationship has been used as a deliberate check upon the wearer. Public school quasi uniforms enlist the general public as surrogate chaperons.

Norm enforcement emphasizes the master status for wearers and facilitates their adherence to it (ibid.). Another essential function is performed when the quasi uniform reminds the public of basic values; its wearer acts as their moral surrogate or symbol bearer. As one nun describes the outlook of the public, "They simply feel that in a world that is so secular that people do want symbols, that they do [want] something to remind them of God, that there are people dedicated to the service of God. . . . people have the right to know who you are when they see you, they have the right to recognize you'' (Int. 1). The nun's habit casts her in the role of a moral scapegoat for the general public, of someone who can justify moral symbols for the community simply by witnessing for them.

The general public then has a stake in the propriety of these moral anchorages in an uncertain world, hence their resentment toward those nuns who discard the habit. A nun in a modified habit and a little veil was once accosted in a super market. "A woman at the checkout counter got very irate, asking if I was a sister and I said 'Yes', and she said: 'You should be ashamed of yourself, if you want to dress like that you should get out! Leave the order! You are a disgrace!'" (ibid.)

In the role set, the stranger or the general public assumes the role of the generalized other described by Mead as the disembodied voice of society. All seemingly interpret the norms and apply it to the quasi-uniform wearer. Whether or not they actually do so is not as important as the fact that the wearer visualizes them as enforcers of the norms. When quasi-uniform wearers voice feelings of obligation as representatives of their organization, they are in effect describing the public's role as a generalized other.

Reciprocally, the quasi-uniform wearer may serve as the generalized other for the public, reminding them of the important values and symbols of a society, and by that very reminder, or witnessing, enabling the viewer to affirm vicariously his own allegiance to those symbols.

That the symbols worn by the service agencies serve this function for the observer as well as the wearer may be seen in the reaction of the public to the contamination of symbols. Wearing of a habit in the theater proved to be more disturbing to the audience than to the nun (ibid.). Similarly, the bathing of a patient by a nursing nun was more embarrassing to the patient (Int. 2). In these instances, the others felt that the quasi-uniform wearer was profaning her symbols. An alternative view of the association of sacred symbols with the profane world is that these symbols are immune from secular contamination. The nun in habit need not fear contamination by the outer world; her habit, way of life, and internal belief are sufficient protection. The lay viewers were disturbed because these symbols structured their universe by dividing it into the sacred and the profane. Bridging the gap created a cognitive and emotional upset. The nuns, on the other hand, were at least partially accustomed to viewing their habits more prosaically as a means of ordinary interaction.

Another set of relationships may arise between the general public in its role as generalized other and the specific client. The interaction between a quasi-uniform wearer, public health nurse, or nun and a specific client may be monitored by an appraising audience voicing approval or disapproval and even intervening in some instances. Bystanders have reproved others for disrespect toward a nun. These relationships are but an extreme form of the monitoring function of the general public vis-a-vis the quasi-uniform wearer.

Though the very use of a quasi uniform implies an acceptance of the role of the general public, acceptance varies with the nature of the occupation. Jobs such as ticket agents, information clerks, and baggage handlers in a passenger terminal are defined primarily as that of extending brief service to a client seen only momentarily. Significantly, the distinction between client and general public is tenuous, since any stranger may elect to become a client. Employees seemed to accept the public scrutiny and objected primarily to the lack of public differentiation between the various types of jobs.

Other groups such as traditional nuns or the Salvation Army may describe themselves as having a vocation and being on perpetual call. Far from resenting the periphery of the public, they welcome them as an opportunity to extend their services and as additional observers of their witnessing.

For those viewing themselves as professionals—contemporary nuns and nurses—the role of the general public is often seen as an encumbrance upon performance. The casting of a worker in the role of pure symbol, as a living embodiment of the virtues lacking in the observer, may be a straitjacket preventing real interaction with clients. As noted earlier a nun could not interact with others freely because of the interference of prevalent sterotypes; the inevitable well-meaning bystander informed her audience that she was a nun even though in ordinary dress and that they should watch their language. The quasi uniform may prevent wearers from choosing their mode of interaction with clients and from interacting on a professional basis rather than as a remote stereotype.

The quasi uniform also serves a protective function, not by concealing the wearer's true status but by boldly proclaiming it. One of the earliest uses of the quasi uniform for this purpose was by Florence Nightingale's nurses who wore ribbons inscribed ''Scutari Hospital'' as protection against the disorderly army (Ewing 1975, 40). The quasi uniform operated as a safety device precisely because it proclaimed their position as members of the nursing corps rather than as camp followers.

For the modern public health nurse, the quasi uniform serves a protective function in a similar fashion by enlisting the aid of the general public. One nursing educator noted that ''[the blue uniform] is a very protective uniform and nurses are rarely assaulted. You know, nurses travel all over the city into the worst neighborhoods, worst buildings. . . . People have a protective feeling towards nurses and public health nurses in particular. The community feels the public health nurses do care'' (Int. 3).

The general public not only reenforces the norms pertaining to uniforms or quasi uniforms but may also protect wearers, partly through the principle of responsibility. Very often the criminal may blame the victim for a crime, such as rape, on the grounds that ''she asked for it''. Blame may also be attached to the victim by the simple act of trespass upon the criminal's territory or turf. The public health nurse is protected by the clear definition of her status and, in the interviews conducted for this study, by her affiliation with a very old and respected organization. The nurse, then, has as much right to be in the area as any resident.

Peers

Quasi uniforms, and uniforms for that matter, permit wearers to identify their peers. Instead of serving as badges of anonymity as they do with civilians, they become highly distinctive complexes of devices which focus attention upon wearers and reveal their unit, rank, and achievements to the most astute observers—their peers.

This form of dress may broaden the definition of peers and extend the feeling of camaraderie even to those of different organizations who also wear quasi uniforms. A doorman who was stopped by a police officer for a traffic violation reported that the officer recognized him and therefore did not write out a traffic ticket, because he was used to seeing the doorman in a quasi uniform (Int. 13). Similarly, a public health nurse received special attention from a passing police car primarily because of her quasi uniform (Int. 7). Perception of a similarity among these diverse groups is rooted in a broad definition of signs—they are all in quasi uniform—and probably of the wearers' common plight in dealing with the public. As we shall see, a similar abstract category of uniform wearers, but with very different emotive undertones, is sometimes employed by public viewers.

The definition and perception of peers may be restricted at times primarily to colleagues within a specific organization.

There are not too many people in the church or out of the church that could tell one religious habit from another, as far as different communities go or were concerned. People would stop you out on the street and know obviously that you were a sister but they seldom asked what kind you were. But I think the communities themselves had this feeling about their *community identity*—Dominican Sisters, Franciscan Sisters, Sisters of St. Joseph's—each one of them had developed parallel evolutionary kinds of habits. . . . So it became not just a universal thing but kind of like Army, Navy, Marines. Everybody had their distinctive dress and took pride in it. (Int. 1)

Resistance to change by older nuns in the order was not due to age but rather to the attachment to the reference group of an individual order rather than the entire calling.[14]

Quasi uniforms are used very often to enhance one's prestige within an organization. To be sure, sartorial differentiation from peers within an organization serves other purposes as well, such as indication of variation in function and rank. Nevertheless, the enhancement of personal position still bulks large. The attempt by People Express Airline to promote internal democracy by omitting the traditional wings and stripes from the quasi uniforms of pilots and renaming them "flight managers" foundered in the face of opposition by pilots who defined themselves as an elite (Rimer 1984).

The signs that indicate internal organizational differences are more subtle than those intended for the public. The civilian is most likely to identify a quasi uniform, or uniform, by its gross characteristics such as bold colors, striking cut, or rows of buttons. The red of employees' dress became the most distinctive and recognizable feature for passengers in a terminal. Peers, however, require much more refined signs to determine the wearer's exact job or unit. When European industrialization threatened the position of medieval craftsmen, one response was to use distinctive dress "to emphasize the dignity of the journeyman's estate" (Schramm 1960, 16). An important item was the stick whose "shape and length gave those in the know an indication of the owner's affiliation" (ibid.).

THE DIFFERENTIAL PERCEPTION OF QUASI UNIFORMS

Clothing as a means of communication works only when the public can recognize occupational dress and the wearer can predict the response of the public. When one or the other of these conditions is not met, sartorial communication breaks down. Either the public or the wearers and their superiors misperceive each other's responses to the proffered signs.

Just as all wearers of quasi uniforms may perceive an affinity among themselves, so do some viewers combine uniforms or quasi uniforms into the general category of "authority". A public health nurse describes her patients' attitudes toward uniforms.

The patients that I deal with are mostly chronic psychiatric patients, who have been in and out of state hospitals most of their lives and they relate uniforms with these state hospitals. A lot of times there is hostility directed at the uniform more than anything else. Besides, the uniform to the psychiatric patient can represent a lot of things, and not just a nurse. If they are violent psychiatric patients they have runins with the police or something. . . . That [police] is another uniform, and there are just uniforms all around, so they just express hostility to uniforms in general. Police, sanitation workers, maintenance people. One patient said it was like they are all together and they know what they are doing and I am not part of it. (Int. 6)

Another public health nurse states that she works "in the____project uptown and I know quite a few people up there with psychiatric problems, and there is a certain threat. A lot of people think of us as military, police, and they have a very negative connotation to that" (Int. 7).

A night watchman is a natural target for those who view all uniforms as a symbol of hated authority. " 'Night and the slowing up of everything separates the world into two kinds of people. . . . Those who are not affected by uniforms and those who are threatened by them. One person stops and chats, glad for company. Another, under cover of darkness, is not afraid to challenge what he feels is a symbol of authority' " (NYT 13 Aug. 1975).

Similarly, a London constable compares contemporary and past attitudes toward the uniform. " 'Younger people, especially, have an unreal attitude about the police now. . . . To them the uniform is abhorrent, a symbol of authority. You're not a person but a symbol to them. . . . The older people remember the war when they see the uniform. They think of service. The younger people resent the uniform' " (NYT 11 Apr. 1972).

In these instances, the viewers are not illogical, for uniforms and quasi uniforms do generally designate an organization with some degree of power vis-a-vis the viewer. The abstraction of sartorial symbols is, however, taken to a level not intended by the wearers. Public health nurses did not expect the public to associate them with the police.

Another frequent type of overgeneralization is the association of a given physical vehicle, color for example, with a specific uniform. Other types of occupational clothing of the same format will be identified with the prototype. Blue is so frequently identified with the police that public health nurses have often been mistaken for police officers. Sophisticated viewers who recognize the public health nurses' quasi uniforms often by extension identify other quasi uniforms as those of the public health nurses. When a religious order added nursing to its duties, it adopted blue dress.

A more common example is the association of medical dress with white and by extension unpleasantness and pain. Children and adults exhibit an uneasiness toward personnel in white which they do not toward the same individuals in pastel or civilian dress. Children display the same abhorrence toward waitresses in white as toward nurses with whom they have had unpleasant experiences (Bradshaw & Cheng 1963). Needless to say, the association would not exist in periods and countries where nurses were not dressed in white, as in Victorian England. Conversely, the association of white with medicine and science has been used by hucksters in white laboratory coats to lend respectability to commercials.

To destroy the association of white with fear and pain, medical personnel have used quasi uniforms of other colors and street clothing. The experiment eases the fears of children who will accept the same medication and treatment from nurses out of uniform that they reject from them in white (ibid.). They do not see those who treat them as nurses but as "friendly ladies" who play with them.

Police forces have performed similar experiments. The original police uniform was adopted by Sir Robert Peel and deliberately patterned after civilian dress to avert the unfavorable connotations of military uniforms. Yet, animosity has been displayed toward the London police and their uniforms (NYT 11 Apr. 1972). Even the blazer which was adopted to replace conventional police uniforms several years ago in some localities has itself encountered hostility (Mauro 1984). A change in signals cannot always alter the relationship to the existential base.

The learning of sartorial symbols has much in common with the acquisition of verbal stereotypes. Psychiatric patients who score lower in tests on stereotypes are better able to view nurses as individuals despite their uniforms (Leff et al. 1970).

Viewers may ignore the niceties of distinction between the several statuses of an organization, mirrored in their dress, and insert everyone into a single category. In the elaborate structure of one terminal, all employees including supervisors, baggage handlers, ticket agents, passenger service representatives, and information clerks are defined as simply railroad employees by some passengers. As we have seen, hospital patients often combine all medical personnel in the same manner.

The public's perception of symbols often lags behind the changes instituted by an organization. The new quasi uniforms of a public health nursing service were still strange to the public, who had been accustomed to the traditional navy blue ones, and no longer served as protection (Int. 5).[15] Adopting the new quasi uniform changed the reading of symbols. The public now seemed to rely even more upon the nurses' bag in the absence of other identifying symbols. When a Filipino nurse averted hostility by placing her bag upon the restaurant table, the bag then became a key symbol attracting both the friendship and the protection of the general public (Int. 8). It also drew the unwanted attention of the street addict who had not yet learned that the bags contained no drugs. Even the bag has lost some of its identifying value, however, because of the prevalent fashion of women's shoulder bags, an example of the loss of the legitimating power of a symbol after wide dissemination and use by outsiders.

The slowness of the public in learning new symbols is not surprising. After all, we are not dealing simply with cognitive signals but also with emotionally laden symbols which may take time to learn and longer to unlearn. Harry Truman's dress blue National Guard uniform still created animosity in his unreconstructed mother a half century after the Civil War.

NOTES

1. Obviously, not every contemporary occupation has a distinctive form of dress. Factory workers in a vast range of activities may share the same general form of dress, unless other distinctions are made for status or department affiliation. At times, it may be useful to think in terms of families or groups of occupations utilizing the same type of clothing.

2. Career apparel provides additional proof that uniformity of dress alone is insufficient to create a uniform in our sense of the term. Since legitimating sartorial insignia are absent, a complementary system of signs—spatial—is required to identify organizational representatives.

3. This paragraph is also based upon Career Apparel Ins. (n.d.); Fashion Career Apparel (n.d.); NYT 28 Feb. 1971; 27 Dec. 1971; 30 Aug. 1975; Portrait Clothes (1979); WSJ 12 Apr. 1977. Career apparel is not worn by upper echelon executives, a pattern reminiscent of general officers who also enjoy a degree of freedom from army uniform regulations.

4. According to Max Weber, the division between home and workplace was one of the essential components in the development of rationality by Western economic enterprise (1978, 957).

5. In sharp contrast, when the cobbler from Kopenick fraudulently donned the uniform of the Kaiser's army, the explicit and precise sartorial symbolism masked his physical deformities. Lofland discusses the importance of familiarity with the locale (1973, 122–27, 141–51).

6. Chief stewards aboard Norwegian and British vessels wear gold braid insignia more frequently than Americans, and chefs on French ships wear up to twenty types of hats in contrast to the three of Americans (Int. 14).

7. Cleanliness or neatness may also indicate formality. A nun pointed out that the Sunday habit was always newer and cleaner than the daily one. After much usage, the Sunday habit would be relegated to daily wear (Int. 1).

8. The class distinction between users and nonusers of symbols is an old one, made by Marx in his division of workers between those who work with their hands and those who

work with their brains, and used extensively since then. Though the clothes of manual workers may reflect status differences, they are generally not used for mobility on the job. Workers may employ leisure clothing for temporary mobility off the job.

9. The Public Relationships Coordinator of Honda stated that "office ladies wear only the smock shown in the [enclosed] picture while all other associates wear the complete uniform, regardless of their position at our company. Our other plants in Japan practice the same uniform rule, except that all uniforms are the same" (Shiffer 1982). The Sony plant in England also promulgated a common master status by abolishing its six cafeterias, differentiated by the rank of employees and executives, and the private parking spaces for senior management. As in its Japanese factory, all ranks wore similar jackets (NYT 14 Dec. 1981; Precker 1982).

10. The separation of workplace and domicile, previously alluded to, did not characterize the relationship between employer and employee for a large part of the nineteenth century. The heads of a pioneering Parisian department store, Bon Marché, attempted to create an internal work community in which they controlled the nonwork activities of their staff by providing for meals, often lodging, education, leisure, and savings (Miller, M. 1981, 7–8, 107–12). These efforts were not due solely to necessity, which might be inferred because of the very long workday, but out of ideology.

11. Today, the attempt to secure employment in other armies on the basis of income, job satisfaction, and conditions of work—factors considered by other professionals—might well earn one the epithet of "mercenary".

12. The bus line dress code in the 1960's specified conservative clothing for employees in contact with the public precisely to reassure passengers. With the advent of the counter-culture in the late 1960's and the increase of youthful passengers, the old dress codes seemed outmoded to the official. He also reported being asked for information in department stores while in a business suit. Formal attire seems to be a sign of authority or officeholding in casually dressed Los Angeles.

13. Personal observation.

14. The quasi uniform in this instance operates contrary to professionalism by fragmenting the corps of quasi-uniform wearers and enabling them to identify with specific organizations within the larger body rather than with the entire profession. Among wearers of military uniforms, a similar outlook leads to the emphasis of individual services or units within them rather than upon the defense establishment as a whole.

15. Since the data was gathered, the public health nursing agency has reverted to its former uniforms.

10

Leisure Clothing: The Alternative to Work

The relationship between the two major areas of our lives, work and leisure, forms an intricate counterpoint. Leisure may be only an escape from the drudgery of earning a living; it may be a variant of work to be pursued with the same intensity and dedication; or it may become an arena for the display of grace and form, values not generally emphasized in work.[1]

Clothing and symbols vary accordingly. Whereas the symbols of uniforms and occupational dress indicate structure, group affiliations, and function, the symbols of leisure clothing announce respite from work, dedication to an activity, social mobility, or the expression of moods and identity. The wider range of symbolism in leisure is made possible by its looser structure and greater autonomy.

Leisure includes a variety of activities such as sports, formal events, informal parties, travel, commercial entertainment, private pursuits, or a state of apathy and collapse. Not all of these activities are accompanied by distinctive clothing or symbols; their very absence is significant as an indication of the amorphous state of leisure and at times a lack of differentiation from other activities.[2]

The use of the same clothing for both work and leisure complicates the study of leisure dress and illuminates some of the characteristics of leisure. Often this is due simply to an inability to afford specialized garb. But sometimes one man's leisure clothing is another's occupational dress; my formal suit is the working clothes of the maitre d' or diplomat, while both the professional and amateur scuba divers wear the same gear.

As will be demonstrated subsequently, the sartorial symbols of leisure indicate a relief from work, a resort to other activities, and the inauguration of a new persona.

LEISURE AS RESPITE FROM WORK

As territorial animals, we use markers such as towels and newspapers to indicate temporary ownership of space on beaches or trains. As temporal animals, we also use markers to organize the chronological rhythms of daily life which pattern our existence. Changes in clothing, often routine and unconscious, may accompany these cycles. The white-collar worker loosens his tie and unbuttons his collar as he leaves the office and so symbolically frees himself from oppressive authority and the obligations of the work role. A railroad employee takes off his uniform jacket during his lunch hour to avoid the importunate traveller (Int. 9); a factory worker puts his on when he leaves for the day. A student nurse will wear a face mask when she attends tubercular patients; the same nurse will remove all protective clothing when she "socializes" with patients off-duty (Roth 1957). Though specific actions vary, the underlying theme is the same. Wearers are entering a new segment of time—their own—and are distancing themselves from their occupational roles.

As an initial definition, leisure clothing, then, is the apparel employed to establish distance from one's primary employment or pursuit.[3] It need not consist only of clothes so labeled nor of clothes worn only for that specific purpose. When the office worker on the way to the parking lot or bus stop removes his suit jacket and tie, his dress becomes leisure attire. At the other extreme, one may adopt clothing suitable only for vacations—formally designated leisure time. Though the same theme of establishing distance underlies all changes from work clothes, the symbols vary with age, class, and the activity to which one is fleeing.

These changes of clothing symbolize the relationship of work and leisure in our society in several ways. First, leisure signifies a surcease from work. An extreme version is depicted in the Marxist concept of alienation best described by C. Wright Mill's statement that the work cycle consists of the worker selling himself during the week to buy a piece of himself back for the weekend. Although work does not always reach such alienation, some components may be universally present.

Apart from alienation the rhythm of work and respite structures the day. A frequent demoralizing result of unemployment or retirement is the partial loss of daily routines based upon changes in signs including those of clothing.

Surcease, whether brief or long, consists of freedom from obligations of the work role and the possibility of gratifying the self and its impulses which have been restricted by work requirements. Picture the resentment of a soldier whose break is infringed upon or of the instructor tracked down during his lunch hour. Others are intruding the demands of a role which is temporarily in abeyance and inapplicable. The intrusion is particularly resented when the trespassers have authority over the individual; the noncom is especially disliked when he intrudes upon free time.

The cycle of work and surcease affects even royalty. The Petit Trianon at Versailles served as a retreat where elaborate charades were enacted by courtiers in pastoral costumes. Relaxation was often signalled by informal clothing; Henry VIII was one of the early users of the dressing gown which was probably adapted from the Islamic caftan (Squire 1974, 106).

Second, the symbols of leisure herald a fresh round of activities, a new stage in the cycle of the day or week. One prepares for it, at times by almost ritualistic activities. In *A Tree Grows in Brooklyn*, the elaborate bathing and careful dressing of a young girl before a date is described by an even younger girl who sees in it an omen of future mysteries (Smith, B. 1943). Preparation for the Christian and Jewish Sabbath is an important part of the weekly cycle for the observant. Portrayals of the preparation for the Jewish Sabbath in the European shtetl contrast the humiliations and deprivations of the secular week with the compensatory joys of the holy day which must be carefully demarcated by clothing. "The Sabbath caftan is usually of 'silk'. It may be sateen if the man is very poor, and the black fabric, whatever it is, may be green with age, frayed and mended. But the Sabbath caftan is made of 'silk' and is a very special garment, stored away during the week" (Zborowski & Herzog 1962, 41).

The most poverty stricken southern sharecropper honored the Sabbath by a change in dress, even if it consisted of nothing more than putting on shoes and a cleaner or newer version of workaday clothes (Agee & Evans 1960, 257–86). In a more secular vein, conservative members of the New York State legislature complained about those legislators who wore casual attire in anticipation of impending adjournment (NYT 9 July 1975).

Third, since free time, unlike working time, is a block of time under one's command, it can be organized by individuals themselves. Planning may encompass nothing more than leaving the time open-ended so that anything can happen. In the classic evening on the town, one places oneself in a position where things can happen; one goes where the action is. Freely organized time is symbolized, in part, by the appropriate clothing—the elaborate or funky dating outfit, the sloppy gardening apparel.

Finally, free time is, above all, that time when individuals are truly themselves, free of the dictates of the outer world and free to assert their identity. The ego is often visualized as possessing a spatial locus; an "I" dwelling in the brain or heart. I suggest an analogous temporal location. Clothing may be used by a part-time hippie to free himself from the demands of daily life and to express his true self on weekends. " 'He dresses fairly conservatively, I mean you see him walking down the street, he usually wears slacks and button down shirt. . . . in terms of drugs, [he] can't be high all the time because of his job. Likes to, you know, cut loose on weekends and wear Levis and sweat shirt' " (Carey 1968, 140).

The assertion of identity during free time is also found in countries subject to the cross pressures of traditional and Western influences. In Japan, Western clothes are worn during the day and on the streets; traditional clothing is used for relaxation during the evening at home, partly because it is more familiar and indicative of one's "true" self.

Reluctance to follow the cycle of work and respite, or to indicate such changes, may result from the greater prestige or protection of an occupational status. A black doorman in a fashionable neighborhood was loath to remove his uniform before leaving his job for the day (Int. 13). The uniform provided a badge of respectability and made it easier to obtain a cab at night. On the other hand, the uniform made him an easier mark for muggers by singling him out as a man with a job and therefore more likely to have money.

Similarly, young physicians may deliberately wear blood-stained uniforms to hospital cafeterias to indicate their professional position (and perhaps for shock value) in sharp contrast to older doctors (Sudnow 1967, 55). Ironically, a black morgue attendant at the same hospital often shunned a uniform of any kind, let alone a bloody one, during his free time to avoid emphasizing his nonprofessional status.

Where a daily cycle of work and free time does not ordinarily exist, then routines may be based upon leisure pursuits. Country weekends of the British elite were structured by an elaborate schedule of activities and meals with the appropriate clothing for each. Nineteenth-century middle-class women without the structure of employment fashioned a similar daily rhythm.

Starting with a morning dress, if she was to receive callers at home, or a housekeeping dress if she has to do menial tasks, she might change to a walking costume, with a skirt 2 inches to 4 inches above the ground, or a tailor-made costume for church or travel. In the afternoon, she might don a carriage dress which was a charming bright-colored silk confection she could display riding with the coach top down, or she might slip into an opera dress for a matinee. . . . dinner gowns should be changed for ball gowns at ten o'clock. (Anspach 1967, 330–31)

LEISURE AS ACTIVITY

Leisure is not simply a respite from work; in modern society, it is usually a time for the pursuit of other activities. Leisure time activities have historical and cultural dimensions; they range from the strenuous life of a Theodore Roosevelt to the artistic or contemplative endeavors of a mandarin. Crosscutting these dimensions is that of social class, and it is the relationship between stratification and leisure clothing and its symbolism that is of prime concern here.

Leisure and Status Symbols

In a complex society, the patterning of leisure activity is most critically shaped by its system of stratification. Like income, status, and power, free time is unevenly distributed. How much leisure one has, and the way it is used, are central components of a style of life. The symbols rooted in leisure activities are demonstrations of the superiority of one status group over another. Just as hand-made Bond Street shoes are symbols of a higher position so too are one hundred and thirty dollar jogging shoes.

The superiority of a group may be demonstrated, first of all, by the sheer amount of time for leisure available to it, the freedom from toil, and the underlying economic resources. Gluttony may be directed toward time as well as food. Time-consuming daily routines are structured around such social rites as visiting and promenading. In fashionable areas of Paris in the early nineteenth century, "large numbers of young elegants could be seen in the afternoon walking up and down, with arms interlinked, coming and going perhaps a hundred times. . . . There were crowds of spectators whose scrutiny no neckcloth arrangement, no set of new-fangled spurs, no detail of the clothes was likely to escape" (Schramm 1958a, 22).

Concomitantly, clothing symbols indicate the availability of large quantities of free time. Beau Brummell "was able to spend some five hours every morning at his toilet: first bathing in milk, eau-de-Cologne and water, then giving an hour to his hair-dresser and another two hours to 'creasing down' his starched cravat until he was satisfied with the perfect shape of its folds (Margetson 1969, 18–19).

Other symbols of free time include extremely long fingernails which preclude work, the ultrawhiteness of clothing dependent on servants and freedom from sweat and soil, and impractical clothing such as crinolines, corsets, and skintight trousers which prevent arduous activities. The wearer of crinolines had great difficulty in avoiding lit candles and bric-a-brac in lavishly decorated Victorian drawing rooms, passing through narrow doorways, or lavishing affection on children (Born 1943, 1674–76). To paraphrase St. Anselm, I wear it because it is absurd.

Symbols and free time, conspicuous consumption and conspicuous leisure in Veblen's terminology, are opposite sides of the same coin; the proper use of symbols requires a period of education in the refinements of fashion. For the nineteenth-century dandy, a knowledge of the proper color of gloves or when to wear buttoned or laced shoes was indispensable. In turn, acquisition of symbols entails shopping, attendance at fashion shows which may become ends in themselves, and curators to tend and advise on symbols (Goffman 1951).

Status may be indicated not only by the possession of free time but also by the type of leisure activity. Sports as a way of spending leisure have been a prime arena for this purpose. In Western Europe, medieval royalty and nobility had their distinctive sports of hawking, hunting, and court tennis, not to mention the martial pursuits of the tournament. These sports and the attendant clothing were protected by sumptuary legislation, the sponsorship of the royal court, and the general rigidities of a feudal class system, thereby severely restricting although not completely eliminating the circulation of symbols outside of their original sphere.

During the Renaissance, symbols of courtly sports reflected the ethos of the cultivated amateur who displayed an esthetic sense, grace, and dedication to sport for its own sake. "Essential to the exercise of the courtier was the sense of *style* in his games playing: victory was sweet, but graceful defeat was preferable to a fashionless triumph" (Brailsford 1969, 81).

Ice skating illustrates the elite spirit in sports. It was introduced into England with the restoration of Charles II who had spent his exile in the Netherlands (ibid., 207–8). Since speed skating was a utilitarian skill requiring little practice and obviously useful in a cold, canal-rich nation, it was primarily a plebian activity. Figure skating, on the other hand, was less useful and required a great deal of practice, skill, and appreciation of form and grace. It therefore became an upper-class sport and eventually, as in the Olympics, was assimilated to the format of ballroom dancing.

The courtly tradition led to a great stress upon sports as an important part of the elite style of life, and to a proliferation of symbols in sports dress and equipment—the elite use of leisure clothes as temporal markers. Sports assumed "a make-believe air of seriousness and moment quite beyond that intrinsic to the activities themselves. They demanded their own costumes and accoutrements, as well as a playing area specifically designed for their use" (ibid., 84).

In harsh reality, the code of the courtier was not always adhered to and upper-class sports often reflected exclusiveness and violence. Court tennis was popular with the elite partially because of the expense of the court and equipment which placed them beyond the reach of the less wealthy; blood sports always had an extensive following.

Leisure clothing of the elite symbolized status or a style of life characterized by high social standing, association with others of similar position, and by certain experiences such as travel, participation in elite sports and "cultural" activities. These symbols, "status symbols" in the true sense of the term, depended upon a closed society where hunting, riding, and similar pursuits were confined to a relatively limited group whose membership was rigorously guarded and easily verified. In the middle of the eighteenth century, for example, the wearing of silk kneebreeches, white silk stockings, shoes with diamond buckles and red heels, and enormously high white cravats—to maintain the dandy's necessary air of aloofness—indicated membership in the "Maccaroni [sic] Club", composed of those young men who had taken the Grand Tour and returned enamored of Italy (Varron 1941, 1375–76).

Leisure and Mobility

Once, however, the rigid stratification system of the ancien régime was replaced by the relatively open class system of modern liberal democracies, sports and their status symbols were organized in a different manner. Except in extreme caste systems, some institutions function as ladders of mobility—the Church in medieval Europe, the civil service of the Chinese Empire, and education in contemporary United States. Sports are a mobility ladder in modern society; Babe Ruth vies with Andrew Carnegie as the archetype of the American success story. But if the successful professional athlete can make the permanent move from working-class origins to middle-class status, sports have the additional virtue of permitting peripheral groups, such as amateurs and spectators, to move temporarily to a higher status. And here clothing plays a key role.

The British worker, especially the younger man, loses his class identity off the job when he associates with others at the race track or at dances (Zweig 1952, 158). He rises, albeit only for the evening, because he can remove his working-class clothes and substitute clothes that are associated with higher status or are, at least, free of a working-class taint. Sometimes this is impossible as in the case of an army that prescribes uniforms for leisure activities—the British Army's walk-ing-out uniform—and then the private is labeled as such even outside of the camp. Yet even the private may shed his low status and achieve at least a classless anonymity when he changes into tennis clothes or the warm-up suit of the dedicated jogger.

Not only is there a standardized dress used for active participation in a sport, but there may be sports clothing specific to the spectator especially if it enhances his position. In eighteenth and early nineteenth century England, the illegal and disreputable sport of boxing fascinated some members of the upper classes whose clothing served to distance them from lower-class participants. Boxers stripped to the waist, wore breeches in the eighteenth century or long trousers in the nine-teenth, and identifying colored neckerchieves (Schramm 1965b, 12–13). Upper-class members of a "Pugilistic Society" sponsoring the bouts wore a distinctive "club uniform" which also separated them from lower-class spectators.

Whether spectators choose clothing that distances them from the participants or clothing that stresses identification with them depends upon the usefulness of the sport as a claim to status. Because not all sports are equally useful as symbols of high status, distinguishing among them is crucial in a relatively open society. Horse racing in the early and mid-nineteenth century, for example, required large sums for the maintenance of horses and gambling, and in its attitude toward money, showed an aristocratic disdain for the rationalized bourgeois pursuit of wealth. Yachting was a similar enterprise, as J. P. Morgan's famous reply to the inquiry about cost indicates. Racing, though, had the added advantage of the aristocratic mystique of the cavalier on horseback. In the democratic nineteenth and twentieth century the spectator can connect himself symbolically with that ancient tradition by the proper choice of clothing. The formal dress of spectators in the Jockey Club, an upper-class sporting club, or at the Royal Enclosure at Ascot proclaims that they are descendants of knights and their ladies (Schramm 1965b, 11).

Other sartorial distinctions arise when spectators create their own subculture and regard the game as a pretext for their activities in the stands or off the field. British soccer fans, largely working class, have established elaborate clothing codes to indicate differences in group roles and geographical origin (Marsh et al. 1978, 58–86, 115–34). These codes also create the context of a moral holiday.

Many types of clothing for participants and spectators, though not necessarily the sports themselves, have gone through a cycle aptly described as the circulation of symbols and their abandonment upon contamination (Goffman 1951). In the first stage, the upper classes adopt a sport and its sartorial symbols in part to display their elite, leisured status (Morris, Desmond 1970, 185–87). These symbols may be worn as ordinary day clothes, even when not actively engaged in the sport, to emphasize one's position. The sport and its symbols then spread to the rest of society as a means of status enhancement until finally the elite abandon the sport, its symbols, or both. Several sports have undergone the process—hunting, riding, polo, yachting, and skiing (ibid.).

The contamination of symbols is related to the paradoxes of an affluent society—a rising standard of living, continuing gross inequities of income, and a strong egalitarian ethos. Affluence permits those of lower status to purchase the symbols of higher status. The safari suit today merely indicates the possession of money and knowledge of the latest fashion rather than adherence to an elite style of life. The Norfolk jacket formerly used for hunting and the safari suit are "dead metaphors" because the intrinsic connection between symbol and activity has been severed. Whereas symbols previously legitimated one's claim to a given status, now they assert membership in an economic class—status symbols have become class symbols.

Because of the blurring of class differences, those of higher rank must search for other symbols of superiority. At this point clothing as a symbol becomes susceptible to commercial manipulation as an item of fashion. One function of fashion, then, is to offer an elite a chance to differentiate itself from others while permitting the latter an opportunity to claim membership in the elite group through the purchase of the same symbols. Manipulation of symbols is easiest in the sphere of leisure time, since status relationships are more difficult to blur in the world of work where the realities of inequality are more apparent. This suggests, in turn, that one is more likely to find attempts to achieve temporary social mobility through appropriate symbols in areas most removed from work—vacations and travel.

Resorts, vacation areas, cruise ships, and especially the recent vacation clubs often create a never-never land of fantasy divorced from reality. A holiday in these areas is also a moral holiday, an occasion for attiring oneself in a new set of symbols. Such places become areas of temporary mobility where individuals abandon the statuses of their everyday life, often with the hope of transforming temporary into permanent mobility. Travel and resorts are channels of mobility only when it is safe to use indicators of wealth—the context of safety.

The symbolism may even be carried over into the working world where suntans, streaked hair, sunglasses worn negligently on the head, and exotic foreign jewelry signify actual or purported vacations. Of course, suntans are the mark of leisure only in industrial societies where workers do not ordinarily have time for outdoor activities; in primarily agricultural societies, suntans indicate lowly origins and are to be avoided. Recent Vietnamese refugees in the United States are careful to shun the sun to avoid being mistaken for peasants (NYT 26 May 1975).

Leisure as a Symbol of Endeavor

Following the Industrial Revolution and the rise of the middle class, the meaning of leisure symbols, particularly in sports, changed. Many current symbols of sport offer images of neither grace nor beauty, and emulation of neither a higher status nor a wealthier class. Instead, "the creed of *play* is replaced by a work-out" (Slusher 1967, 134). Leisure comes to symbolize a struggle for success as grim and determined as any in the business world, and, to paraphrase Clausewitz, sport becomes work pursued by other means.

The Protestant Ethic is an ideological source of this outlook that portrays leisure as of only instrumental value. Sports should fulfill only the rational purpose of promoting the physical well-being essential to efficient labor. Beyond that, any other function, such as enjoyment, was suspect. "Impulsive enjoyment of life, which leads away both from work in a calling and from religion, was as such the enemy of rational asceticism, whether in the form of seigneurial sports, or the enjoyment of the dance-hall or the public-house of the common man" (Weber, M. 1930, 167–68). This view was reinforced by the injunction against the waste of money for frivolous aims (anything other than the struggle for additional wealth), the suspicion of the body as a vehicle of sin, and the association of sports with the aristocratic vices of drink and gambling.

An appropriate end of sport is good health. Under the prodding of eighteenth- and nineteenth-century reformers who condemned the physically inactive bourgeoisie as enervated, the middle class became interested in physical exercise. Predictably enough, this interest was pursued in the highly rationalized form of gymnastics, a disciplined, nonspontaneous approach to exercise. One of its nineteenth-century founders, the schoolmaster Frederich Jahn, stressed not only its salutary effects but its promotion of liberal democracy and eradication of class lines. He therefore prescribed an inexpensive gymnastic dress in his classes, and this eventually led to his dismissal by a class-conscious headmaster (Schramm 1965a, 22). Part of the dress consisted of long trousers—symbolic of a liberal outlook.[4]

The result of the movement to convert the bourgeoisie to a more active way of life was reflected in popular literature. "In half a century [from early to late nineteenth] the hero of fiction had changed from being a languid exquisite in scented silk, exhausted by dissipation, to the clean-limbed athlete of the Nineties in Norfolk jacket and knickerbockers, smelling of tobacco" (Cunnington & Cunnington 1959, 28).

The definition of leisure as a serious pursuit employing the same symbols as those of the workaday world is evidenced today in the Black Forest of Germany. "On Sundays, even the thickest forest is populated with city dwellers, clad in suits and ties, on their obligatory afternoon Spaziergange, or outing" (NYT 15 Sept. 1975).

Another nineteenth-century manifestation of the instrumental attitude toward sports was "muscular Christianity" which saw an identity between the goals of sports and religion in fostering the growth of moral and worthy citizens. The outlook became characteristic of the British public school where "Games reenforced the chapel because the ideal of moral integrity and self-control could be practiced on the playing field" (Weinberg 1967, 45).

In a further development of the identification of religion and sports, athletic activity becomes a mystic communion with God. "Buddy Edelsen, one of the marathon runners of the United States, . . . was asked, due to his long training regime, when he has time to go to church. [He said] 'I was closer to God out there on those roads than most people get to Him in a lifetime' " (Slusher 1967, 135). An advocate of holistic running describes it as "indeed a form of worship, an attempt to find God, a means to the transcendent" (Clecak 1983, 149).

Even short of mystical experiences, sports may assume a key role in civic religion and become an excellent preparation for citizenship and service in the armed forces. A former Notre Dame football coach wrote that the "Stars and Stripes have never taken second place on any battlefield" because of the qualities of our fighting men. " 'These traits are something that cannot be found in textbooks nor can they be learned in the lecture room. It is on the athletic fields that our boys acquire these winning ways that are as much a part of the American life as are freedom of speech and of the press' " (Arens 1975, 77). Athletes become enshrined as the fittest representatives of the nation; American participants in recent Olympics served as the focus for a resurgence of feelings of national pride.[5] Athletes thereby assume the role of exemplars for the young. The use of parts of their uniform or equipment as fetishes for the young is an established custom.[6] Autographing baseballs for young patients, though perhaps once a public relations ploy, has become a practice among professional athletes.

The dress of the athlete assumes some of the symbolic properties of knightly dress. Honor becomes attached to the sports outfit, perhaps best indicated by the permanent retirement of the sports clothing and number of a particularly outstanding athlete. The rite assumes even greater significance when compared with the lack of comparable ceremony for any other occupational dress—which admittedly might be difficult, however, in the absence of identifying individual numbers.

Another characteristic middle-class attitude, stemming from the Protestant Ethic, as well as a pervasiveness of rationality, views sports as work to be pursued with similar dedication and perseverance. Whereas the earmark of the aristocratic sportsman was grace and effortless perfection, the emphasis of the bourgeoisie is upon achievement and winning, even at the cost of displaying obvious effort. The change is a movement from sports to athletics; the emphasis is primarily upon winning, organization and, above all, rationality (Guttmann 1978, 16–55; Vanderzwaag 1972, 66–74).

Rationality—the careful evaluation of the effectiveness of means and the desirability of ends—has led in sports to the development of an elaborate technology for training and performance. As random cases in point, note the development of new types of poles in vaulting, filming games for didactic purposes, and the elaborate weight- and labor-saving devices for yachts contending in the America Cup races.

Rationality also includes the examination of goals toward which action is oriented rather than their acceptance on a sentimental basis or as a tradition. In contemporary America there is not only a stress upon winning rather than grace in performance or enjoyment, but also a displacement toward the objective and quantitative indices of winning. The sports cognoscenti have at their fingertips the batting averages of baseball players, the hang times of punters, and the shooting percentages of basketball players. The individual applies the same criteria to his own performance; the score in today's golf game is measured against one's achievement in yesterday's round (Guttmann 1978, 47–54).

Leisure and sports today are serious pursuits which are no longer spontaneous fun but enterprises in which one's abilities are tested. Leisure is regarded as work, a career for which one prepares diligently, often beginning with the Little Leagues. The ethos and standards of the athlete and virtuoso performer have taken over even if the sportsman does not intend to become a professional. These standards are applied to all aspects of our leisure, not only to sports but to singing, dancing, and the playing of musical instruments (Davis, F. 1967, 13–14).

These new values are symbolized by the attire of the participants. The jogger shows his dedication and earnestness by purchasing jogging pants, shirt, and jacket in addition to the latest "scientifically" designed running shoes. He is only emulating earlier generations of part-time golfers and tennis players who appeared on tees and courts in appropriate clothes endorsed by the stars of those sports. Here, as elsewhere, a dialectical process is at work; attire can also symbolize distance and alienation from the dominant values. Black American athletes during the award of Olympic medals in 1972 appeared shoeless or with one black glove on the winners' podium and offered a black salute during the playing of the national anthem.

The cultural pressure to perfection creates a strain of its own; we become embarrassed when we fall short of perfection. One mode of coping with antici-pated embarrassment is to disclaim any attempt at perfection. The popularity of the self-deprecatory "fun clothing" such as aprons decorated with self-mocking slogans so dear to suburban backyard chefs stems from the aprons' function as a defense mechanism. Yet this defensive maneuver testifies to the power and pervasiveness of virtuoso standards; it is the homage amateur ineptitude pays to professional skills.[7] Compare the attitudes toward occupational dress which signal that one is engaged in remunerative work and is to be taken seriously.

LEISURE CLOTHING AS SYMBOLS OF PERSONA

The symbolic functions of leisure clothing drastically changed in the cultural revolution of the 1960's and 1970's. Instead of serving primarily as a means of social placement and mobility, or as the expression of earnest resolve, leisure clothing also acted as a means of describing moods or portraying identities. Concomitantly, dress codes which specified the occasions for work, leisure, and other pursuits weakened, permitting the development of all-purpose clothing which transcended role demarcations. The dual emphasis on the portrayal of freely changing personae and on ignoring the boundaries between activities and roles was reflected in the trends of "youthful display" and the "casual look".[8]

One of the best explanations of youthful display is offered by Lifton who described "protean man" as the hypothetical contemporary man who is malleable vis-a-vis the tremendous forces of today's world which expose him to far greater change than his ancestors ever encountered (1968). This individual may undergo many ideological changes in his lifetime, in sharp contrast to his Victorian counterpart who would agonize over only one change of conscience. Indeed, the very term "change of conscience" has an anachronistic ring.

The new personality combines elements of seriousness and nonseriousness in all areas of life. Even when political protest was made in all sincerity, an element of self-mockery for making such a protest still persisted. The "Free Speech Movement" at Berkeley was rapidly followed by the "Filthy Speech Movement." On the serious side of the coin, sincerity was elevated to a cardinal virtue which compensated for a great many shortcomings. Sincerity to the point of inarticulateness was much more important than adhering to the sham and artificiality of modern society.

The adult world, in short, is hypocritical; the use of clothing to mark boundaries between roles and events is not only artificial and meaningless but insincere.[9] The conventional symbolism, therefore, may be safely ignored especially when its observance threatens to violate one's identity. Dress is a means to express that identity regardless of context—jeans become the standardized dress for work, classrooms, theater, and often formal occasions like school proms.

> The whole picture has changed from a few years ago. . . . The last time we even had girls in blue jeans with American flags sewed on their behinds sitting on the floor and drinking beer out of cans to mock the whole thing. . . . Proms were looked down upon— people used to feel that they couldn't get dressed up and do frivolous things with the war and other things going on and still retain their radicalness. Half of them only used to come to goof on it anyway, wearing tuxedos with T-shirts and tennis sneakers. (NYT 20 Apr. 1974)

But by 1974 senior proms and formal wear were returning to favor (ibid.).

A current channel for the expression of sincerity is a renewed preoccupation with nature; what is "natural" is clearly superior to the typical urban, industrial culture and its products.[10] Plastics, the deity of modern technology immediately after World War II, have become an epithet. "Natural" foods are preferred to more conventional fare just as natural fibers are more esteemed than man-made material. "Natural" activities such as hiking, camping, and running are also signs of sincerity and virtue; hiking boots, running shoes, along with down vests

and jackets proliferate in the leisure wardrobes of the urban young. More significantly, they also spilled over into other spheres of life; the hiker's day pack
became the ubiquitous bookbag of students while jogging shoes replaced more
conventional shoes for many occasions.

Rejection by the young of the conventions of dress that serve to demarcate
roles and activities became a convention of its own in the casual look of the
1970's. Whereas Victorian women changed dresses frequently to signal changes
in role and activity, the solution for the 1960's and 1970's was the all-purpose
dress, adapted from casual leisure clothing, that could meet all contingencies
with a few changes in accessories.

A subtle modification of the philosophy of the casual look led to another,
perhaps more basic, change. Clothes no longer signalled shifts in roles but
instead described changes in feelings and identity—the expression of persona
through dress. Expression of the inward is more sincere and important than
hypocritical conformity to the outward convention. "Casual clothes are young
clothes. In them you *do* go 'to places', 'do things', 'have fun' . . . [one can]
create his own aura of 'make-believe'. In blue jeans and shirt, 'she' can become
'he'; the 'size 16' girl may be any age; the housewife is queen one minute, slave
the next" (Anspach 1963, 255).

The vehicle that bears the designation of "fun clothing" varies over time.
What is significant for our purposes is not the specific item of attire or design but
rather the transformation of some vehicles from the category of class or status
symbols into symbols of fun, perhaps another form of the adulteration of symbols. Although undoubtedly partially the result of marketing strategy, fashion
shows of the 1970's and advertisements which stressed "fun furs" indicated that
the new reason for wearing leisure clothes was self-expression rather than status
or class. As part of the fun fur pattern, fur-lined denims were advertised and one
dealer stated that mink was no longer a status symbol (NYT 28 Sept. 1975).

One of the results of the casual look and the use of clothes to express persona
was the weakening of the relationship between scenes and signs. In the Victorian
era the range of dress permissible for a given occasion was severely restricted
and the rules of dress were well known, particularly among the elite; in the
1970's the spectrum of appropriate clothes for the same evening event ranged
from formal evening attire to leisure or sportswear (NYT 20 Oct. 1975). During
the heyday of the counterculture, young professional musicians, and even some
of their elders, appeared at concerts dressed informally as did many in the
audience. If formal specialized clothing accentuated the distance between the
professional and those who take him as their model, the informally clad musicians seemed to be attempting to close the gap between themselves and their
audience. Clothes now designated the individual's impression of himself rather
than his definition of the situation, the latter being of secondary importance.

The change in relationship between scene and signs was well illustrated by a
clash between the casual look and a traditional culture which prescribed elaborate
role changes in dress. Asian guests wearing rich silk for a diplomatic dinner in

their country were shocked when they met American women who dressed for the occasion in "neat wool dresses and discreet jewelry" to offset the local impression of the United States as extremely "materialistic" (Anspach 1963, 257). Evidently, the Americans felt that dressing in good taste and in an essentially casual style indicated sincerity and honesty that carried far greater weight in winning friends than meaningless formalities. The Asians, laying great store on ceremony, felt that the simple American dress did not confer sufficient honor on the host and was therefore insulting.

The diffusion of leisure and casual clothing into other areas was partly due to the structure of the clothing industry which depends upon popular whim and where havoc may be wreaked by faulty predictions of future fashion trends. One solution has been the manipulation of trends by the labeling of clothing, and this has made the designer and manufacturer silent participants in the interaction between viewer and wearer of clothes.

Labeling clothes as casual has been used as a device to order a chaotic field.[11] Contemporary manufacturers reenforced a trend toward casual clothing by using that designation as much as possible. "Sportswear" became a catch-all category. "Sportswear is what has saved Seventh Avenue in the last three years when dresses and coats gave way. . . . And sportswear—such is the rush to get on the bandwagon—may be as much semantics as product. 'Sportswear', a buyer said last week, 'is everything today—including what is not sportswear' " (NYT 24 Mar. 1974).

Some of the effects of the clothing revolution of the 1960's and 1970's may be vanishing and more formal clothing may be becoming popular; the three-piece suit of the contemporary "yuppy" is a case in point. More significant than the fashion cycles, however, is the change between the relative importance of persona and scene.

NOTES

1. The relationship between work and leisure changes with the society. Indeed the question arises, which cannot be answered here, as to whether or not leisure in the modern sense can exist in a preindustrial society (Dumazedier 1968; Turner, V. 1983, 135).

2. As an example of undifferentiated leisure activities, the games of English villagers before the nineteenth century—football, handball, and hockey—were not separate activities but part of general festivals in which villagers participated en masse without organization into teams, special clothing, or equipment (Cunnington & Mansfield 1970, 354). Symbols denoting participation in games were ephemeral and consisted of the removal of coats or the adaptation of ordinary clothing, such as the wearing of extra stockings in early cricket matches as protection. Later the elite, under the aegis of the public schools, organized these activities into sports by formal rules, specialized clothing and equipment.

3. For a discussion of the association of leisure time with "freedom-from" and "freedom-to", see Victor Turner (1983, 139–40).

4. The connotations of gymnastics differed greatly from those of organized or team

sports. The former, prevalent in Germany and other continental countries during the nineteenth century, enlisted the masses and carried overtones of service to the nation-state. Organized sports, more characteristic of the English in the same era, carried elitist connotations (Weber, E. 1971).

In an inventory of clothing types, which this study does not purport to be, the dress of organized sports, as distinguished from that of leisure, would be analyzed. Some of the relevant questions are: the interplay of the military and organized sports, and their clothing, as societal metaphors; and the function of organized sports and its dress as socializing or control devices for the young, labor, and immigrants.

5. An American gold medal winner in the 1984 Olympics said in an interview that the victory made the United States a world power in the sport.

6. In a television commercial, a professional football player gives his jersey to a young fan who had offered him a soft drink as solace for leaving the game.

7. The counterculture movement led to the substitution of more realistic and attainable standards for musicians, writers, and artists for the virtuoso standards of professionals (Davis, F. 1967).

8. The dynamics of the change consist of breaching the boundaries between roles and activities by transporting the symbols appropriate for the one into the other: in the nineteenth century, wearing riding clothes for formal occasions; in the twentieth, wearing swimming clothes in the dining rooms of resort hotels. The 1960's and 1970's differed from earlier periods in the large number of individuals engaged in the change.

9. This outlook is exemplified by a group of British hippies.

All their clothes seemed to be permanently out of joint with the immediate environmental determinations of their situation. . . . Particularly rich items of clothing were soiled or dirty, or creased to deny their role in any consistent class notion of dress. Poor materials, colourless shirts, threadbare jeans, denim jackets or waistcoats were thoroughly washed and cleaned to deny their associations with poverty. Bare feet braved the coldest days, but great sheepskin coats, heavy cloaks and ankle-length cardigans were worn on the hottest days. (Willis 1978, 97–98)

10. Superiority of the natural is an old theme in Western thought. In the nineteenth century, it consisted of a Social Darwinian belief in the virtues of individualistic competition and of the superiority of handicrafted furniture, books, and other items over mass-produced commodities.

11. Categories of clothes may differ subtly and often overlap. In nineteenth-century England, there was a large number of ordinary coats for the middle- or upper-class male—morning, dress and lounge—each showing only a slight variation (Cunnington & Cunnington 1959, 227–39). The meaning of a given category might also change with time. A frock coat originally designated a cheap peasant garment, then a comfortable, informal middle-class jacket, and finally a conventional, formal coat. The labeling of clothes, as of humans, structures an ambiguous area and gives the labeler leverage to shape events.

11

Costumes

The use of exotic clothing by youth in our society to proclaim their affiliation with the déclassé, or resentment of the establishment, has often been noted as an expression of deviation through dress. I am of course referring to the *incroyables* of the French Revolution who dressed as guillotine victims, and to the choirboys of medieval cathedrals who annually masqueraded as "boy bishops" during the Feast of Fools (Chambers 1903, 336–71; Grana 1967, 73). The use of clothing as costume to signal a departure from conventional interaction occurs frequently enough among all ages, classes, and cultures to form a distinctive and important pattern.

Costume symbolizes the abrogation of ordinary social relationships—behavior under unusual conditions when the conventional social structure vanishes. It encompasses the moral holiday of a carnival, the status reversal of a rite of rebellion, or the feeling of brotherhood during the Mardi Gras.[1]

Costumes convey an awareness that their wearers are engaged in extraordinary and very spontaneous behavior.[2] Our first task is to examine the symbolism and its embodiment in several types of costume.

Costumes further denote a change in social relationships which results from a suspension of the usual norms or, obversely, an extraordinary status claim by groups or individuals. The patterns of interaction, their influence upon the wearer's identity and their function for the individual will then be analyzed. Finally, the ambivalent attitudes toward a dangerous servant will be seen reflected in the group controls and functions of costume.

CHARACTERISTICS OF THE COSTUME

Costume as a Symbol of the Extraordinary

The characteristic of a costume that differentiates it from all other forms of apparel is its open proclamation of departures in behavior. Whereas ordinary dress and uniforms declare their wearer's group affiliations and statuses, costume announces that the wearer is stepping out of character and into a new constellation of imaginary or unusual social relationships.

The symbolism which proclaims the new constellation has an extraordinary quality which is indispensable for its operation. The Gogo of Tanzania engage in temporary transvestism to impress upon the cosmic forces that the world is awry and must be restored to its customary cycles (Rigby 1968, 159–60, 170–73). In these rituals, married women wear male dress and perform tasks usually done only by men and indeed often forbidden to women.

Thus, when unusual or unnatural events occur in the reproductive processes or general health and productivity of humans or animals . . . in spite of the men's constant efforts, 'time' is reversed and a bad ritual state . . . is created. The complementary opposition between the sexes as social categories now provides the 'model' for the *manipulation* of ritual symbols to attain a desired end. That end is a 're-reversal' of time and a return to the previous ritual state and events. . . . In order to bring this about, this reversal of time and thus a return to the previous state, a ritual involving role reversal presents itself as the model for symbolic action. (Rigby 1968, 172)

Transvestism would lose its efficacy in this rite if it were customary.

Closer to home, flag-bedecked clothing, unisex dress, jeans, and male long hair, symbols of the counterculture, also depended upon their extraordinary quality for effect. As soon as these symbols became commonplace, the shock value of the exotic was lost and countercultural costume became ordinary dress.

The symbolism of costume creates an impression of the extraordinary in several ways. First, it may indicate a status that is inappropriate for the individual purporting to hold it—the transvestite claiming the status of female. Second, the status depicted by the costume may be nonexistent. In our society, this includes anthropomorphic animals such as the inhabitants of Disneyland, secularized saints such as Santa Claus, and fictional heroes such as Superman. That societies themselves often recognize the fictitious, or at least unusual, quality of these statuses is indicated by the unreality, exaggeration, and grotesquerie of tribal masks and costumes created for didactic purposes (Turner, V. 1967, 103–6). Finally, costumes and masks circumvent the usual processes of interaction and avoid accountability for behavior.

The symbolism of costumes is an essay in playful dramaturgy, a quality illustrated by carnival costumes in Trinidad. Before emancipation, Trinidadian planters expressed their superiority over slaves at carnival time by wearing slave dress, performing slave dances, and participating in street processions simulating slave chores. They played out a symbolic status reversal, consisting in part of *canboulay* or *cannes brules,* the burning of sugar cane (Hill 1972, 11). In later years, the freed slaves and their descendants reversed the status reversal by reenacting the same routines in costumes, this time to commemorate their freedom (ibid., 23–30).[3]

Costume Spontaneity

Spontaneity can appear to some extent in all types of apparel. Even in uniforms, the most standardized of all dress, the desire for self-expression has ranged from the flamboyance of a General Custer to the antiwar symbols of troops in Vietnam. Spontaneity, however, is basically antithetical to the purpose of uniforms and must be kept within very narrow bounds. Though greater freedom is permitted in ordinary clothing, even here limits are set by group norms and ultimately by law. Costume, on the other hand, may be defined as "institutionalized spontaneity" through dress.

The use of costume to assume nonexistent, imaginary statuses is associated with spontaneity or the free expression of impulse, an important component of costume. In modern society, such spontaneity expresses the whim of the individual. Prizes are awarded for the most original costumes in festival parades; a basic theme of the counterculture is dressing for self-expression (Cameron 1972; Welch 1966; Wills 1972). Simone De Beauvoir gives a sensitive description of the use of costume by an author to express evanescent moods. "I took a large shawl of Mother's, I cut a hole for my head and sewed the side together. This shawl, falling in classic folds, gave me an Oriental, Biblical, exotic air" (1961, 502–3).

In a simple society, spontaneity in costume functions on behalf of the community rather than the individual. The artist expresses his vision of the collective representation of gods and demons (Turner, V. 1983, 156–57). Even within a complex society, spontaneity may be the province of group leaders in the organized activities of a masquerade ball and Mardi Gras. Here the right to spontaneity has been partially surrendered to leaders of Mardi Gras krewes and directors of balls who select themes for the costumes.

Costume Types

Paradoxically, the first costume device is rooted in the questioning of the reasons for the existence of clothing itself and in the subsequent resort to nudity as protest. This device does not borrow from or modify any status but questions the conventional social structure by disputing the fundamental clothing norms regulating modesty. In a novel about China in the 1920's, radical Chinese girls,

ordinarily very modest, paraded in the nude as witnesses for political change
(McKenna 1963). In this instance of projective behavior, they performed an act
which brought the utmost disgrace upon themselves, thereby demonstrating the
sincerity of their beliefs and shaming those who forced them to resort to this
device. Canadian Doukhobors have also used nudity to protest against the establishment. Unlike the Chinese, they do not feel disgrace or shame; instead, they
use the authorities' embarrassment as a weapon (Dixon 1955, 213–15; Shulman
1955, 144–46).

This mode of dissent loses its dramatic impact when nudity is more widely
accepted. As an aftermath of the streaking craze in the early 1970's, professional
models were hired to streak at a conventional fashion show, apparently without
protest from the audience (NYT 26 Mar. 1974). A policeman in Truro, Cape
Cod, threw up his hands in dismay at the prospect of arresting 6,000 nudes on a
public beach in order to enforce a Massachusetts law against indecent exposure
(NYT 3 Sept. 1974). In the former instance, nudity had lost its shock value and
was coopted as a form of fashionable titillation or chic. In the latter, it changed
public conventions at least temporarily.

Status reversal is a universal and dramatic device that borrows the clothing, in
part or in toto, of other and radically different statuses such as the opposite sex,
sharply different social classes (the adoption of proletarian dress by militant
middle-class members of the counterculture, or masters' dress by slaves), and
other age groups (the dressing up of the young in their elders' clothing).[4] In all of
these instances, costume signals either a desired change in social position or
relationships, or a celebration of one's superiority to the status reenacted.

Several types of rationale underlie status reversal. First, the act of reversal
itself seems a form of idiocy or laughable incongruity as in the wearing of female
clothes by the Trockaderos, a ballet ensemble of rugged males whose appearance
obscures the actual skill of their performance (Croce 1974). The absurdity of the
contrast between the actual social position of wearers and their attire creates a
spirit of burlesque.

Second, status reversal may be rooted in a cosmology which depicts the world
as fashioned in man's image. The dynamics of the universe may therefore be
stated in terms of statuses and social relationships, the functional equivalent of
our mathematical astronomical equations. Changes in the abstract and impersonal universe may be encouraged by a ritual change in social relationships, a form
of sympathetic magic, as in the instance of the Gogo. The cracker barrel philoso-
pher who uses simple down-home homilies to express profound truths exemplifies this form of native metaphysics.

Third, the attributes of other statuses may be borrowed. Wiko men dress as
women to indicate that they too help nurture the young (Gluckman 1963a, 160).
The Philadelphia Shooters, predecessors of the contemporary Mummers, wore
women's clothing on New Year's Day to assume an anomalous social position
which permitted them a moral holiday (Glah 1952; Welch 1966).[5] And of course
transvestism can always be used for sexual purposes. In our society, the dress of

inferior classes or minorities is adopted to absorb their purported spontaneity and lack of inhibition (Matza 1961, 112).

Borrowing the clothes of another status is not necessarily status reversal. Twelfth-century women wore masculine riding habits for their greater physical freedom (Garland 1970, 36). Medieval transvestism did occur as a device for women to achieve mobility by masquerading as monks or clergy. The reverse, men pretending to be nuns, was interpreted as a desire for sexual adventure and condemned (Bullough 1974).

The symbolic meaning of each reversal may be read only within the relevant social context which includes the norms governing holidays, the locus of activity and, as we shall see, the type of social structure. The British police, for example, suspended laws against transvestism on stipulated moral holidays; one should not accost King Neptune's consort for homosexual purposes during naval rites marking the crossing of the equator (Withington 1918, 8).[6] Some contexts may be accepted by the entire society (Lupercalia, Halloween, and Mardi Gras); others may be known to and accepted by only a smaller segment, for example Miss Fannie's Drag Ball in St. Louis, an interracial event organized by blacks (Humphreys 1972, 84–85).

Status reversal may also compensate for status inconsistency, a function that is especially apparent for black fraternal organizations such as Prince Hall Freemasonry which is recruited from the black middle class (Williams 1980, 49–50, 78–111). Like all fraternal groups, these organizations have internal hierarchies with appropriate costumes and insignia which may compensate for the lack of recognition in the external world.

Another costume type, the dress of other nations and cultures, has long been used by groups ranging from Bohemians to upper-class elites to express the allure of the distant and mysterious. The underlying process is similar to status reversal with an uninhibited and erotic existence being imputed to the mysterious stranger. The upper-class masquerade balls of earlier eras frequently used Oriental costume to avoid the constraints of conventional morality (Laver 1954b, v). Bohemians of various periods have adopted the clothing of exotic peoples to proclaim their new position as liberated individuals. The upper-class English of the late nineteenth century attended masked Bohemian balls for a moral holiday (Davidoff 1973, 66).

The "other culture" adopted through costume may be one's own past, often distorted out of historical recognition. Folk dress of the past, for instance, has been revived in Scotland, Switzerland, the United States, and elsewhere as contemporary costume. Whereas folk dress was based upon standards of practicality, economy, fashion, and sometimes sumptuary legislation, its use as costume relies upon some form of group identification and enhancement such as nationalism, political movements, or gender loyalties. The symbolism is often historically inaccurate. Imported culture traits have been seen as indigenous; widespread currency has been ascribed to dress originally severely restricted in time or place; and great antiquity has been imputed to styles devised only in the middle or late nineteenth century. The capriciousness of symbols is however irrelevant to their identification with a bygone golden age.

The dashiki, originally a cheap cotton garment from Lancashire mills, was later adopted by nineteenth-century Africans as practical clothing and became an emblem of militancy in the 1960's and 1970's. Mboya stresses the lack of authenticity of the symbol.

What is unrealistic about the proposal is the ease with which some black Americans think that they can throw off their American culture and become African. For example, some think that to identify with Africa one should wear a shaggy beard or a piece of cloth on one's head or a cheap garment on one's body. I find here a complete misunderstanding of what African culture really means. An African walks barefoot or wears sandals made of old tires not because it is his culture but because he lives in poverty. We live in mud and wattle huts and buy cheap Hong Kong fabrics not because it is part of our culture but because these are conditions imposed upon us today by poverty and by limitations in technical, educational, and other resources. White people have often confused the symbols of our poverty with our culture. I would hope that black people would not make the same error. (1970, 411–12)

Mboya's excerpt indicates another characteristic of costume symbols. Since costume, like uniforms, pertains primarily to an external aspect of behavior, to the facade of a status or social relationship, it lends itself easily to stereotyping and the assimilation of the whole into the part.

The folk costume is rooted in part in Western romanticism which has long glorified the peasant—the child of the soil as symbolic of a lost pristine purity. Among German youth of the nineteenth century, the *wandervogel* tried to recapture a preindustial era and express their displeasure at French "effeminacy" by hikes in the forests, self-reliance in the wilderness, and wearing their version of rough peasant garb (Becker, 1946, 75–79; Gillis 1981, 73–74, 152–54).

In another costume type, the relationships or statuses symbolized by costumes are literally "out of this world". To suggest supernatural or superhuman forces, men have often resorted to the impersonation of deities or animals with extraordinary powers. A contemporary example of the evocation of deities through costume, in this case a comic strip, movie, and television deity, is the dedication of Metropolis, Illinois to Superman. To rescue its faltering economy, the city remolded itself in his image. The local newspaper was renamed the *Metropolis Planet;* a Superman museum was established; his image was depicted on the water tower and signs; costumed reenactments of episodes from his life were staged. The thrust of these activities was of course the stimulation of tourism (NYT 8 Aug. 1972).

A traveler reports a synthesis of ancient gods and contemporary comic strip deities in Mexico.

Two groups of boys are fighting each other in a mock dance. The first group wears satin Batman costumes. . . . and on the back of the Batman cloaks I see embroidered the old feathered symbol of the Bird-God Quetzalcoatl. Batman has been taken over by the Indians as the latest reincarnation of their old winged God, who came to them once as the white Spaniards, then as the Angel Gabriel, then as a Protestant pirate operating out of the jungles and now as Robin transformed. (NYT 30 Sept. 1973)

Costumes may rely on statuses based upon anthropomorphic animals, sympathetic magic, or the evocation of the dead. Great use has been made of the characters created by Walt Disney which are borrowed even, or perhaps especially, by adults for their fantasies (NYT 6 May 1973; 18 Oct. 1973). Leather is worn by fetishists to borrow the virile attributes of the original animal while costumes suggesting ghosts have been employed by groups such as the Ku Klux Klan (Popplestone 1966).

Finally, the utopian visions of science fiction employ futuristic dress, costumes which describe nonexistent statuses and relationships. Even in such flights of fancy, the symbolism necessarily reflects contemporary society since it is an extrapolation of present tendencies and states of the art such as the use of plastics, functional design, and unisex dress.

COSTUME AND THE INDIVIDUAL

Interaction and Identity

The spontaneity embodied in costume as well as the exotic nature of its symbolism give rise to a distinctive form of interaction that contrasts sharply with those of uniforms and ordinary dress. Costumed rites of tribal societies, contemporary carnivals, and costume balls exemplify the underlying processes of costumed interaction.

The prerequisite for costumed interaction is a suspension of disbelief. Without such suspension, the contradictions between the status symbolized by the costume and other statuses which are incompletely suppressed by it would prevent any interaction with the wearer. The literally minded little boy who saw the unclothed emperor is outside our paradigm but defines its limits.

In some instances, the interaction facilitates forms of sociability, a social relationship for its own sake rather than as an instrument (Simmel 1950, 40–57). The three-foot astronaut and the adult enjoy their Halloween conversation because each pretends to believe in the reality being projected while each knows that the other is not deceived. The very young learning the rules of interaction may need reassurance that the costume wearer is a fraud or that the child itself in costume is not being taken at face value.

In costumed interaction, actors operate outside of their usual anchorage of statuses. They are in effect footloose in social time and space and no longer subject to the usual norms. Such interaction permits friendship between people of different social classes who would not otherwise interact; it permits the suspension of the rules regulating morality, sexuality, and religion. The process is that of induced anomie accomplished through the elimination of symbols associated with conventional dress.

Identity is similarly reshaped by the loss of former anchorages. Removal from previous statuses may also weaken the internalized norms originating with the groups incorporating these statuses. The social looking-glass in which one sees oneself reflected has been altered. A participant in the Easter procession of Seville, Spain, who undergoes self-inflicted penitence, wears a costume similar to that of heretics condemned by the medieval inquisition (Michener 1968, 316–20). Don Francisco endures a twelve-hour ordeal of marching in the procession barefoot and bound by chains. "As he lays aside his cross and unbinds his chains, he says with his mask off, 'I feel that the Virgin was very close to Sevilla this day. I could sense her nodding as she accepted my penance' " (ibid., 320). His mystical experience seems to have been aided by the change of identity created in part by costume as well as the solemnity of the occasion and rituals.

In many instances, the anomie of costume has been institutionalized. In some cultures, the loss of anchorage serves as the basic principle of rites of passage. The individual undergoing drastic status change is in a state of liminality where he is suspended for a time in a social no-man's-land, devoid of his former social ties and stranded between the status he has just left and the status he is yet to assume (Turner, V. 1969, 95). The initiate cannot function as a child, where the transition is to adolescence or adulthood, because he is removed from his former surroundings. He does not interact with parents or peers and is reminded on every hand by the symbols of apparel and ceremony that he is no longer to consider himself a child. Yet he is not ready to assume his new status until additional changes have occurred. Costumes are an indispensable part of the rites.[7]

Liminal entities, such as neophytes in initiation or puberty rites, may be represented as possessing nothing. They may be disguised as monsters, wear only a strip of clothing, or even go naked, to demonstrate that as liminal beings they have no status, property, insignia, secular clothing indicating rank or role, position in a kinship system—in short, nothing that may distinguish them from their fellow neophytes or initiands. (ibid.)

Where several individuals are in a similar liminal position, a bond of communitas may develop among them which is based upon common social isolation, an "Ur-relationship" free of all artificial contrivances of rank and role (ibid., 96–97). The feeling of communitas occurs among the cohort subjected to initiation rites, army draftees during the interval between deprivation of civilian status and complete assimilation into their first military unit, and carnival celebrants.

In our society, Mardi Gras mythology is replete with accounts of individuals who found their true love during the festival, love made possible only through the liberation by costumes and festivities from the fetters of social status which obscure true worth (Tallant 1948). Liminality may also be achieved in a doomsday situation such as the survival of a shipwreck, or the hopefully fictitious encounter among the last men on earth.

An individual may employ costumes to establish distance from the rest of society. Even such individualistic use may be institutionalized as with the fool's or jester's clothing which was patterned after that of medieval mental defectives (Swain 1932, 2). The use of the costume and status of a defective to permit criticism of the community with impunity was institutionalized insofar as it became an accepted and standardized pattern. The costume of the mental defective is an important component of the immunity of the jester from those he criticizes. His dress makes him ambiguous; since he is a mental defective, one need not take his criticism seriously. The costume symbolizes the saving ambiguity of his speech.

Costumed interaction is particularly suitable for moral holidays, almost by definition. In a situation where norms are drastically changed and one is encouraged to behave in an abandoned manner, what better clothing device than one based upon the renunciation of accustomed statuses? The type of moral holiday that ensues is dependent upon the social context. It may occur in a community at large as in Renaissance Venice where carnival time became one of extreme debauchery. Or the moral holiday may be limited to a group as in an office party, festivities in a mental hospital, or the hazing of ship's officers upon crossing the equator (Goffman 1961, 97–112).

The epitome of costume is a mask which denies one's identity as an individual, or even as human if one is disguised as a god or demon (Crumrine 1983, 2). A Japanese warrior's helmet is "more mask than hat, it is a disguise to transform the wearer into a personage of otherworldly ferocity. Intended to frighten the enemy, an even more subtle function may be to transform the wearer. . . . He is the samurai dedicated to death. . . . The mask of terror becomes the man himself" (Noguchi 1985, 13).

A mask results in the elimination of interaction with an individual ego, one of the components of ordinary two-sided behavior. Instead interaction occurs with literally a nonentity. The other has disappeared and, along with his disappearance, his accountability for his actions has also vanished. Simmel describes the loss of accountability in some tribal masked societies whose representatives may commit all violations against anyone they meet. "He is not held responsible for his crimes—obviously because of his mask. The mask is the somewhat clumsy form in which these groups let the personalities of their members disappear, and without which the members would undoubtedly be overtaken by revenge and punishment" (1950, 374).

Interaction with a masked individual is a one-sided relationship with someone who is not there.

If we ourselves are unmasked, we feel at a distinctive disadvantage in talking to a masked person. To some extent the same effect may be produced by any garment (such as the veil) that tends to conceal the face, and even by spectacles or eye-glasses, since these make it more difficult to note the direction and movements of the gaze. The present writer must confess, too, that he always feels a little embarrassed and uncomfortable in talking to women whose hats are so low over their foreheads as more or less to hide the eyes. (Flugel 1969, 52)

Interaction with a masked or costumed nonbeing may free one from the constraints attendant upon interaction with humans and permit the venting of aggression upon these beings. People portraying Santa Claus on city streets during Christmas, or such characters as the Mad Hatter, Dumbo, and Mickey Mouse in Disney World complain of being shot, stabbed, kicked, and punched by adults and children (NYT 29 Nov. 1975; 30 Sept. 1981; WSJ 16 Oct. 1975). According to a Disney World actor, "They punch us around like they see Donald Duck on television getting run over by a truck or hit with a sledgehammer without getting hurt. I don't think they think we're real people" (WSJ 16 Oct. 1975).

Obversely, Flugel argues that the loss of accountability changes the identity of the masker.

When we wear a mask, we cease, to some extent, to be ourselves; we conceal from others both our identity and the natural expression of our emotions, and, in consequence, we do not feel the same responsibility as when our faces are uncovered; for it appears to us that, owing to our unrecognisibility and the alteration in our personality (*persona* = mask), what we may do in our masked state cannot be brought up as evidence against us when we resume our normal unmasked lives. The masked person is, therefore, apt to be freer and less inhibited, both in feeling and in action, and can do things from which he might otherwise be impeded by fear or shame. Hence the highwayman, the burglar, and the executioner have frequently worn masks and a masked ball permits of less restrained expression of certain tendencies, notably the erotic ones, than is otherwise possible. (1969, 51–52)

The mask utilizes the principle of the looking-glass self in reverse. Instead of reading our identity in the eyes of others, we blind them by our masks and may thereby shape our personalities free of external constraints. Masks free stutterers from their customary roles; the resultant anonymity eliminates their stuttering (Pollaczek & Homefield 1954). The quizzing fan of earlier centuries had an inset of mica or gauze which enabled a lady to screen her face while watching risque plays and preserve her modesty (Binder 1954, 193). Masks have always enabled actors to submerge their identity under an outer covering. Kim Hunter, the actress, describes her disguise as a chimpanzee in a series of motion pictures as "putting on someone else's cloak in a sort of total way" and as "really quite freeing" (NYT 13 Dec. 1970).

The loss of accountability and identity does not always result in acts inimical to the community and may instead enable the masked individual to portray a prototypical character in a wide range of dramatic forms. Here again the individual has lost components of his ego, not to indulge his id but rather to enlist his super-ego in the service of the community, to submerge his personal identity for the good of the group which he now personifies. In the riots and protests described later, the masked participants acted in the name of economic and social justice.

Sunglasses are used as a contemporary version of the mask. Their departure from the ostensible function of protection from the sun is indicated by their use indoors where they are much more likely to be used to evade accountability or deny identity. They have been employed to hide the dilation of pupils caused by drugs or to disguise a celebrity. In variation, they have been adopted by nonusers of drugs and by the nonfamous to pretend membership in sophisticated elites, another example of the hipster "in the know". Even the outdoor use of sunglasses may serve to evade responsibility when they permit discreet ogling on the beach. These functions of sunglasses are suggested by the term frequently applied to them, "shades", which carries the connotation of concealment.

An actor who had portrayed the Lone Ranger for thirty years lost the role because of age and was forbidden to wear in public appearances the mask identified with the character. He resorted to sunglasses as a functional equivalent of the mask (NYT 7 Sept. 1979; 10 Mar. 1981).

Functions for the Individual

For the individual, the patterns of interaction serve several functions, among which the ludic is of great importance. Costumed interaction permits one to express a capacity for play—the construction of new social worlds with distinctive norms and the participation in them for the sheer pleasure of creation and manipulation (Turner, V. 1983). Dressing up has a vital function for play. "Here the 'extra-ordinary' nature of play reaches perfection. The disguised or masked individual 'plays' another part, another being. He *is* another being. The terrors of childhood, open-hearted gaiety, mystic fantasy and sacred awe are all inextricably entangled in this strange business of masks and disguises" (Huizinga 1950, 13). Players range from eighteenth-century shepherdesses at the Petit Trianon to small boys in space suits.

Simmel also emphasizes play as interaction often engaged in for its own sake (1950, 42–43). His discussion of secrecy and the tension it immediately creates for betrayal or disclosure suggests the dynamics underlying the eroticism or coquetry of the mask (ibid., 333–34). Its secrecy gives both wearer and viewer a desire to perpetuate the concealment and yet to abandon it. The result at a masked ball may be a partial revelation and immediate concealment, a facial striptease as it were.

Costumes may be employed as rhetoric. Perhaps the simplest example is their bearing witness to one's beliefs, the blue denim work clothes worn by the original leaders of the black militant movement in the United States to announce their affiliation with agricultural workers, and the colored shirts of political organizations between the two world wars before they became established ruling groups. Here the costume is used as an external manifestation of one's ideology, often that of sympathy with the déclassé. The costume proclaims its message by the incongruous use of symbols and distortion of communication. A flag made into a shirt, Abbie Hoffman's dress during a television program, expresses attitudes toward the establishment far more effectively than conventional communication (NYT 29 Mar. 1970).

Counterculture used the ludic and rhetorical functions of costume in counterpoint. The costume of these protestors was ludic when it expressed a desire to "do one's own thing" (Berger 1967; NYT 25 June 1972). In contrast, antiuniforms or flags made into shirts expressed a strong desire to "épater la bourgeoisie" (IHT 22 June 1971; NYT 29 Mar. 1970). In trials of protestors, sacred secular symbols such as judicial robes were used as costumes (NYT 5 Dec. 1973). Guerrilla or street theater used costume and drama in a highly organized manner to convey political messages (Falconer 1972; Wills 1972).

The costume of student-members of the counterculture reflects their position as individuals who are not firmly anchored in society but are part of a temporary constellation of social relationships.

Everyone knows what to wear to a prom but what does one wear to the Revolution? Patty Graham and Robert Caplan . . . college students from New Rochelle, New York, have chosen the Pepsi Proletariat costume. This consists of overalls, flannel shirt, and heavy work boots, the traditional accouterments of the working class. . . . To adopt the Pepsi Proletariat guise is to express one of the more euphoriant pipe dreams of the counterculture; the hope that a coalition may someday be fashioned out of workers and freaks. "Revolution?" says the couple. "We guess you can say we're into revolution—we've got nothing else to do". (Sabol & Truscott 1971, 124)

The tentative and uncertain nature of the last statement in the quotation, they are "into" revolution in lieu of any alternative, indicates a renunciation of past statuses coupled with the nonassumption of permanent positions.[8]

When the oppressed wear the apparel of the oppressor, costume serves a cathartic function. Classic examples include women in male attire to discharge their resentment of masculine superiority, and the assumption of the clothing of superiors in an organization or society to express resentment over caste restrictions. In Trinidadian carnivals, "Dame Lorraine" was a stock figure used by black celebrants to satirize the pretensions of the white upper classes (Hill 1972, 40). Most bizarre of all, some inmate leaders in concentration camps who had internalized the values of their guards modified their prison garb to simulate SS uniforms (Bettelheim 1960, 170–72). "The lengths prisoners would go to was sometimes hard to believe, particularly since they were sometimes punished for trying to look like the SS. When asked why they did it, they said it was because they wanted to look smart. To them looking smart meant to look like their enemies" (ibid., 171).

As previously indicated, clothing may be imposed upon others as an extension of one's ego. Similarly, costume may serve as a means of vicarious gratification. An employer or official may use outmoded dress as livery for domestics, as working clothes for the staff of a museum village, or as uniforms for the members of anachronistic military units. Whereas for wearers, the clothing may be an occupational or military uniform, for viewers the clothing becomes a costume to which they react as such.

Personal power is most significantly displayed over children who are frequently selected as personal symbol bearers. As in other areas, they make admirable pawns and can be utilized to express feelings one dares not voice directly. One cause of male transvestism is that of mothers dressing their young sons in female clothing out of a desire for revenge against males which cannot be overtly stated (Stoller 1968, 183–84). Here, personal power serves as a vicarious proclamation of protest. Other attributes of children enhance their vicarious role in more conventional fashion. Since they are "innocents"—cognitively and morally—and representatives of the future, they are most fit to wear costumes incorporating sacred symbols of a culture. It is therefore the children who are singled out to wear costumes denoting patriotism, ethnic pride, and religious piety in pageants and parades.

Dressing in adult clothes may be used for anticipatory socialization and other functions by children (Stone, G. 1970). The incongruity between the status limned by the costume and the children's actual position may be reassuring; they can experiment with the adult position while aware that they are not subject to its responsibilities.[9]

The spontaneity of costume permits the recognition and satisfaction of erotic impulses more easily than conventional attire.[10] Costume may draw upon the design of ordinary dress from other periods and cultures with contrasting codes of modesty. The definition of the erogenous zones of the body varies with the culture. Whereas members of one society may cover up their genitals when surprised in the nude, in others they may be more embarrassed by exposed faces or limbs. Ordinary dress reflects these perspectives.

Dress of peoples considered exotic, primitive, or natural by another society may have erotic connotations due to association. The clothing of the shepherd figured for a long time in the sexual play of the French and English courts (Huizinga 1954, 137). In more recent times, gypsy and folk costumes have served similar purposes.

Contemporary clothing of the opposite sex may also be used as an erotic costume. Paradoxically such costumes may work either by heightening or suppressing one's own sexual characteristics. The woman in outsized masculine attire gives piquancy to her femininity by contrast, a logic similar to the mixture of sweet and sour seasoning in many cuisines. On the other hand, transvestites use costume to assume the outer identity of the opposite sex, a suppression of their own gender.

COSTUME AND THE GROUP

Social Contexts and Control

Costumes are a Promethean gift which must be hedged about by restrictions. They promise the liberating and innovative influences of "anti-structure", the temporary lack of a conventional and restrictive normative structure; yet they may also induce or facilitate revolt as in the agrarian Rebecca riots of Britain and the Stamp Act Riots described later (Turner, V. 1983, 130–31). Control must be exerted, not to insure the precision and legitimacy of signs as with uniforms, but to contain a dangerous servant. Even in costume, social constraints are manifested; even in the realm of the imagination, we are not entirely free.

The social history of costume is in part the transfer of control over it. Control is exerted directly by the community, groups acting as community surrogates, formal or informal groups for intramural purposes, and societal regulation. No necessary sequence of development is implied.[11]

In the first context, control is exercised primarily by the community—usually small and simple—during agricultural or calendrical festivals, rites, or ceremonies. While costumes are only part of the event, they are nevertheless indispensable. Here, the costumed event serves a function for the entire community and enlists the participation of all members to varying degrees (ibid. 144–46).

In medieval and renaissance Europe, religious holidays, agricultural festivals, and carnivals provided numerous occasions for community-wide use of costume in many nations. Over twenty such holidays existed in preindustrial England (Bryant 1951, 279–82). The core of these celebrations was often mumming, a complex of costumed activities which included singing, dancing, and amateur theatricals in well-defined folk roles (Aries 1962, 79–82; Chambers 1903, 116–22, 207–17). Largesse dispensed to costumed celebrants was an integral part of the festivities. The atmosphere of a moral holiday pervaded these occasions (Laver 1954b, v–viii). Participation varied with class, the lower classes engaging more in the theatricals of mumming, the upper classes giving gifts.

In a second type of social context, control by community surrogate, a group organizes and controls costumed events on behalf of the community. The New Orleans Mardi Gras is directed by krewes, secret carnival societies; the medieval Feast of Fools was led by ad hoc youth guilds; and the Philadelphia Mummers parade is organized by marching clubs.

The organization of costumed events becomes more complex in this second context and allows for greater differences in participation. In the contemporary Mardi Gras the structure of the festival is provided by the krewes which furnish the floats and paraders and, more importantly, stage the restricted formal balls (Tallant 1948). The rest of the community may participate but as spectators or as casual nonorganized celebrants.

Since the Industrial Revolution, the community and its surrogates have gradually lost much of their former control over costumed activities in the developed areas of the world. Costume itself has not disappeared; only the manner and intensity of control has changed. The contemporary use of costume is much less likely to be a communal enterprise and, instead, occasions for its use are defined by the organization, informal group, or the individual.

In the United States only a few costumed communal events such as the Mardi Gras and the Philadelphia Mummers still survive.[12] The many ritual activities originally connected with mumming have also disappeared, leaving the atmosphere of a moral holiday—the begging and pranksterism associated with Halloween or the Philadelphia Shooters (Welch 1966). Participants may be self-selected. Whereas "in tribal ritual, even the normally orderly, meek, and 'law-abiding' people would be *obliged* to be disorderly in key rituals, regardless of their temperament and character", in St. Vincent "only *certain types* of personalities are attracted to the Carnival as performers . . . the rude and sporty segment" (Turner, V. 1983, 146).

A third social context is the intramural where the significance and functions of the event do not extend beyond the group or organization. These include renaissance court masques, ceremonies on crossing the equator and lately the Arctic Circle and International Dateline, office parties, and costumed events in total institutions.

A fourth context occurs when costume is used on an individual basis outside of any structural framework as in informal masquerade parties, costumes of the counterculture, or individual deviance. This also occurs in simple societies as seen in the use of transvestite costume on an individual basis—as opposed to a communal ceremony—by the Mohave berdache (Devereux 1937). Even in this context, there is of course social guidance but not direct control as in structured events.

Costumed events may shift from one social context to another. The Feast of Fools was originally a community event with Roman origins; it later became an intramural occasion for the medieval Church with fringe participation from the community. Banned by the Church because of excesses, it was then taken over by ad hoc guilds and transformed into an event organized by a community surrogate (Chambers 1903, 274–332).

Societal control over costume is still essential in modern times. Costumes may be sacrilegious—the wearing of sacred symbols by unauthorized personnel, on unauthorized occasions, or in a derogatory manner. In contemporary society, flags have been incorporated into costumes, military uniforms have been worn improperly by civilians, and judges' robes abused by members of the counterculture on trial (NYT 29 Mar. 1970; 26 May 1970; 5 Dec. 1973). Costumes have violated the sanctity of ceremonies such as commencements when modified gowns served as symbols of protest.

The suitability of commencements, court trials, and similar occasions as forums for protest stems from their customary use as public reaffirmation of basic values. In turn, this creates an excellent opportunity to advocate contrary values. The decline in protest after the 1960's and 1970's made academic caps and gowns acceptable again (NYT 22 June 1972).

Costumes are also taboo if they violate the customary methods of control. Hoods and masks may be forbidden because they circumvent the usual processes of accountability and wrap the perpetrator in a cloak of anonymity. Ironically, the ruling groups may themselves adopt lack of accountability or anonymity when suitable. Witnesses before investigating bodies who fear for their safety have at times worn disguises. The use of disguises by police and other agents of control is also familiar.

Social Class and Costume

The relative importance of class and community in determining the use of costume varies greatly and depends upon the context. In a communal event, all classes participate to some degree in common festivities—one of the differences between a simple and a complex social context is precisely the greater importance of social classes in the latter.

The influence of social class upon the use of costume has been heightened by the growth of sophistication or cosmopolitanism, an outlook stemming from industrialization, urbanization, and secularization. As a result of their greater sophistication, the upper and middle classes led in the movement away from agricultural festivals as fertility or magical rites to occasions for communal carnival.

Whereas the very early mummers' plays were ritual in intent, they later became the occasion primarily for celebration. The festivities were communal and participated in by all members of the community. Costumes and masks were used by all classes and became so integral a part of ordinary life that during the sixteenth to eighteenth centuries the wealthy sometimes had portraits painted in their favorite costume (Aries 1962, 99).

Subsequently the carnival was abandoned as communal play in many parts of Western Europe by the upper and middle classes who became disenchanted with the leisure pursuits of the lower classes and children (ibid., 92–99; Burckhardt 1954, 300). They also became less tolerant of the begging of the lower classes on some holidays. In Philadelphia and New Orleans, at the end of the eighteenth century, legislation declared masqued balls, mummery, and shooting of guns to be common nuisances (Welch 1966). Only after the festivals were reorganized in a community surrogate context and directed by krewes and marching societies did they become respectable and again supported by all classes.

In addition to these general factors, a more immediate cause for the change was the overshadowing of play by the work ethic (Huizinga 1950, 179–92; Weber, M. 1930, 168–69). The carnival, however, has persisted as a communal event in Southern Europe and Latin America.

Costume was not abandoned in the nineteenth century by the elite who continued to wear it at their masquerade balls (Laver 1954a). Costumes were now used on a class-segregated rather than communal basis. As previously suggested, the revival of the New Orleans Mardi Gras may stem from its restructuring in the early nineteenth century as an event in which the upper and middle classes could participate on an exclusive basis by means of krewes with limited membership and private balls.

Costumed activities may be used by social classes as a mode of differentiation just as fashion in ordinary dress. The extent to which class outweighs communal considerations depends upon the period and place.

Functions for the Group

The symbolism of costumes has important functions for a group. In the broad area of status regulation, costumed ceremonies of rites of passage, as previously mentioned, insure the proper transition through the statuses structuring one's life. Again, costume functions as an effective means of institutionalizing deviance to the advantage of both society and the individual. The status of the costumed berdache in American Indian societies clarified for transvestite and society the position of homosexuals.

Of equal importance is a topic alluded to in the discussion of class, the integration or divisiveness engendered by costumed activities. A most strategic instance is status reversal which reveals a controversy over its function. Some anthropologists, anticipated by Trotsky, state that rituals of rebellion serve as catharsis for feelings of resentment engendered by a rigid social system among groups of inferior position (Babcock 1978, 22–24). These "seasonal folk rebellions [serve] as steam valves preserving the established order and thereby hindering the emergence of a revolutionary consciousness" (ibid., 22).

Roman slaves and lower classes used the costumed festivities of Lupercalia and Saturnalia to discharge their resentment. Similar festivities permit women of many cultures to express their opposition to male domination (Bateson 1958; Gluckman 1963b). Costumed rituals of rebellion among the tribes of South East Africa allowed subjects to express hostility toward their rulers (Gluckman 1963a, 110–36). The lower orders of the medieval clergy, who were often barely literate and of peasant origins, retaliated against their superiors on the Feast of Fools. "Priests and clerks may be seen wearing masks and monstrous visages at the hours of office. They dance in the choir dressed as women, panders or minstrels. They sing wanton songs. They eat black puddings at the horn of the altar while the celebrant is saying Mass. They play dice there" (Chambers 1903, 294). The laity engaged in status reversal on the same occasion by wearing priestly robes (ibid., 295).

In sixteenth-century France, costumed activities also functioned as social control by humiliating wrongdoers such as wife or husband beaters, cuckolds, and remarrying widows or widowers (Davis, N. 1950). Medieval youth guilds censured older men who took young wives (Gillis 1981, 30).

Other students of dress, including Marx, believe that by providing a channel for the expression of resentment, these costumed rituals may lead instead to change or even revolution (Babcock 1978, 22–24; Davis, N. 1978, esp. 178–81). The Stamp Act Riots of August 1765 in the American colonies were rooted in an old folk tradition of mumming (Shaw 1981, 9–12, 204–26). Participants included gentry who dressed as workers in trousers and jackets to show solidarity with the working class. In the rural riots of the 1830's in England and Wales to protest economic and social injustice, participants drew upon rural tradition and dressed as "Rebeccas", men wearing women's clothing and blackening their faces, or as the mythical figure "Swing" in very fine clothing (Gillis 1981, 45). An antimilitia movement of the 1830's in the United States was a forerunner of antiuniform protest in the 1960's and 1970's. Demonstrators dressed in mock uniforms, carried wooden "swords" and pipe "guns", and held burlesque parades (Cunliffe 1973, 186–92; Gero & Maples 1980; Harrington, R. 1977).

Youth groups have used costume to symbolize a variety of conflicts; the British mods, rockers, skinheads, and hippies have worn Edwardian clothing, bizarre hairdos, and hippie dress in their class-based feuds (NYT 9 Dec. 1971). Costume is a highly visible medium by which contemporary youth can express its rebellion against the older generation (Sebald 1968, 221–22; Scott & Lyman 1970, 133–34).

Costumed activities may serve as a source of divisiveness rather than of integration. When the entire community is not permitted to participate, such events may emphasize the cleavages within it. In New Orleans, the exclusion of Jews from the Mardi Gras krewes, some of which were founded by the Jews themselves, creates polarization. Prominent Jews may leave the city during Mardi Gras to avoid social snubs (Trillin 1971, 155).

Other costumed activities integrate the community by providing a communal channel for recreation or leisure. After the agricultural and fertility festivals of Western Europe lost their original function, they became an outlet for the social classes and age groups who participated in them jointly—the community context (Aries 1962, 65–81). Costumes formed an integral part of the activities. "In the society of old, work did not take up so much time during the day and did not have so much importance in the public mind. . . . On the other hand, games and amusements . . . formed one of the principal means employed by a society to draw its collective bonds closer, to feel united" (ibid, 72–73).

Costumes have furthered cultural nationalism by providing the easily identifiable national emblems of the American cowboy and Indian and the great variety of folk clothing in Europe and elsewhere (Fairservis 1971, 19). These are costumes inasmuch as they do not accurately depict current statuses but refer instead to a reconstructed past.[13] In Switzerland, folk costume was revived as a unifying symbol in the face of external threat and isolation in World War I (Pfister-Burkhalter 1947, 2012). The revival was selective chronologically and geographically since it was the dress of eighteenth-century Berne that was primarily emphasized.

Folk costume, when it becomes firmly rooted as a symbol, may function as more than a tourist attraction and instead become a national emblem. Swazi delegates to a constitutional convention in London during a bitterly cold English winter insisted upon wearing their traditional clothing even though it was unsuited for the climate (Kuper 1973, 359).

As with uniforms, costumes may also serve as propaganda. Nineteenth-century interest in folk clothing in central and eastern European states originated in the desire of intellectuals and ruling groups to create national symbols for newly emerging nations, a process still at work today (Snowden 1979, 13). The price paid may have been the creation of a "false consciousness" in clothing based upon a falsification of the past and a lack of appreciation of the requirements of the lower rural classes. Nationalism originated among intellectuals and "involved the peasantry and their folk arts in a political patriotism which they did not necessarily share and of which they were potential victims. . . . You cannot detain people in sub-standard houses for the sake of their picturesque dresses and they do not transplant naturally to a new environment" (ibid.). Folk clothing may lead to a perception of greater unity than actually exists.

NOTES

1. The extraordinary quality of costumes is further indicated by the lack of, or confusion in, temporal location; costumes state that the time is out of joint. Saturnalia, a moral holiday, originated in the intercalary period inserted by the Romans to fill the gap between the lunar and solar years (Willeford 1969, 69). In masked tribal rituals, the wearer is transformed into his own ancestor (Halpin 1983, 224). Victor Turner describes the ambiguity of costumed activity in terms of social structure (1983).

2. Who is aware of the unusual nature of the status claim or drastic change in the rules of behavior, the wearer or the viewer of costume? This chapter deals with bilateral awareness where both parties realize that costume is being worn. In unilateral awareness, only one party perceives apparel as costume, for example the viewer who perceives the ordinary dress of a stranger from another culture as an exotic costume. In another type of unilateral costume, only the wearer—the imposter—knows that he is in costume; the traditional transvestite attempts to pass as a female and to be accepted at face value by the straight world. In contrast, the wearer of radical drag intends to defy the establishment by revealing that he is a transvestite through, for example, visible facial hair.

3. In the United States, minstrelsy, organized by slaves as a satire of the white plantation class, was taken over and transformed by white showmen. What started out as ridicule of whites was inverted and turned into ridicule of blacks (Williams 1980, 96).

4. Another dimension of costume is its duration which may vary from an evening at a ball to a long sojourn in a counterculture commune.

5. Flugel discusses the nonsexual aspect of transvestism (1969, 119).

6. I am not resorting to the perspective of depth psychology which would inquire into an individual's motives for adopting costume.

7. The liminality of status passages has been described by Goffman (1961, 14–35), Strauss, A. (1962, 63–85), and Turner, V. (1983).

8. See Scott & Lyman (1970, 133–34) on costumes and student revolt.

9. The use of costume for the anticipatory socialization of children is possible only in societies where childhood exists as a separate status with distinctive apparel. This would not apply to medieval Europe when "as soon as the child abandoned his swaddling-band—the band of cloth that was wound tightly around his body in babyhood—he was dressed just like the other men and women of his class" (Aries 1962, 50).

10. Costume eroticism should not be confused with that of ordinary dress—tight clothing, decolletage, farthingales, codpieces, or bustles.

11. These changes are a movement from the liminal stage of simple societies which emphasizes communal and obligatory characteristics to the liminoid stage of complex societies which stresses the individualistic and voluntary aspects of these activities (Turner, V. 1983, 156–59). From another perspective, societies are proceeding from a communal basis of organization, gemeinschaft, to an associational one, gesellschaft (Toennies 1957). Durkheim's mechanical and organic solidarities reflect the movement from the universal rule of norms in tribal cultures to the latitude granted the individual in contemporary cultures (1933, 109–10, 127–32).

12. The Department of Commerce has listed over 700 festivals which include an indeterminate number of costumed events (U.S. Travel Service 1973). Many, of course, are primarily oriented toward tourism.

13. The disclosure of ideological premises underlying costume may not always lead to its rejection. Even when the fictitious nature of their supernatural costume was revealed to the Wiko, they still believed in the power of the costumes and dances (Gluckman 1963b, 160–61). The need for ideological underpinnings may be more important than accuracy.

12

Retrospect and Prospect

RETROSPECT

In this study, several types of clothing were analyzed, each representing a different strategy in the use of signs, the control of individuals, and the forms of interaction. Uniforms enabled rigorous control of the individual by means of very precise sartorial signs, the dominance of the organizational status within the individual's status set, and the presence of third parties in interaction. The distinguishing characteristics of leisure clothing were their indication of the individual's release from the dictates of work or organizational obligations, engagement in activity subject to other norms, and freedom to express one's persona. Costumes were the antithesis of the uniform in that the former described statuses in a deliberately obfuscating manner and signified freedom from customary norms.

Though the procedure enabled us to focus upon specific relationships, in so doing, we may well have lost sight of the forest. This reprise, summarizing repeatedly encountered themes and emphasizing common contextual factors, will reestablish a broader perspective. Since any analysis inevitably opens more avenues than can be explored, this stocktaking also includes discussion of fruitful extensions of research and furthers a sociology of clothing.

Clothing and Social Change

Clothing, as a social artifact, cannot be understood apart from the vast changes in Western society over the past few centuries. Among the most important has been a multifaceted movement from a gemeinschaft to a gesellschaft society, or a transition from a communally to an institutionally based social structure.[1] Some of the connotations of this dichotomy are caught up in Weber's distinction between patrimonial organizations rooted in personal and traditional ties, and bureaucracies based upon impersonal and rational relationships.

The movement from patrimonial to bureaucratic modes of organization was accompanied by a transition in the meaning of military dress from indicating personal ties to an overlord to denoting service in an impersonal governmental bureaucracy.[2] Within occupational dress, the advent of quasi uniforms similarly denoted service to an impersonal corporation rather than to a master or employer.

As bureaucracy developed, the importance of stratification as a principle of organizational structure, for example the patrimonial army or business enterprise, declined. The history of sartorial signs in Western society for the past few centuries is in part that of the interplay between the rationality of bureaucratic organization and the nonrationality of stratification within organizations and in extraorganizational activities.

The emergence of specialized institutions, a component of the transition to a gesellschaft pattern of organization, has important consequences for clothing. Formerly, a societal function such as charity, warfare, policing, or nursing would be the obligation of individuals at large or the community as a whole rather than of any specific organization. Alternatively, organizations might serve several functions; the medieval church furnished nursing care and charity in addition to its other tasks. Contemporary organizations are much more likely to be highly specialized and serve fewer functions. As part of this trend, the standing army, the military as a permanent and separate organization, emerged from the civilian community only within the last few centuries. This institutional change was indicated by the advent of the modern uniform.[3] The navy separated from the merchant marine in terms of personnel and the creation of a distinctive uniform only within the last century. Similarly, the police uniform developed parallel with the emergence of an organization separate and distinct from the military. Nursing and its dress became differentiated from their ecclesiastical origins.

Growing urbanization, another component of the inclusive historical trend, has meant the weakening of community bonds, or the change from a communal to an institutional society. The trend is reflected in costume usage which is no longer a communal activity serving communal functions but has instead passed into the control of individuals or voluntary groups and now functions largely as entertainment and a means of personal mobility.

As compensation for the loss of gemeinschaft within the community, attempts have been made to create a feeling of brotherhood within organizations such as the military, schools, and factories partly through uniforms and quasi uniforms and taboos on the indication of other organizational affiliations such as unions.[4] The group may become egalitarian by the removal of distinctions of rank among officers—or even between officers and enlisted men—in some military organizations, and among the several strata in factories or commercial organizations such as the Honda automobile plant and the People Express Airline. As one of its functions, career apparel promotes egalitarianism by limiting the competition for mobility through the manipulation of clothing.

Urbanization has facilitated rapid and anonymous secondary relationships in which the intrusion of actors' identities is a handicap. Uniforms and quasi uniforms facilitate such interaction by eliminating personal considerations and reducing the individual to a faceless, and at times even genderless, representative of an organization.[5] Urbanization has also led to a need for visual landmarks for safety and information which is often fulfilled by quasi uniforms and other types of clothing.

Clothing and Social Structure

Clothing must be seen in relation to societal and group structures which form indispensable contexts for the interpretation of signs. Indeed, many types of contemporary clothing dynamics, such as conspicuous and vicarious consumption or the use of status symbols, are possible only within the contexts of safety.

The uniform is a strategic category for explaining the relationship between social structure and signs. This type of dress provides the clearest picture of clothing as a means of communication and control within a group, in this instance, bureaucracy. Other forms of organization and other institutions utilize clothing in their own manner.

Through metaphor and metonymy, sartorial signs generated by groups and organizations are used by others to perceive and make sense of the world. At one time or another, nuns and clergymen have employed the statuses of peasants, widows, and academicians as metaphors to locate themselves socially and to organize their perceptions of themselves and others.

Expressive statuses and stock characters, the outward manifestations and custodians of symbols, are essential components of communication. Women and children in our society display the social status of their families; uniformed figures ranging from Rogers' Rangers to the French paratrooper and the American marine have served as stock characters.

Other categories of clothing not only enable wearers to carry on their activities but also supply perceptual categories for the rest of society. A complex of occupational clothing, that of the cowboy, has been transmuted into an important American and even international set of symbols. Costumes in earlier centuries provided such categories as the buffoon or jester who were important not only in the popular imagination but also in literature and drama.[6] The hippie was a pervasive and important symbol of the times both in popular and political imagery. Leisure clothing has similarly furnished class and national symbols such as the fox-hunting John Bull, the yachtsman, the polo player, the quintessential juvenile sand lot baseball player, and the nude Norman Rockwell water hole swimmer.

Clothing as communication can create distorted perceptions and definitions of reality either unwittingly or through deliberate intent as in the propagandistic use of clothing. The Continental soldier became a staple of propaganda for nativistic Americans in the nineteenth century; the picture of George Washington in his Continental uniform was utilized by the Nazi German-American Bund in the 1930's.

Values

Rationality. The change to a gesellschaft society, and from a patrimonial to a bureaucratic system of organization, entailed corresponding changes in underlying values, perhaps the most essential of which was an increased emphasis upon rationality. These trends were accompanied by changes in clothing, especially in the emergence of uniforms and quasi uniforms. The acceptance of rationality as a dominant value is evidenced in the status set of uniformed individuals where the organizational status predominates to the exclusion of all other affiliations.

An extreme form of the rational outlook is the utilitarian in which clothing is seen purely as a physical vehicle for carrying out one's duties to which everything else must be subordinated. The drawback of utilitarianism is its equation of the functional with the nonsocial, overlooking the importance of indicators of position, achievement, and group affiliation.

The influence of rationality is also reflected in leisure pursuits, some of which are as rational as any contemporary work endeavor, for example the great precision and calculation demonstrated in modern athletic equipment and training. On the other hand, some leisure activities such as fox-hunting stress traditional values; still others, such as parties or individual drinking, denote sheer individual nonrationality and spontaneity.

Costumes attempt to express the inexpressible and to rationalize the nonrational. From a social point of view, costume wearers strive to institutionalize and routinize the paradoxical.

Witnessing vs. Internalization. Throughout the analysis, whether of nuns, soldiers, or nurses, we found that a significant component of the values governing the use of sartorial signs was the individual's basic mode of indicating beliefs. Individuals may stress either witnessing, the overt display of beliefs by dress, or internalization, the refusal to engage in such display.[7] Which tactic to adopt, witnessing or internalization, is determined by other social values such as the responsibility attributed to individuals for their actions, and the degree of privacy to which one is entitled.

Nonrational Values. Because the uniform was used as a point of departure, the values initially discussed were those associated with bureaucracy. One cannot proceed very far in the analysis of clothing, however, before encountering other values which intrude upon even bureaucratic structure and are also the key principles to other clothing categories such as patrimonial dress, costume, and many forms of leisure clothing.

Even the uniform reflects nonbureaucratic values. At times, uniforms have been worn primarily to do homage to the controller of these symbols. The uniform shares these characteristics with other items such as livery which display the power of an individual through vicarious consumption.[8] The sartorial signs used within bureaucracy are not always those of bureaucracy.

Some nonrational values are elite in origin and include the grace of the accomplished amateur who performs with seeming lack of effort in direct contrast to the bourgeois who makes a virtue of earnest striving. Many leisure activities— diving, figure skating, and riding—still incorporate this outlook.

Other important values are rooted in patrimonial organization and stress honor and therefore pride of place within an organization. These values make it difficult to submerge oneself in a group effort; the individual warrior-hero of patrimonial armies contrasts sharply with the contemporary colorless but efficient bureaucratic military leader.

Still other values which have arisen in recent years as a result of the counterculture, and are also antithetical to middle-class values, stress sincerity, originality, and self-fulfillment. Their residual effect on modern clothing is indicated by the decline in the use of formal clothing.

Values, both rational and nonrational, are shaped to a great measure by class which bridges work and leisure by providing a common set of values for both. For example, the elite values of personal honor are operative not only in feudal or patrimonial military units but also characterize the use of leisure. Similarly, the rationality of the middle class was manifested not only in bureaucratic organization but also in the bourgeois use of leisure which very often assumed the guise of work under other circumstances.[9] The working class, as previously noted, does not use clothing to obtain job mobility, although it does so in leisure pursuits.

Social Control: Conformity and Deviance

Clothing not only operates as a means of social control but also signifies the individual's resistance to group forces and deviations from group expectations. This duality is most apparent in the uniform which converts wearers primarily into group representatives, makes the individual subject to organizational norms, and renders deviation even more visible. Still deviation occurs; uniforms fail to meet all exigencies and satisfy individual needs. Uniforms also reflect conflicts between the demands of the bureaucracy and other affiliations of the individual.

Even in the realm of strict controls, some leeway for the individual, however slight and surreptitious, exists. In time, these deviations are often recognized by the heads of organizations and institutionalized into new uniform regulations.

Both leisure clothing and costume are in part attempts to escape from the controls of work and organizational duty, although they themselves often involve arduous labor and conformity to other sets of norms. Leisure clothing is difficult to characterize since it covers so wide a variety of activities. Nevertheless, this type of dress denotes an escape or a respite from work, permanently in the instance of the leisure class, temporarily for others. Leisure clothing of all varieties, therefore, incorporates an indication of freedom from the norms of the workplace.

Leisure clothes represent, if not a lack of control, at least a change of group control insofar as leisure is a respite from work. Constraints persist because even the private use of leisure is shaped by social factors, especially social class. Whereas the advent of bureaucracy meant a decline in the use of class as a determinant of organizational structure, class has continued to be of great importance in leisure pursuits and clothing.

Leisure pursuits may be an alternative to work in the attainment of temporary or permanent mobility. The elite uses it to gain advantages, the working class for temporary mobility outside the area of work. But here again leisure is regarded as an alternative to work.

Turning to leisure as an activity rather than respite from work, such pursuits are very much subject to group determination as in the clothing prescribed for elite hunting clubs which approximate uniforms (Mackay-Smith 1984, 35–39). Aside from these organized group activities, leisure clothing is determined by fashion which is used to justify one's position, to achieve mobility, or to pursue sports as a means of earnest endeavor. Here group control is in evidence but not as rigorously as in the instance of uniforms. Indeed, some latitude in the use of leisure clothes is indispensable to meet the criteria of good taste or self-fulfillment.

The final aspect of leisure, the use of leisure clothes in the last two decades as the outer sign of inner sincerity, consisted of the refusal to acknowledge the need to change roles with activities. This led to the breaching of sartorial demarcations between formal and informal occasions.

Costumes are a societal effort to depict and institutionalize the paradoxical, to describe the topsy-turvy nature of the universe, to protest against injustice, to portray an anomalous position, or to vent otherwise inexpressible feelings. Though costumes permit greater freedom of behavior, even they establish limits by prescribing the pattern of dress and also the occasions for breaching the barriers of the norms of the workaday world. In medieval Europe, the dress of the fool adhered to the set patterns of cowls, asses' ears, baubles, and motley (Welsford 1966, 204–7; Willeford 1969, 15–22). Other costumes consisted of an inversion of signs such as the transvestism of gender or of social status—the borrowing of the insignia of ecclesiastical superiors by lowly clergy. Later, the transvestism of minorities in the Boston Tea Party and minstrel shows, where the guises of Indians or blacks were assumed, also revealed social constraints.

Clothing and Interaction

The several types of clothing create varying degrees of awareness of peripheral, and even unseen, participants in interaction and of accountability to others. Uniforms lead to a realization by both actor and audience that interaction occurs primarily for the sake of the group rather than its representative. Indeed the uniform operates to preclude the intrusion of personal considerations.

In any type of interaction, actors never confront each other directly or completely but only through a filter of socially acquired meanings. With uniforms, the social component is felt more immediately. We know that third parties, in the form of superiors, are present; that is precisely why we accept the uniform as a badge of legitimacy. The public also acts as a third party by enforcing uniform norms. In effect, the uniform makes visible the generalized other that is operative for all adults.

Leisure clothing signals a transfer of accountability from the work place. At an extreme, in solitary pursuits one is accountable primarily to the internalized dictates of values acquired from class and other affiliations. In the group pursuit of leisure, the group may enjoin traditional values or one may pursue leisure with the same earnestness and rationality as in work. Finally, one may, especially with the drastic change in clothing of the 1960's and 1970's, use the opportunity to alter one's persona. But under any circumstances, one is still aware of a change of accountability, an awareness which is put to good use when leisure situations are utilized to achieve business goals difficult to attain in the ordinary office setting.

Costume signifies the cessation of customary forms of interaction in work or leisure by removing the usual types of responsibility or accountability.

Power, the ability or the potential to achieve one's goals against the resistance of others, is the reciprocal of accountability. Livery, in the era of feudalism and bastard feudalism, indicated the ability of a magnate to achieve his political ends despite opposition of fellow magnates, courts, or at times even kings. In later periods, livery, through the mechanisms of conspicuous or vicarious consumption, denoted the economic power or prestige of the master.

Power also operates on a group level. Internally, within organizations, clothing may advance the objectives of one group over another as in the jockeying for power through the attempts to secure mobility by components of military services. The relative lack of power is displayed by the reluctance of liaison officers from the military to congress to wear uniforms while on duty. On an intergroup and societal level, it has been displayed by the power or threat implicit in the mass formations used by the police or military and by nongovernmental groups in the courtroom or the street.

PROSPECTS

The delineation of new avenues of investigation, which were opened in the course of study but could not be explored, suggests a future course for the sociology of clothing. The most promising areas of research include the examination of changes in the use of clothing types and alterations in social structure.

Changes in Clothing Types

Uniforms. A most unexpected finding was the large number of incidents, described later, in which modifications in the appearance or use of uniforms or quasi uniforms failed. Taking advantage of these natural experimental situations, we should inquire into the limitations of uniforms as a means of control, a system of communication, and a form of rhetoric or propaganda. More broadly, we should expect to learn more about the relationship between social structure and signs and the existential limits to the use of signs.

The first category of questions concerns the personal factors which determine the wearer's receptivity to the influence of the uniform. Some limited data in this area emerged in the course of study, the railroad terminal agent who was a reservist and stated a liking for uniforms in general, and the nun who was both a nurse and an air force officer and therefore very familiar with uniforms (Ints. 2, 11). Even in the landmark study by Zimbardo, differences within the ranks of both "guards" and "convicts" emerged (1972). Clues may be provided by the literature on the authoritarian personality which was intensively studied several decades ago. However, the underlying personality factor may not necessarily be only authoritarianism in the strict sense but also the stability provided by the precise structuring of the world given by the uniform. Our aim should be to determine the groups to whom the uniform is most congenial on a personal level.

Personality factors blend into group affiliations. We already know that uniforms do not influence all wearers to the same extent but must instead contend with class, gender, race, and other affiliations.[10] Among these extraorganizational affiliations are those of professional associations or communities which at times establish norms at odds with those of the uniformed organization. I have suggested the influence of these groups upon nurses. Extrapolating, one wonders about the influence of military unions upon the armed forces in Sweden and the Netherlands where they have been established.

A closely related set of factors which influences the wearer's attitudes toward his uniforms is the receptivity of his family. Wives of sanitation workers have insisted upon their husbands changing into civilian clothes before returning home (NYT 23 Apr. 1979); a nun was moved by the reaction of her relatives upon her abandonment of the traditional habit (Int. 1). One lacuna is the lack of information about the attitudes of relatives toward the uniforms of female personnel and their influence upon wearers.

Another broad area of inquiry concerns the resistance to uniforms displayed by the wearers' clients and the public. Rejection includes first, the resistance to the underlying social referent of the uniform as in the black community of Menlo Park, California which was less favorably disposed than others to the police regardless of whether they wore traditional uniforms or green blazers (Mauro 1984). Clothing engineering has reached its limits in this case and cannot offset the reality of the underlying social structure.

Another type of rejection consists of those who resist innovation, as in the laity protesting against the abolition of traditional nuns' habits or naval bell-bottom uniforms. They do not object to the underlying social organization but to its change of signs and they are a group for whom the symbolism of traditional uniforms is important. The key questions then concern their social location (class, education, and particularly relationship to the organization), personality characteristics, and political outlook.

Other instances of rejection may fall into either category and include those based upon gender such as the public's discrimination against uniformed women. The public preferred to ask questions of male park rangers rather than of their female colleagues even though the latter were better informed (NYT 15 Mar. 1976). Female airline pilots in uniform aboard an airline bus were regarded as bus company employees (WSJ 19 July 1978).

In another area, changes in uniforms and quasi uniforms should be studied as the result of a decision making process within formal organizations including military services, corporations, and public service groups. The first order of questions concerns the sources of change in a hierarchy. In the course of discussion, we have seen many instances of their origins in the lowest echelons of the military services. In the instance of changes from below, we should ascertain the conditions necessary for the acceptance or rejection of such change by the upper echelons; when are they regarded as useful innovations and when as punishable deviations. The differences between military and civilian organizations should also be of interest.

Movement of change upwards in a hierarchy implies channels by which the upper echelon obtains knowlege of innovations. Some of these channels are integral to the organization as in the standard, prescribed chain of command. Another pipeline for information consists of extraorganizational groups which means sharing the making of decisions about symbols with outsiders. Vehicles in the nineteenth-century American army included service journals—which probably still serve the same purpose—and letters from junior officers to journals. The interplay of these vehicles and organizations should be examined.

On the other hand, change may be instituted by the upper echelon. One would like to know the difference in the criteria for change of symbols used by upper and lower echelons. To what extent are the several groups motivated by considerations of the uniform or quasi uniform as a symbol, sign, or as a convenient tool for the performance of the wearer's functions? Changes in organizational dress may at times be intended primarily as a public relations ploy, for example the corporate quasi uniform as advertisement. This suggests the importance of organizational symbols for the outer world.

No organization is an isolated entity but is related to other groups economically, politically, and symbolically. A promising avenue of inquiry is the investigation of outside agencies in the promotion or rejection of changes in symbols. What role does the media play in informing outside groups of these changes; how is support amassed? The rejection of the proposed abandonment of bell-bottoms by the navy of the German Federal Republic may well have been the result of a letter-writing campaign to the newspapers.

Finally, cross-cultural comparisons should determine the relative emphasis upon the military institution, the status of its wearers (the two are not necessarily synonymous), and the stress upon the uniform. The function and importance of the military varies with nations. For some, it serves an educational and assimilating function; for others, it is a ladder of mobility. How does the variation in function influence attitudes toward the uniform?

The development of bureaucracy is determined in part by rationality in other institutions and in societal outlook. One wonders about the use of bureaucracy and uniforms in a new society where a governmental bureaucracy has been recently introduced. To what extent does the use of uniforms conform to the model presented in this analysis?

Costumes in Modern and Simple Societies. The contemporary scene offers many intriguing leads for the investigation of the role of costumes in modern society where they are still surprisingly prevalent. On the individual level, where costumes are under the control of the wearer, these include neighborhood and community parades on festivals and the reenactment or commemoration of historical events.[11] Individuals also wear the costumes of fictional heroes at conventions of space or science-fiction fans or at film premieres.

On an organizational level, costumed groups consist of fraternal orders such as the Masons and Elks, groups whose sole purpose is participation in festivals such as the Mardi Gras krewes, and extremist organizations such as the Ku Klux Klan. In addition, some organizations attempt to reproduce the life style of past eras such as classical Greece or Rome, medieval Europe, and the American Revolution and Civil War by adopting their dress, cuisine, and activities such as banquets, jousting, and warfare.

Of particular interest are those organizations that reconstruct the past, because some enlist the participation of entire families. The question inevitably arises as to the motivation for these time-devouring activities. One also wonders about the reasons for seceding from one's own culture, the "Miniver Cheevy syndrome". Furthermore, why do some voluntarily select the role of "enemy" losers, the simulated "Tory" units of the American Revolution?

Costumes may of course serve as compensation for urban anonymity and, for costumed fraternal orders, as an alternative source of prestige. For the young, particularly, they may enable identification and the worship of heroes.

All of the instances cited above, especially those of subcultural or organized groups, describe cultural rejection or an attempt to join another culture, this time of one's own choosing. What occurs, however, if the costume wearer takes an additional step and tries to change the society, and the cultural rejection or rebellion becomes a political one?

In the past, some costumed activities criticized the prevalent state of affairs. These activities at times became political protest as in the early opposition of the "Rebeccas" (a form of rural festival) to British industrialization, and the Boston Tea Party.[12]

In modern times, the use of costumes as political protest faces a quandary. Most of the communally recognized costumed activities and functions, including social criticism, have disappeared; costumed activities are now voluntary and serve few functions other than those of commerce, entertainment, or self-gratification. Costumes and costumed activities, therefore, have to be invented to express political dissent. The most noteworthy of these are the Ku Klux Klan and similar groups, and the politicalization of the countercultural movement of the 1960's and 1970's. Relevant areas of research concern the processes by which contemporary costumed activity becomes political protest.

These problems suggest a link between costumes in simple and complex societies. In simple societies based upon mechanical solidarity, the costume serves communal functions such as rites of passage, catharsis, censorship of the deviant, and propitiation; it is therefore under communal control and participated in actively by all. In sharp contrast, in modern society based upon organic solidarity, costumes are more likely to be a voluntary activity, participated in by a self-selected group, who may differ from others in some measure by personality. Though the mechanism or dynamics may be the same in both societies, change of accountability varies.

The question then comes to mind whether it is possible to capture the change in the functions and use of costume in developing countries undergoing transition to modern societies. Within the United States, what are the functions of contemporary American Indian rituals? Have they any remnant of their original religious-symbolic function; do they serve as a channel for the expression of contemporary cultural-political protest; or do they function primarily as tourist attractions?

There is a dispute over the functions of costumed criticism, whether they serve as a conservative force by their cathartic effect or as a revolutionary force by providing a channel for the organization of opposition to injustice. A suitable field of study might be a comparison of the functions of costume in newly emerging nations, especially in relationship to the political structure. One wonders if costumed activities have the same political tinge in Marxist and non-Marxist nations.

Change of Social Structure

Bureaucratic Organization. The movement toward bureaucratic organization in our society over the past few centuries has at times been controverted by efforts to make organizations more egalitarian and democratic through changes in structure or the use of uniforms and quasi uniforms. Contemporary examples of these attempts provide an opportunity to study the operation of clothing in naturally experimental settings. Internal changes in these organizations consist of the compression or even elimination of the hierarchical structure, and the abolition of sartorial and other signs indicating differences in rank or function, such as insignia or uniforms, reserved parking, and segregated cafeterias and locker rooms.

A related but not identical effort has been the attempt to create a feeling of brotherhood, or gemeinschaft, within elite units or commercial and industrial establishments.[13] Needless to say, feelings of brotherhood do not necessarily involve the abolition of hierarchy; one may feel a communal spirit toward those of different strata.

Other changes consist of attempting to draw closer to the public by altering the uniforms or quasi uniforms that have erected a barrier between wearers and viewers. These include the well-publicized examples of the use of blazers instead of the traditional military style uniform by police, the nonwhite uniforms or street clothes of nurses, especially pediatric or psychiatric, and the abolition of traditional habits in some orders of nuns.[14]

The most important aspect of these changes for a study of the sociology of clothing is the complete or partial rescinding of them in many instances, police departments, the United States and West German navies, the Canadian armed forces, and corporations such as the People Express Airline.[15] These reversions to previous types of dress suggest some constraint on the extent of departure from bureaucratic structure in modern organizations. If this is so, then several avenues of investigation become apparent.

We should first determine which of these changes are real and which are feigned; the real hierarchical structure may exist but in a disguised fashion, using other types of signs. Some of the changes may actually be publicity ploys. If so, then how does one detect the difference between actual and cosmetic changes in bureaucratic structure? One should like to know, for example, the alternatives to uniforms that indicate continuing differences in rank or function.

If the structural change is actual, then the next set of problems concerns the methods by which an organization performs the tasks of transmitting orders and information and the other functions of a bureaucratic structure. Again, we are interested in the concomitant alterations in sartorial signs.

Any sociological study of clothing must take into account the informal structure that parallels the formal within any organization. The study of People Express indicates very intense informal interaction extending to off-duty hours and perhaps constituting a subculture; this is augmented by a decentralization of activities and a consequent reliance upon small work teams (Rimer 1984; Whitestone 1983). Drawing upon a knowledge of similar informal structures within formal organizations, one wonders about the insignia which may be adopted by these small groups to differentiate among themselves.

The traditional bureaucracy satisfies several functions for its members including the provision for a career and upward mobility; the signs of mobility include increased income, changes in uniforms or quasi uniforms, and other symbols of position. Does a decentralized, nonhierarchical, and egalitarian organization provide substitutes for conventional bureaucratic devices? Conceivably, dedication to a common goal may enable individuals to submerge personal considerations in favor of a group cause. Furthermore, mobility is not a universal drive but varies with social class and other factors. Whether one can so immerse oneself in the group will depend upon the strength of familial and other affiliations, or the extent to which the organization approaches a total institution.[16]

Some of the efforts to alter the relationships between the organization and the community, as well as alterations of internal structure, seem not to have assessed fully the public perception of, or stake in, organizational uniforms and quasi uniforms. First, the public may not always even be aware of the changes.[17] Furthermore, the sartorial signs worn by an individual may not overcome the antipathy toward his organization by outsiders. On the other side of the coin, the public may be so attached to organizational symbols as to resent and resist any effort at alteration as in the example of the opposition by some to the abandonment of traditional nuns' habits.

Change does occur however, organizational structure and uniforms have been greatly altered over the decades, but change may not occur easily or automatically and the factors facilitating or retarding change must be overcome. "Clothing engineering", whether on the individual or group level, is not a universal panacea; the underlying reality must be considered as well as the appearance.

Incorporation of New Statuses into an Organization. The incorporation of new statuses into organizations offers another excellent opportunity to extend our findings. When such statuses are problematical because they are new to the organization or are recruited from new or different sources, then we may ask how an organization manages the status sets of its members to avoid discordance and keep the organizational status dominant.[18] The problem becomes even more intriguing with the advent of recruits such as racial groups and women whose visibility may at times conflict with that of clothing, especially uniforms and quasi uniforms.[19] The organization must then revise its sartorial signs to take account of these changes or else engage in the charade of ignoring them. When uniforms or quasi uniforms are used, changes are much more apparent due to the precision of the signs which compel a description of the newcomers without evasion; authority cannot avoid the issue. Since the process of incorporating statuses is still continuing, its examination should shed light on the methods of altering signs.

In recent times, the advent of female clergy has led to a resurgence of the problem in another form which makes it worth investigating. It differs from preceding instances in that the wearer is more in control of her dress than her military counterpart. In one solution, a woman cleric adopted the traditional vestment worn by males and added an apron, seemingly to incorporate the female nurturance role. The ensemble suggests the reconciliation of ambiguity through the creation of a new definition for the status position. Another approach has been to adopt the hostess or cocktail gown which suggests the assimilation of the clerical position to that of the female as hostess. The metaphor chosen offers an insight into the definition of the role by the occupant as a modification of the male role or as an assimilation into a female role.[20]

At issue is a potential tug-of-war or dialectic between the new recruits to institutional statuses and the institution itself. Instead of merely providing an additional source of professionals, they have also reformulated the role of the clergy in an effort to adapt to a hitherto all-male preserve. The examination of the newly redefined role as described by the quasi uniforms would be of great value.

Structurally, what would be of interest is a determination of how their changes influence others in the organization. Because they wear quasi uniforms rather than uniforms, they may be freer to change their sartorial signs.

Changes in signs concern not only the wearers themselves but also reach far beyond them and affect colleagues, whose role interpretations are also at stake, and the public—the invisible third party—for whom the wearers also serve as symbol bearers. One wonders about the reactions of these individuals; to what extent will the reformulated dress meet the same range of responses as those of innovative nuns?

NOTES

1. See chapter eleven on the social contexts of costume.

2. Other important trends which I have not considered in detail are the development of modern economy and technology.

3. Another indicator of the separation of the military from the civilian population was the establishment of permanent barracks instead of billets among civilians during the nineteenth century.

4. The long history of such attempts includes efforts by all parts of the political spectrum to convert commercial enterprises and occupational and professional associations into broad social and political units. These include the proposals of syndicalists, fascists, and others. I am not asserting that compensation for the ills of urbanization is the sole cause of all efforts at instilling camaraderie within organizations.

5. A similar change has been noted in the growth of the importance of clothing and other external markers as status symbols in fluid urban settings where groups of anonymous strangers interact.

6. The clown, court jester, and fool have been discussed extensively (Swain 1932; Welsford 1966; Willeford 1969).

7. The religious origins of this dichotomy, which received great impetus from the Protestant Reformation, are apparent but not within our scope.

8. Lord Cardigan, commander of the ill-fated Light Brigade of the Crimean War, would give his smartest men the day off and five shillings each to go to London and salute him as he strolled through the streets (Woodham-Smith 1953, 57). He also spent 10,000 pounds annually out of his own pocket on uniforms and equipment for his regiment. Sartorial honorifics are not confined to uniforms and livery but may assume other forms as in the coordinated dresses of bridesmaids which are carefully subordinated to the bride's gown. Ordinary clothing, more likely of a formal or festive nature, is also used as honorifics by, for example, spectators at the processions of dignitaries.

9. I am oversimplifying. Though the middle class may have been responsible in large measure for bureaucracy, its use is not restricted to them. Furthermore, some elite leisure activities, such as yachting, may be pursued with a great deal of rationality and precision.

10. Bidwell points out the young professional who keeps reminders of his status above his bunk to resist the influence of his military surroundings (1961). Moskos describes the enthusiastic combat soldier who voluntarily wears his uniform on leave in contrast to the company clerk who does not (1970, 73–74). The resistance of aristocrats to the military code is yet another example. Alex noted the greater importance of the uniform to the black policeman both on and off duty (1969, 171–83).

11. The Easter "Parade" in New York City is not a parade at all but a promenade to display spring finery and fantastic costumes.

12. The transition from cultural to political dissent is facilitated by costumes in several ways. First, costumes may symbolize permissible dissent where the wearer is simply using an institutionalized means of expressing grievances. Furthermore, these symbols indicate that the times are out of joint and something is amiss. Finally, costume symbols identify the wearer not as a rebel but rather as a legitimated community representative with a constituency and the power of numbers.

13. Examples of these in nonmilitary organizations include the early New England mills, the factories established by early socialist industrialists, and department stores such as Bon Marché.

14. Recent changes in uniforms have other causes. The United States and West German navies abolished bell-bottoms for economy as well as to lessen the distance between military and civilian; the Canadian armed forces adopted a common uniform for economy and to integrate the services.

15. Rescinding was partial for People Express Airline pilots who were allowed to wear wings and stripes on their uniforms and complete for police departments and navies where uniforms had been abolished or greatly changed.

16. Dissatisfaction exists in People Express Airline with the lack of indication of mobility and with the overabsorption into company activities, leading at times to marital discord and physical illness (Rimer 1984; Whitestone 1983). The company has attempted to increase identification with it by obligating all employees to become stock holders and has minimized the emphasis on mobility by stressing personal self-development as an alternative.

17. Many members of the black community in Menlo Park, California who were hostile to police were unaware of the change from the traditional police uniform to blazers (Mauro 1984).

18. To review previous analysis, organizations on occasion had to incorporate new statuses into an existing structure, partly because of technological change. The steam engineer was first segregated from line officers in the navy and then integrated. When organizations incorporated minorities or women, these externally derived statuses were often defined as conflicting with group membership.

19. Women have presented problems to uniformed organizations attempting to incorporate them into their ranks. One approach has been to ignore gender as far as possible and to issue uniforms on a male pattern with the barest modifications essential to accommodate anatomical differences. The uniforms of early policewomen and female yeomen (clerical workers) in several navies of World War I fall into this category. Another approach has been to acknowledge the femininity of the new recruits and issue uniforms specifically tailored for them, often employing fashion designers. Although some of the differences in signs may be due to the exigencies of the moment, a great many probably stem from the definition of the roles of women. They may be regarded simply as male substitutes or else the differences in gender and in potential contribution may be acknowledged.

One mode of incorporating racial and ethnic minorities into uniformed groups has been their segregation into separate units with distinctive uniforms which may be honorific, as in the instance of martial races, or stigmatic, as with the black Union troops previously described. The alternative is to ignore racial and ethnic differences, to integrate minorities into all units and indeed to suppress as antithetical to organizational control indications of other affiliations such as turbans and yarmulkes. Obviously combinations of the two approaches exist.

20. The Israeli army offers another example of changes in role definition and accompanying sartorial signs. "The shift from actual front-line assignments to rear-echelon work was accompanied by a change in the image and style of CHEN [Women's Army]. From baggy, shapeless khaki drill pants and government-issue brassieres, the women soldiers have moved on to the bare-leg look, tapered blouses and personalized lingerie" (Schiff 1974, 119).

Interviews

Interviews were open ended and were conducted from 1972 to 1974.

Bibliography

Aaron, Daniel. 1961. *Writers on the Left*. New York: Avon.

Agee, James, and Walker Evans. 1960. *Let Us Now Praise Famous Men*. Boston: Houghton Mifflin.

Ahrenholz, Ray et al. 1979. "Company A, Milwaukee Light Guard, 1858–1861". *Military Collector and Historian* 31:23.

Aimone, Alan, and Barbara Aimone. 1976. "Organizing and Equipping Montgomery's Yorkers in 1775". *Military Collector and Historian* 28:53–63.

Alex, Nicholas. 1969. *Black in Blue: A Study of the Negro Policeman*. New York: Appleton-Century-Crofts.

Alpern, David. 1980. "The New FBI is Watching". *Newsweek* 25 Feb.

Altman, B. & Co. 1977, 1978. Training Dept. (Dress Codes for Employees).

Ambrose, Stephen. 1972. "The Military and American Society: An Overview". In *The Military and American Society*, eds. Stephen Ambrose and James Barber. New York: Free Press. 3–18.

Am. Fed. Gov't. Emp. (*American Federation of Government Employees, Local 1712 and H.Q., Fort Richardson, USA, Alaska*). Arbitrators Opinion and Award. Mar. 1, 1972.

Anderson, Olive. 1971. "The Growth of Christian Militarism in Mid-Victorian Britain". *English Historical Review* 86:46–72.

Anspach, Karlyne. 1963. "The American in Casual Dress". *Journal of Home Economics* 55:255–57.

_____. 1967. *The Why of Fashion*. Ames, Iowa: Iowa State Univ. Press.

Aran, Gideon. 1974. "Parachuting". *American Journal of Sociology* 80:124–52.

Arens, William. 1975. "The Great American Football Ritual". *Natural History* Oct.:72–81.

Aries, Phillippe. 1962. *Centuries of Childhood: A Social History of Family Life*. New York: Vintage.

Assoc. Civ. Tech. (*Association of Civilian Technicians, Aaron B. Roberts Chap. and Savannah Chap. and Adj. Gen. State of Georgia*). Asst. Sect. for Labor-Management Relations, U.S. Dept. of Labor, Case No. 40-3147 (CA26). Official Report of Proceedings. Feb. 9, 1972.

Atkinson, Charles Francis. 1910–11. "Uniforms". *Encyclopaedia Brittanica*. 11th ed. 27:582–93.

Babcock, Barbara, ed. 1978. "Introduction". In *The Reversible World: Symbolic Inversion in Art and Society,* Ithaca, N.Y.: Cornell Univ. Press. 13–36.

Bailey, Anthony. 1975. "Our Far Flung Correspondents: 'Island Walk' ". *New Yorker* 8 Sept.

Baker, Margaret. 1979. *Folklore of the Sea*. London: David & Charles.

Ball, Donald. 1973. *Microecology: Social Situations and Intimate Space*. Indianapolis, Ind.: Bobbs-Merrill.

Banton, Michael. 1965. *Roles: An Introduction to the Study of Social Relations*. New York: Basic Books.

Barber, Bernard. 1949. "Place, Symbol and Utilitarian Function in War Memorials". *Social Forces* 28:64–68.

Barnes, R.M. 1951. *A History of the Regiments and Uniforms of the British Army*. London: Seeley Service.

Barnett, Correlli. 1970. *Britain and Her Army, 1509–1970*. New York: William Morrow.

————. 1978. *Bonaparte*. New York: Hill & Wang.

Barshay, Shirley. 1979. (Copy writer). Letter 16 Nov.

Barthes, Roland. 1968. *Elements of Semiology,* trans. Annette Lavers and Colin Smith. New York: Hill & Wang.

————. 1972. *Critical Essays,* trans. Richard Howard. Evanston, Ill.: Northwestern Univ. Press.

Barthorp, Michael. 1983. "Britain's Colonial Wars in the Nineteenth Century". In *Battledress: The Uniforms of the World's Great Armies, 1700 to the Present*, ed. I.T. Shick. London: Peerage. 137–56.

Bateson, Gregory. 1958. *Naven*. 2nd ed. Stanford, Calif.: Stanford Univ. Press.

Baxter, Richard. 1951. "So-Called 'Unprivileged Belligerency': Spies, Guerrillas, and Saboteurs". *British Yearbook of International Law*. 28:322–45.

Becker, Howard. 1946. *German Youth: Bond or Free*. New York: Oxford Univ. Press.

Bendix, Reinhard. 1960. *Max Weber: An Intellectual Portrait*. Garden City, N.Y.: Doubleday.

Berger, Bennett. 1967. "Hippie Morality—More Old Than New". *Transaction* 5:19–27.

Berlin, Isaiah. 1982. *Against the Current*. New York: Penguin.

Bernstein, Carl, and Robert Woodward. 1974. *All the President's Men*. New York: Warner.

Best, Geoffrey. 1980. *Humanity in Warfare*. New York: Columbia Univ. Press.

Bettelheim, Bruno. 1960. *The Informed Heart*. Glencoe, Ill.: Free Press.

Bickman, Leonard. 1971. "Effect of Different Uniforms on Obedience in Field Situations". *Proceedings, 79th Annual Convention, Amer. Psych. Assoc.* 359–60.

Bidwell, Charles. 1961. "The Young Professional in the Army: A Study of Occupational Identity". *American Sociological Review* 26:360–72.

Binder, P. 1954. *Muffs and Morals*. New York: William Morrow.

Black, Max. 1962. *Models and Metaphors*. Ithaca, N.Y.: Cornell Univ. Press.

Blackman, C.M. 1971. "Comments". In *Command and Commanders in Modern Warfare*, ed. William Geffen. Washington, D.C.: Office of Air Force History. 108–10.

Bliven, Bruce Jr. 1964. *Battle for Manhattan*. Baltimore: Penguin.

Bogatyrev, Petr. 1971. *The Functions of Folk Costume in Moravian Slovakia*. The Hague: Mouton.

Born, W. 1943. "The Crinoline". *Ciba* 4:1669–81.

Bradshaw, Carol, and Nancy Chen Cheng. 1963. "Pastels in Pediatrics". *Nursing Outlook* 2:361–63.

Brailsford, Dennis. 1969. *Sport and Society: Elizabeth to Anne*. London: Routledge & Kegan Paul.

Braudel, Fernand. 1981. *Civilization & Capitalism: 15th–18th Century*. Vol. 1, *Structures of Everyday Life*. New York: Harper & Row.

Braun-Ronsdor, M. 1962. "Travel Clothes". *Ciba Review* 3:12–30.

Brett-James, Anthony. 1972. *Life in Wellington's Army*. London: George Allen & Unwin.

Brown, Anne S. 1952. "Some San Francisco Uniforms of 1870". *Military Collector and Historian* 4:1–7.

————. 1974. "Introduction". In *Military Uniforms in America*. Vol. 1, *The Era of the American Revolution, 1755–1795*, ed. John R. Elting. San Rafael, Calif.: Presidio. v–ix.

Brown, Anthony C. 1976. *The Secret War Report of the OSS*. New York: Berkley.

Brown, Esther. 1966. "Nursing and Patient Care". In *The Nursing Profession: Five Sociological Essays*, ed. Fred Davis. New York: John Wiley. 176–203.

Brown, Julia, and Lester Goldstein. 1968. "Nurse-Patient Interaction Before and After the Substitution of Street Clothes for Uniforms". *International Journal of Social Psychiatry* 14:33–43.

Brownlow, Kevin. 1978. *The War, The West and The Wilderness*. New York: Knopf.

Bryant, Arthur. 1951. *The Age of Elegance*. New York: Harper.

————. 1972. *Jackets of Green*. London: Collins.

Buller, Lynn. 1975. "The Encyclopedia Game". In *Life Styles: A Diversity in American Society*, 2nd ed., eds. Saul Feldman and Gerald Thielbar. Boston: Little, Brown. 74–86.

Bullough, Vern. 1974. "Transvestites in the Middle Ages". *American Journal of Sociology* 79:1381–94.

Bultzingslowen, R.F. von. 1957a. "Evolution of the Shirt". *Ciba* 11:11–22.

————. 1957b. "The Shirt in Folklore". *Ciba* 11:23–29.

Burckhardt, Jacob. 1954. *The Civilization of the Renaissance in Italy*. New York: Random House.

Burke, Kenneth. 1945. *A Grammar of Motives*. New York: Prentice-Hall.

CMH (Center of Military History). 1976. *Soldiers of the American Revolution—A Sketchbook*. Washington, D.C.: Dept. of the Army.

Cameron, Lawrence. 1972. "Working Class on Parade". *Transaction* 10:90–93.

Camman, Schuyler. 1952. *China's Dragon Robes*. New York: Ronald.

Career Apparel Institute. n.d. "Guide to Career Apparel". 3rd ed.

Carey, James. 1968. *The College Drug Scene*. Englewood Cliffs, N.J.: Prentice-Hall.

Carman, William. 1957. *British Military Uniforms from Contemporary Pictures, Henry VII to the Present Day*. London: Leonard Hill.

Chambers, Edmund. 1903. *The Medieval Stage*. Oxford: Oxford Univ. Press.

Chapman, Frederick, and Tom Parker. 1974. "The Virginia Regiment, 1754–1762". In *Military Uniforms in America*. Vol. 1, *The Era of the Revolution, 1755–1795*, ed. John R. Elting. San Rafael, Calif.: Presidio. 20.

Chevalier, A. 1947. "Medieval Dress". *Ciba Review* 5:2061–75.

Clecak, Peter. 1983. *America's Quest for the Ideal Self*. New York: Oxford Univ. Press.

Coffey, Thomas. 1969. *Agony at Easter: The 1916 Irish Uprising*. Toronto: Macmillan.

Cohen, Alfred. (Psychologist). Conversation.

Consol. Dec. (*Consolidated Decision on Negotiability Issues*). U.S. Federal Labor Relations Council. (76A-16, 76A-17, 76A-40, 76A-43, 76A-54). Jan. 19, 1977.

Copeland, Peter. 1973. "Our Ancestors as Fashion Plates". *Smithsonian* Oct.

———. 1977. *Working Dress in Colonial and Revolutionary America*. Westport, Conn.: Greenwood.

Corvisier, Andre. 1979. *Armies and Society in Europe: 1494–1789*. Bloomington, Ind.: Indiana Univ. Press.

Coser, Rose. 1962. *Life in the Ward*. East Lansing, Mich.: Michigan State Univ. Press.

Craighead, Alexander. 1963. "Military Art in America, 1750–1914". *Military Collector and Historian* 15:35–40, 73–79.

Croce, Arlene. 1974. "The Two Trocaderos". *New Yorker* 14 Oct.

Cross, James. 1975. *Conflict in the Shadows: The Nature and Politics of Guerrilla War*, 2nd ed. Westport, Conn.: Greenwood.

Crumrine, N. Ross. 1983. "Introduction". In *The Power of Symbols: Masks and Masquerades in the Americas*, eds. N. Ross Crumrine and Marjorie Halpin. Vancouver, B.C.: Univ. of British Columbia Press. 1–11.

Cunliffe, Marcus. 1973. *Soldiers and Civilians: The Martial Spirit in America, 1775–1865*. New York: Free Press.

Cunnington, Cecil, and Phillis Cunnington. 1951. *The History of Underclothes*. London: M. Joseph.

———. 1959. *Handbook of English Costume in the 19th Century*. London: Faber & Faber.

———. 1975. *Handbook of English Costume in the 18th Century*. London: Faber & Faber.

Cunnington, Phillis, and Catherine Lucas. 1967. *Occupational Clothing in England from the 11th Century to 1914*. London: Adam & Charles Black.

———. 1978. *Charity Costumes of Children, Scholars, Almsfolk, Pensioners*. New York: Barnes & Noble.

Cunnington, Phillis, and Alan Mansfield. 1970. *English Costume for Sports and Outdoor Recreation: From the 16th to the 19th Centuries*. New York: Barnes & Noble.

Davidoff, Leonore. 1973. *The Best Circles: Women and Society in Victorian England*. Totowa, N.J.: Rowan & Littlefield.

Davis, Brian. 1980. *German Uniforms of the Third Reich, 1933–1945*. New York: Arco.

Davis, Fred. 1967. "Why All of Us May Be Hippies Some Day". *Transaction* 5:10–18.

———. 1972. *Illness, Interaction, and the Self*. Belmont, Calif.: Wadsworth.

Davis, Kingsley. 1940. "The Sociology of Parent-Youth Conflict". *American Sociological Review* 5:523–34.

———. 1942. "A Conceptual Analysis of Stratification". *American Sociological Review* 7:309–21.

Davis, Natalie. 1950. "The Reasons of Misrule: Youth Groups and Charivaris in Sixteenth Century France". *Past and Present* 50:31–47.

――――. 1978. "Women on Top". In *The Reversible World: Symbolic Inversion in Art and Society,* ed. Barbara Babcock. Ithaca, N.Y.: Cornell Univ. Press. 147–90.

Dayan, Yael. 1967. *Israeli Journal: June 1967.* New York: McGraw Hill.

De Beauvoir, Simone. 1961. *The Second Sex.* New York: Bantam.

Deetz, James. 1969. "The Reality of the Pilgrim Fathers". *Natural History* Nov.

Deighton, Len. 1979. *Fighter: The True Story of the Battle of Britain.* New York: Ballantine.

Devereux, George. 1937. "Institutionalized Homosexuality of the Mohave Indians". *Human Biology* 9:498–527.

Dickens, Sir Gerald. 1977. *The Dress of the British Sailor.* London: HMSO.

Dixon, William. 1955. "Public Administration and the Community". In *The Doukhobors of British Columbia,* ed. Harry Hawthorn. Vancouver, B.C.: Univ. of British Columbia Press. 184–220.

Donovan, James Jr. 1967. *The United States Marine Corps.* New York: Praeger.

Draper, G. 1971. "The Status of Combatants and the Question of Guerrilla War". *British Yearbook of International Law* 45:173–218.

Dumazedier, J. 1968. "Leisure". In *Encyclopedia of the Social Sciences* 9:248–54.

Dunbar, Telfer. 1964. *History of Highland Dress.* Phila.: Dufour Ed.

Durkheim, Emile. 1933. *Division of Labor in Society,* trans. George Simpson. New York: Macmillan.

――――. 1947. *The Elementary Forms of the Religious Life,* trans. John W. Swain. Glencoe, Ill.: Free Press.

Edwards, Anne. 1977. *Vivien Leigh: A Biography.* New York: Simon & Schuster.

Ehrlich, Blake. 1966. *Resistance: France 1940–1945.* New York: Signet.

Ellis, John. 1980. *The Sharp End: The Fighting Man in World War II.* New York: Charles Scribner.

Ellis, Joseph, and Robert Moore. 1974. *School For Soldiers: West Point and the Profession of Arms.* New York: Oxford Univ. Press.

Elting, John. 1960. "The Thompson Westcott Descriptions Descriptions of Military Dress during the American Revolution". *Military Collector and Historian* 12:1–5.

Emerson, William. 1983. *Chevrons: Illustrated History and Catalog of U.S. Army Insignia.* Washington, D.C.: Smithsonian Institution.

Enloe, Cynthia. 1980. *Ethnic Soldiers: State Security in Divided Societies.* Athens, Ga.: Univ. of Georgia Press.

Erdmann, Carl. 1977. *The Origin of the Idea of Crusade,* trans. Marshall Baldwin and Walter Goffart. Princeton, N.J.: Princeton Univ. Press.

Etzioni, Amitai. 1959–60. "Israeli Army: The Human Factor". *Jewish Frontier* 26:4–9; 27:9–13.

Ewing, Elizabeth. 1975. *Women in Uniform Through the Centuries.* Totowa, N.J.: Rowan & Littlefield.

――――. 1977. *History of Children's Costume.* New York: Charles Scribner.

Fairservis, Walter Jr. 1971. *Costumes of the East.* New York: American Museum of Natural History.

Falconer, Barbara. 1972. "Revolution or Tomatoes?". In *Side-Saddle on the Golden Calf,* ed. George Lewis. Pacific Palisades, Calif.: Goodyear. 358–67.

Farwell, Byron. 1976. *The Anglo-Boer War.* New York: Harper & Row.

――――. 1980. *Mr. Kipling's Army.* New York: Norton.

Fashionaire Career Apparel. n.d. (Trade Brochure by Hart, Schaffner & Marx).

Feuer, Lewis. 1969. *The Conflict of Generations*. New York: Basic Books.

The Figgie Report on Fear of Crime: America Afraid. Part 1, *The General Public*. 1980. Sponsored by A-T-O Inc. Willoughby, Ohio.

Finke, Detmar. 1956. "Insignia of Rank in the Continental Army, 1775–1783". *Military Collector and Historian* 8:71–73.

Finke, Detmar, and H. Charles McBarron Jr. 1962. "Continental Army Uniform and Specifications, 1779–1781". *Military Collector and Historian* 14:35–41.

Finlay, J.L. 1970. "John Hargrave, the Green Shirts, and Social Credit". *Journal of Contemporary History* 5:53–71.

Firth, Charles. 1962. *Cromwell's Army*. 4th ed. London: Methuen.

Firth, Raymond. 1973. *Symbols: Public and Private*. Ithaca, N.Y.: Cornell Univ. Press.

Flugel, J.C. 1969. *The Psychology of Clothes*. New York: Intl. Univ. Press.

Form, William, and Gregory Stone. 1955. "The Social Significance of Clothing in Occupational Life". Technical Bulletin 247 (June). Michigan State College Agricultural Experiment Station.

Frazier, George. 1967. "The Art of Wearing Clothes". In *Esquire Fashions for Men*, eds. John Berendt et al. New York: Harper & Row. 201–9.

Friedrich, Otto. 1981. "Kingdom of Auschwitz". *Atlantic Monthly* Sept.

Fussell, Paul. 1977. *The Great War and Modern Memory*. New York: Oxford Univ. Press.

Garland, Madge. 1970. *The Changing Form of Fashion*. New York: Praeger.

Gasnick, Jack. 1976. "Sans Regalia". Letter to *New York Times Magazine* 1 Feb.

Gavin, James. 1978. *On To Berlin*. New York: Viking.

Geraghty, Tony. 1982. *Inside the S.A.S.* New York: Ballantine.

Gero, Anthony, and Philip Maples. 1980. "Fusileering in Western New York, 1830 to 1840". *Military Collector and Historian* 32:117.

Gero, Anthony, and Barry Thompson. 1979. "The First Samoan Battalion, U.S.M.C. Reserve, 1940 to 1944". *Military Collector and Historian* 31:167–69.

Gerrish, Theodore. 1882. *Army Life: A Private's Reminiscences of the Civil War*. Portland, Me.: Hoyt, Fogg & Donham.

Gessler, E.A., and H. Schneider. 1952. "Uniforms". *Ciba Review* 93:3330–59.

Gerster, Patrick, and Nicholas Cords. 1977. *Myth in American History*. New York: Glencoe.

Gillis, John. 1981. *Youth and History*. New York: Academic Press.

Ginzberg, Eli et al. 1961. *Occupational Choice: An Approach to a General Theory*. New York: Columbia Univ. Press.

Girouard, Mark. 1978. *Life in the English Country House*. New Haven: Yale Univ. Press.

———. 1981. *The Return to Camelot: Chivalry and the English Gentleman*. New Haven: Yale Univ. Press.

Glah, Robert. 1952. "The Philadelphia Mummers: A New Year Pageant". *New York Folklore Quarterly* 8:291–300.

Gluckman, Max. 1963a. *Order and Rebellion in Tribal Africa*. New York: Free Press.

———. 1963b. "The Role of the Sexes in Wiko Circumcision Ceremonies". In *Social Structure: Studies Presented to A. R. Radcliffe-Brown*, ed. Meyer Fortes. New York: Russell & Russell. 145–167.

Goffman, Erving. 1951. "Symbols of Class Status". *British Journal of Sociology* 2:294–304.

———. 1959. *Presentation of Self in Everyday Life*. Garden City, N.Y.: Doubleday Anchor.

_____. 1961. *Asylums*. Garden City, N.Y.: Doubleday Anchor.

_____. 1963. *Stigma: Notes on the Management of Spoiled Identity*. Englewood Cliffs, N.J.: Prentice-Hall.

_____. 1972. *Relations in Public*. New York: Harper Colophon.

Goodman, W.E. Jr. 1954. "Development of Designs for Shoulder Sleeve Insignia". *Military Collector and Historian* 6:7–9.

Gouldner, Alvin. 1970. *The Coming Crisis of Western Sociology*. New York: Basic Books.

Graicunas, V.A. 1937. "Relationships in Organization". In *Papers on the Science of Administration*, eds. Luther Gulick and L. Urwick. New York: N.Y. Inst. of Public Admin. (Columbia Univ.) 183–87.

Grana, Cesar. 1967. *Modernity and Its Discontents: French Society and the French Man of Letters in the Nineteenth Century*. New York: Harper & Row.

Graves, Robert, and Alan Hodge. 1941. *The Long Weekend*. New York: Macmillan.

Green, Martin. 1976. *Children of the Sun*. New York: Basic Books.

Greenspan, Morris. 1959. *The Modern Law of Land Warfare*. Berkeley: Univ. of California Press.

Grose, Francis. 1812. *Military Antiquities*. London: Stockdale.

Gross, Edward, and Gregory Stone. 1964. "Embarrassment and the Analysis of Role Requirements". *American Journal of Sociology* 70:1–15.

Gulick, Luther. 1937. "Notes on the Theory of Organization". In *Papers on the Science of Administration*, eds. Luther Gulick and L. Urwick. New York: N.Y. Inst. of Public Admin. (Columbia Univ.). 3–40.

Guttmann, Allan. 1978. *From Ritual to Record: The Nature of Modern Sports*. New York: Columbia Univ. Press.

Halbert, Sara. 1978. (Attorney). Letter 14 Apr.

Halpin, Marjorie. 1983. "The Mask of Tradition". In *The Power of Symbols: Masks and Masquerades in the Americas*, eds. N. Ross Crumrine and Marjorie Halpin. Vancouver, B.C.: Univ. of British Columbia Press. 219–26.

Harder, Mary et al. 1972. "Jesus People". *Psychology Today* Dec.

Harries-Jenkins, Gwyn. 1977. *The Army in Victorian Society*. London: Routledge & Kegan Paul.

Harrington, Michael. 1972. *The Other America*. Baltimore: Penguin.

Harrington, Richard. 1977. "The United States Militia Caricatured". *Military Collector and Historian* 29:186–87.

Harrod, Frederick. 1978. *Manning the New Navy*. Westport, Conn.: Greenwood.

Haythornthwaite, Philip. 1976. *Uniforms of the Civil War, 1861–1867*. New York: Macmillan.

Hecht, J.J. 1950. *The Domestic Servant Class in 18th Century England*. London: Routledge & Kegan Paul.

Hellyer, Paul. 1966. (Minister of National Defence. Canada). Address on The Canadian Forces Reorganization Act. Dec. 7.

Herr, Michael. 1978. *Dispatches*. New York: Avon.

Herwig, Holger. 1973. *The German Naval Officer Corps: A Social and Political History*. London: Oxford Univ. Press.

Hicks, Marjorie. n.d. *Clothing for Ladies and Gentleman of Higher and Lower Standing*. Washington, D.C.: GPO.

Hill, Errol. 1972. *The Trinidad Carnival*. Austin, Tex.: Univ. of Texas Press.

Hine, Robert. 1973. *The American West*. Boston: Little Brown.

Hines, Comdr. R. Jr. USN. 1980. (Special Assistant for Navy Uniform Matters). Letter 8 July.

Hobshawn, Eric. 1969. *Bandits*. New York: Delacorte.

Hollander, Anne. 1980. *Seeing Through Clothes*. New York: Avon.

Holt, Edgar. 1961. *Protest in Arms: The Irish Troubles, 1916–1923*. New York: Coward-McCann.

Honda (Honda of America and International Union, United Automobile, Aerospace and Agricultural Workers of America (UAW)). 1981. 260 NLRB No. 97. Oct. 19.

Howarth, David. 1969. *Trafalgar: The Nelson Touch*. New York: Galahad.

Huggett, Frank. 1977. *Life Below Stairs: Domestic Servants in England from Victorian Times*. London: Book Club Assoc.

Hughes, Everett. 1945. "Dilemmas and Contradictions of Status". *American Journal of Sociology* 50:353–59.

Huizinga, J. 1950. *Homo Ludens: A Study of the Play-Element in Culture*. New York: Roy.

———. 1954. *Waning of the Middle Ages*. New York: Doubleday Anchor.

Humphreys, Laud. 1972. *Out of the Closets: The Sociology of Homosexual Liberation*. Englewood Cliffs, N.J.: Prentice-Hall.

Huntington, Samuel. 1957. *The Soldier and the State*. Cambridge, Mass.: Belknap.

Hutchins, James. 1976. *Boots and Saddles at Little Big Horn*. Ft. Collins, Col.: Old Army Press.

Irwin, John. 1977. *Scenes*. Beverly Hills, Calif.: Sage Publications.

Jaffe, Morris. (Printing Executive). Conversation.

Jakubovskis, Eleonora. 1968. "Uniforms Versus Street Clothes". *Canadian Nurse* 64:37–39.

Janowitz, Morris. 1960. *The Professional Soldier*. Glencoe, Ill.: Free Press.

———. 1977. "From Institutional to Occupational: The Need For Conceptual Continuity". *Armed Forces and Society* 4:51–55.

Jarrett, Dudley. 1960. *British Naval Dress*. London: J.M. Dent & Sons.

Johnson, J.E. 1957. *Wing Leader*. New York: Ballantine.

Jones, James. 1976. *WWII*. New York: Ballantine.

———. 1979. *The Pistol*. New York: Dell.

Jones, Maxwell. 1953. *Therapeutic Community*. New York: Basic Books.

Jones, Tom, and John Elting. 1977. "Texas Rangers, 1823". *Military Collector and Historian* 29:177.

Joseph, Nathan, and Nicholas Alex. 1972. "The Uniform: A Sociological Perspective". *American Journal of Sociology* 77:719–30.

Just, Ward. 1972. *Military Men*. New York: Avon.

Kannik, Preben. 1968. *Military Uniforms*. New York: Macmillan.

Katcher, P.R.N., and Dennis Martin. 1974. "13th Pennsylvania Regiment, Continental Line (The Pennsylvania Regiment), 1776–1778". In *Military Uniforms in America*. Vol. 1, *The Era of the American Revolution 1775–1795*, ed. John Elting. San Rafael, Calif.: Presidio. 86–87.

Katz, Comdr. Hans, German Navy. 1978. (Assistant Naval Attaché of the Federal Republic of Germany). Letter 2 May.

Keegan, John. 1977. *The Face of Battle*. New York: Vintage (Random).

———. 1980. "A Love Affair with Khaki". (Review of *Mr. Kipling's Army* by Byron Farwell). *New Republic* 27 Dec.

Keen, M.H. 1965. *The Laws of War in the Late Middle Ages*. London: Routledge & Kegan Paul.

Kennett, Lee. 1967. *The French Armies in the Seven Years War*. Durham, N.C.: Duke Univ. Press.

Kephart, William. 1982. *Extraordinary Groups: The Sociology of Unconventional Lifestyles*. 2nd ed. New York: St. Martin's.

Kern, Stephen. 1975. *Anatomy and Destiny: A Cultural History of the Human Body*. New York: Harper & Row.

Kett, Joseph. 1977. *Rites of Passage: Adolescence in America, 1790 to the Present*. New York: Basic Books.

Kidwell, Claudia, and Margaret Christman. 1974. *Suiting Everyone: The Democratization of Clothing in America*. Washington, D.C.: Smithsonian Inst.

Kiefer, Thomas. 1974. "Guns of the Tau Sug". *Natural History* June/July:45–51.

Kitchen, Martin. 1975. *A Military History of Germany from the Eighteenth Century to the Present Day*. Bloomington, Ind.: Indiana Univ. Press.

Kitching, Gen. Wilfred. n.d. "The Salvationist and His Uniform". *The War Cry-Eastern Territory*.

Klein, D.B. 1940. "Colored Shirts and Politics: A Psychological Analysis". *Journal of Social Philosophy* 5:326–37.

Knapp, Mark. 1978. *Non-Verbal Communication in Human Interaction*. 2nd ed. New York: Holt Rinehart & Winston.

Knoetel, Herbert et al. 1974. "Hesse-Cassel Field Jaeger Corps, 1776–83". In *Military Uniforms in America*. Vol. 1, *The Era of the American Revolution. 1775–1795*, ed. John Elting. San Rafael, Calif.: Presidio. 7–11.

Knoetel, Herbert, and Frederick Todd. 1954. "Hesse-Cassel Field Artillery, 1776–1786". *Military Collector and Historian* 6:68.

Kornblith, Alice. 1975. Symbolic Aspects of the Uniform as a Function of the Race and Occupation of Its Wearer: A Status Inconsistency Approach. Unpub. Ph.D. Diss. CUNY. Psych. Dept.

Kossoy, Edward. 1976. *Living with Guerrillas*. Geneva: Library Druz.

Kramer, Jane. 1980. *The Last Cowboy*. New York: Pocket Books.

Kuper, Hilda. 1973. "Costume and Identity". *Comparative Studies in Society and History* 15:348–67.

LC (Library of Congress). 1947. *An Album of American Battle Art*. Washington, D.C.

Lane, Robert. 1959. *Political Life*. Glencoe, Ill.: Free Press.

Lane, Roger. 1967. *Policing the City: Boston, 1822–1885*. Cambridge, Mass.: Harvard Univ. Press.

Langley, Harold. 1980. (Curator/Supervisor. Division of Naval History. Smithsonian Inst.). Letter 31 Oct.

Laqueur, Walter. 1962. *Young Germany: A History of the German Youth Movement*. New York: Basic Books.

———. 1975. "The Origins of Guerrilla Doctrine". *Journal of Contemporary History* 10:341–82.

Latham, Aaron. 1978. "The Ballad of the Urban Cowboy: America's Search for True Grit". *Esquire* 12 Sept.

Laver, James. 1948. *British Military Uniforms*. London: Penguin.

———. 1951. "The Evolution of Footmen's Liveries". *Country Life Annual* 126–28.

———. 1954a. "The Poiret Ball (1910)". In *Memorable Balls*, ed. James Laver. London: Derek Verschoyle. 106–16.

———. 1954b. "Preface". In *Memorable Balls*, ed. James Laver. London: Derek Verschoyle. v–viii.

Lawson, Cecil. 1941. *History of the Uniforms of the British Army*. Vol. 2. London: Peter Davies.

Leach, Edmund. 1976. *Claude Levi-Strauss*. Rev. ed. New York: Penguin.

Leff, H. Stephen et al. 1970. "Effect of Nurses' Mode of Dress on Behavior of Psychiatric Patients Differing in Information-Processing Complexity". *Journal of Consulting and Clinical Psychology* 34:72–79.

Leliepvre, Eugene, and John Elting. 1974. "The Soissonnais Infantry, 1780–1783". In *Military Uniforms in America*. Vol. 1, *The Era of the American Revolution, 1755–1795*, ed. John Elting. San Rafael, Calif.: Presidio. 114.

Lewis, Michael. 1948a. *England's Sea-Officers*. London: George Allen & Unwin.

———. 1948b. *The Navy of Britain: A Historical Portrait*. London: George Allen & Unwin.

———. 1957. *The History of the British Navy*. Baltimore: Penguin.

Lewis, N.B. 1968. "The Organization of Indentured Retinues in Fourteenth-Century England". In *Essays in Medieval History*, ed. Richard Southern. London: Macmillan. 200–212.

Liebknecht, Karl. 1917. *Militarism*. New York: B. W. Huebsch.

Lifton, Robert. 1968. "Protean Man". *Partisan Review* 35:13–27.

Little, Roger. 1967. "Buddy Relations and Combat Performance". In *The New Military*, ed. Morris Janowitz. New York: John Wiley. 195–224.

Lloyd, Christopher. 1970. *The British Seaman, 1200–1860: A Social Survey*. Rutherford, N.J.: Fairleigh Dickinson Univ. Press.

Lofland, Lyn. 1973. *A World of Strangers*. New York: Basic Books.

Ludvigsen, Eric. 1978. "Hats, Hats Everywhere". *Army* 28:12.

Lurie, Alison. 1976. "The Dress Code". *New York Review of Books* 25 Nov.

———. 1981. *The Language of Clothes*. New York: Random House.

Luttwak, Edward, and Dan Horowitz. 1975. *The Israeli Army*. New York: Harper & Row.

Lyman, Stanford, and Marvin Scott. 1970. *A Sociology of the Absurd*. New York: Appleton-Century-Crofts.

McBarron, H. Charles et al. 1974. "Grenadier Company, 38th Regiment of Foot, 1775–1776". In *Military Uniforms in America*. Vol. 1, *The Era of the American Revolution, 1775–1795*, ed. John Elting. San Rafael, Calif.: Presidio. 34.

———. 1977a. "Chatham Light Dragoons, Georgia Volunteer Militia, 1811–1816". In *Military Uniforms in America*. Vol. 2, *Years of Growth, 1796–1851*, ed. John Elting. San Rafael, Calif.: Presidio. 8.

———. 1977b. "U.S. Army Garrison Prisoners, 1812". In *Military Uniforms in America*. Vol. 2, *Years of Growth, 1796–1851*, ed. John Elting. San Rafael, Calif.: Presidio. 46.

McBarron, H. Charles, and John Elting. 1977a. "Kentucky Militia, River Raisin, January 1813". In *Military Uniforms in America*. Vol. 2, *Years of Growth, 1796–1851*, ed. John Elting. San Rafael, Calif.: Presidio. 48.

———. 1977b. "Musicians, 1st U.S. Infantry Regiment, Winter Uniform, 1812–1813". In *Military Uniforms in America*. Vol. 2, *Years of Growth, 1796–1851*, ed. John Elting. San Rafael, Calif.: Presidio. 26.

———. 1979. "Thirtieth Anniversary Plate. American Rifle Dress, 1775–1783". *Military Collector and Historian* 31:181.

McBarron, H. Charles, and Philip Katcher. 1974. "5th Pennsylvania Regiment, Continental Line, 1777–1783". In *Military Uniforms in America,* Vol. 1, *The Era of the American Revolution, 1775–1795,* ed. John Elting. San Rafael, Calif.: Presidio. 84–85.

McBarron, H. Charles, and Frederick Todd. 1954. "New York Rifle Corps, 1809–1815". *Military Collector and Historian* 6:12–13.

McCarthy, Carlton. 1882. *Detailed Minutiae of Soldier Life in the Army of Northern Virginia, 1861–1865.* Richmond, Va.: Carlton McCarthy.

McClellan, Elisabeth. 1977. *Historic Dress in America, 1607–1870.* 2 vols. in 1. New York: Arno.

McFarlane, K.B. 1973. *The Nobility of Later Medieval England.* London: Oxford Univ. Press.

Mackay-Smith, Alexander. 1984. "Man and the Horse: The Evolution of Riding and Its Influence on Equestrian Costume". In *Man and the Horse,* eds. Alexander Mackay-Smith et al. New York: Met. Museum/Simon & Schuster. 10–58.

McKee, Alexander. 1964. *Last Round Against Rommel: Battle of the Normandy Beachhead.* New York: Signet.

McKenna, Richard. 1963. *The Sand Pebbles.* New York: Harper & Row.

McMaster, Fitzhugh. 1979. "James Walker's Painting". *Military Collector and Historian* 31:28.

McNeill, William. 1982. *The Pursuit of Power.* Chicago: Univ. of Chicago Press.

Macy's. 1973. (Dress Code for Employees).

Maher, George. 1977. (Chief of Headquarters, Nassau County Police Dept). Letter 6 June.

Manchester, William. 1978. *American Caesar: Douglas MacArthur, 1880–1964.* Boston: Dell.

———. 1982. *Goodby Darkness: A Memoir of the Pacific War.* New York: Dell.

Manders, Eric, and George Snook. 1965. "British Navy, 1704–1714". *Military Collector and Historian* 17:19–20.

Mannheim, Karl. 1940. *Man and Society in an Age of Reconstruction.* New York: Harcourt & Brace.

Mansfield, Alan, and Phillis Cunnington. 1973. *Handbook of English Costume in the Twentieth Century: 1900–1950.* London: Faber & Faber.

Marder, Arthur. 1961. *From the Dreadnought to Scapa Flow. The Royal Navy in the Fisher Era: 1904–1919.* Vol. 1, *The Road to War.* London: Oxford Univ. Press.

Margetson, Stella. 1969. *Leisure and Pleasure in the Nineteenth Century.* New York: Coward-McCann.

Margetts, Donna. 1978. (Training Department B. Altman & Co.). Letter 25 July.

Marsh, Peter et al. 1978. *The Rules of Disorder.* London: Routledge & Kegan Paul.

Marshall, S.L.A. 1965. *Battle at Best.* New York: Pocket Books.

Martin, Paul. 1963. *European Military Uniforms: A Short History.* London: Spring.

Masefield, John. 1937. *Sea Life in Nelson's Time.* London: Methuen.

Masland, John, and Laurence Radway. 1957. *Soldiers and Scholars: Military Education and National Policy.* Princeton, N.J.: Princeton Univ. Press.

Mastai, Boleslaw, and Marie-Louise D'Otrange Mastai. 1973. *The Stars and the Stripes.* New York: Knopf.

Masters, John. 1968. *Bugles and a Tiger.* New York: Ballantine.

Matza, David. 1961. "Subterranean Traditions of Youth". *The Annals of the American Academy of Political and Social Science* 338:103–18.

Mauro, Robert. 1984. "The Constable's New Clothes: Effects of Uniforms on Perceptions and Problems of Police Officers". *Journal of Applied Social Psychology* 14:42–56.

May, W.E. 1966. *The Dress of Naval Officers*. London: HMSO.

Mayer, Egon. (Brooklyn College Sociology Dept.). Conversation.

Mboya, Tom. 1970. "The American Negro Cannot Look to Africa for an Escape". In *Americans from Africa: Old Memories, New Moods,* ed. Peter Rose. New York: Atherton. 411–12.

Mead, George. 1934. *Mind, Self and Society*. Chicago: Univ. of Chicago Press.

Menettrier, Rear Adm. P. 1978. (French Naval Attaché). Letter 6 Nov.

Meredith, Roy. 1955. *The American Wars: A Pictorial History from Quebec to Korea, 1755–1953*. Cleveland: World Publishing.

Merton, Robert K. 1946. *Mass Persuasion*. New York: Harper.

———. 1957. *Social Theory and Social Structure*. Rev. ed. Glencoe, Ill.: Free Press.

Messing, Simon. 1978. "The Non-Verbal Language of the Ethiopian Toga". In *The Body Reader: Social Aspects of the Human Body,* ed. Ted Polhemus. New York: Pantheon. 251–57.

Michener, James. 1968. *Iberia: Spanish Travels and Reflections*. New York: Random House.

Milgrom, Jacob. 1981. "The Tassel and the Tallith". The Fourth Annual Rabbi Louis Feinberg Memorial Lecture in Judaic Studies. Univ. of Cincinnati.

Miller, Michael. 1981. *The Bon Marché*. Princeton, N.J.: Princeton Univ. Press.

Miller, Richard. 1975. *The Law of War*. Lexington, Mass.: D.C. Heath.

Mollo, Andrew. 1977. *Army Uniforms of World War 2*. Poole, England: Blandford.

Mollo, John. 1972. *Military Fashion*. New York: G.P. Putnam.

———. 1975. *Uniforms of the American Revolution*. New York: Macmillan.

Morris, Brian. 1970. "Ernest Thompson Seton and the origins of the Woodcraft movement". *Journal of Contemporary History* 5:183–94.

Morris, Desmond. 1970. *The Human Zoo*. New York: Bantam.

Morris, Donald. 1965. *The Washing of the Spears*. New York: Touchstone (Simon & Schuster).

Morrison, Col. L.C. 1971. (Director, Information Services, Dept. of National Defence, Canada). Letter 25 Nov.

Moskos, Charles. 1970. *The American Enlisted Man: The Rank and File in Today's Military*. New York: Russell Sage.

———. 1977. "From Institution to Occupation: Trends in Military Organization". *Armed Forces and Society* 4:41–50.

Mosse, George. 1979. "National Cemeteries and National Revival: Cult of the Fallen Soldiers in Germany". *Journal of Contemporary History* 14:1–20.

Mossman, B.C., and M.W. Stark. 1971. *Last Salute: Civil and Military Funerals*. Washington, D.C.: Dept. of the Army.

Mostert, Noel. 1975. *Supership*. New York: Warner Books.

Mumford, Emily. 1970. *Interns: From Students to Physicians*. Cambridge, Mass.: Harvard Univ. Press.

Munday, John. 1979. (Keeper, Dept. of Weapons and Antiquities, National Maritime Museum, London, England). Letter 11 Oct.

Musgrove, F. 1965. *Youth and the Social Order*. Bloomington, Ind.: Indiana Univ. Press.

Myerscough, Mary. 1978. (Administrator, Divisional Training, Macy's). Letter 17 Aug.

NHD (Naval History Division). 1966. *Uniforms of the United States Navy 1776–1898*. Washington, D.C.: GPO.

NYTM (*New York Times Magazine*). 1976. Editor's Note. 14 Mar.

Nat. Gd. Bur. (National Guard Bureau). 1977. Brief to Federal Labor Relations Council. 22 Feb.

Neeson, Eoin. 1966. *The Civil War in Ireland*. Cork, Ire.: Mercier.

Neumann, Franz. 1942. *Behemoth: The Structure and Practice of National Socialism*. New York: Oxford Univ. Press.

Newsome, David. 1961. *Godliness and Good Learning*. London: Murray.

Newton, Esther. 1972. *Mother Camp: Female Impersonators in America*. Englewood Cliffs, N.J.: Prentice-Hall.

Niederhoffer, Arthur. 1969. *Behind the Shield: The Police in Urban Society*. New York: Doubleday Anchor.

Noguchi, Isamu. 1985. "No Division Between Artist and Mask". In *Spectacular Helmets of Japan: 16th–19th Century*, ed. Alexandra Munroe. New York: Japan Society. 13.

Oakes, Alma, and Margot Hill. 1970. *Rural Costume: Its Origin and Development in Western Europe and the British Isles*. New York: Van Nostrand Reinhold.

Oleson, Virginia, and Elvi Whitaker. 1968. *The Silent Dialogue*. San Francisco: Jossey-Bass.

O'Malley, Ernie. 1937. *Army Without Banners*. Boston: Houghton Mifflin.

O'Neil, Paul. 1979. "Folk heroics of rodeo have become organized, mechanized—and profitable". *Smithsonian* Mar.

Orwell, George. 1961. *The Road to Wigan Pier*. New York: Berkley.

Osanka, Franklin. 1971. "Social Dynamics of Revolutionary Guerrilla Warfare". In *Handbook of Military Institutions*, ed. Roger Little. Beverly Hills, Calif.: Sage. 399–416.

Paddock, Alfred Jr. 1982. *U.S. Army Special Warfare: Its Origins*. Washington, D.C.: National Defense Univ. Press.

Palliere, Aime. 1928. *The Unknown Sanctuary*. New York: Bloch.

Patai, Raphael. 1947. *Man and Temple: In Ancient Jewish Myth and Ritual*. London: Thomas Nelson & Sons.

Pear, Thomas. 1935. "Suggested Parallels Between Speaking and Clothing". *Acta Psychologica* 1:191–201.

Pa.NG (*Pennsylvania National Guard and Pennsylvania State Council, Association of Civilian Technicians*). Federal Service Impasses Panel. Case No.75 FSIP-7. Hearing Transcript. Aug. 27, 1975.

Perrott, Roy. 1968. *The Aristocrats: A Portrait of Britain's Nobility and Their Way of Life Today*. New York: Macmillan.

Pfister-Burkhalter, M. 1947. "The History of Swiss Peasant Costumes". *Ciba Review* 5:1980–86, 2011–12.

Plant, James. 1950. *The Envelope*. New York: Commonwealth Fund.

Polhemus, Ted, ed. 1978. *The Body Reader: Social Aspects of the Human Body*. New York: Pantheon.

Pollaczek, P.P., and H.D. Homefield. 1954. "The Use of Masks as an Adjunct to Role-Playing". *Mental Hygiene* 38:299–304.

Popplestone, John. 1966. "Horseless Cowboys". *Transaction* 3:25–27.

Portrait Clothes. 1979. (Trade Brochure by Barco of California).

Precker, Prof. Joseph. 1982. (Sophia University, Tokyo). Letter 31 Oct.

Prentice-Hall Executive Report. 1976. P-H Survey: Dress and Grooming Standards in Business and Industry. Special Report, Section 3. March 27.

Preston, Richard. 1978. Comments. In *The American Military on the Frontier, Proceedings of the 7th Military History Symposium*. Washington, D.C.: Office of Air Force History/USAF Academy. 56–66.

Preston, Richard et al. 1956. *Men in Arms*. New York: Frederick Praeger.

Preuschoft, Capt., German Navy. 1978. (Federal Ministry of Defense, Federal Republic of Germany). Evaluation of Press Reports about "Jackets Versus Sailor Uniforms" and Letter 22 Aug.

Renbourn, E.T. 1964. "The Body and Clothing in Retrospect". *Ciba Review* 4:2–11.

Res. Cons. (Resource Consultants). 1980. *Reactions of Active Duty Male E-5's to Proposed Uniform Changes*. Prepared for: Asst. for Navy Uniform Matters, Navy Military Personnel Command, U.S. Navy. McLean, Va.

Richardson, James. 1970. *The New York Police: Colonial Times to 1901*. New York: Oxford Univ. Press.

Richie, Donald. 1973. "The Japanese Art of Tattooing". *Natural History* Dec.

Rickey, Don Jr. 1963. *Forty Miles a Day on Beans and Hay*. Norman, Okla.: Univ. of Oklahoma Press.

———. 1976. *$10 Horse, $40 Saddle: Cowboy Clothing, Arms, Tools and Horse Gear of the 1880's*. Ft. Collins, Colo.: The Old Army Press.

Rigby, Peter. 1968. "Some Gogo Rituals of Purification: An Essay on Social and Moral Categories". In *Dialectic in Practical Religion*, ed. E.R. Leach. Cambridge: Cambridge Univ. Press. 153–78.

Rimer, Sara. 1984. "The Airline that Shook the Industry". *New York Times Magazine* 23 Dec.

Robin, Gerald. 1964. "The Executioner: His Place in English Society". *British Journal of Sociology* 15:234–53.

Rogers, H.C.B. 1977. *The British Army of the 18th Century*. New York: Hippocrene.

Rossi, William. 1976. *The Sex Life of the Foot and Shoe*. New York: Saturday Review Press/E.P.Dutton.

Roth, Julius. 1957. "Ritual and Magic in the Control of Contagion". *American Sociological Review* 22:310–14.

Rubinstein, Jonathan. 1973. *City Police*. New York: Ballantine.

SD (Stamps Division). U.S. Postal Service. 1979. *United States Postage Stamps*. Washington, D.C.: GPO.

SSA (Social Security Administration) and N.Y.-N.J. Council of District Office Locals of American Federation of Government Employees, AFL-CIO. Grievance Arbitration. Nov. 26, 1975.

Sabol, Blair, and Lucian Truscott IV. 1971. "The Politics of the Costume". *Esquire* May.

Salvation Army. n.d. "Ye Are My Witnesses". Brochure.

Sapir, Edward. 1931. "Fashion". In *Encyclopedia of the Social Sciences* 6:139–44.

Sarkesian, Sam. 1975. *The Professional Army Officer in a Changing Society*. Chicago: Nelson-Hall.

Savage, William Jr. 1979. *The Cowboy Hero: His Image in American History and Culture*. Norman, Okla.: Univ. of Oklahoma Press.

Scherer, Joanna. 1975. "You Can't Believe Your Own Eyes: Inaccuracies in Photographs of North American Indians". *Studies in the Anthropology of Visual Communication* 2:67–79.

Schiff, Zeev. 1974. *A History of the Israeli Army (1870–1974)*, trans. Raphael Rothstein. San Francisco: Straight Arrow (Simon & Schuster).

Schneider, Louis, and Sanford Dornbusch. 1953. "The Deferred Gratification Pattern: A Preliminary Study". *American Sociological Review* 18:142–49.

Schramm, H. 1958a. "Fops and Dandies". *Ciba Review* 11:20–23.

_____. 1958b. "Men's Dress from the French Revolution to 1850". *Ciba Review* 11:7–14.

_____. 1960. "Occupational and Festive Costumes in Pre-Industrial Times". *Ciba Review* 12:2–17.

_____. 1965a. "Sports and the Common Man". *Ciba Review* (4) 22–34.

_____. 1965b. "Sports and the Upper Classes". *Ciba Review* (4) 11–21.

Schwartz, Barry. 1981. *Vertical Classification*. Chicago: Univ. of Chicago Press.

Scott, Marvin, and Stanford Lyman. 1970. *The Revolt of the Students*. Columbus, Ohio: Charles E. Merrill.

Sebald, Hans. 1968. *Adolescence: A Sociological Analysis*. New York: Appleton-Century-Crofts.

_____. 1977. *Adolescence: A Social-Psychological Analysis*. 2nd ed. Englewood Cliffs, N.J.: Prentice-Hall.

Sennett, Richard. 1978. *The Fall of Public Man*. New York: Vintage.

Shaw, Peter. 1981. *American Patriots and the Rituals of Revolution*. Cambridge, Mass.: Harvard Univ. Press.

Shibutani, Tamotsu. 1978. *The Derelicts of Company K*. Berkeley, Calif.: Univ. of California Press.

Shiffer, Bonnie. 1982. (Public Relations Coordinator-Honda of America). Letter 13 Dec.

Shipp, John. 1894. *Memoirs*. 2nd ed. London: T. Fisher Unwin.

Shulman, Alfred. 1955. "Personality Chracteristics and Psychological Problems". In *The Doukhobors of British Columbia*, ed. Harry Hawthorn. Vancouver, B.C.: Univ. of British Columbia Press. 122–60.

Sigal, Clancy. 1961. *Weekend in Dinlock*. Garden City, N.Y.: Anchor.

Sigelman, Carol, and Lee Sigelman. 1976. "Authority and Conformity: Violation of a Traffic Regulation". *Journal of Social Psychology* 100:35–43.

Sillitoe, Alan. 1977. *The Widower's Son*. New York: Harper & Row.

Simmel, Georg. 1950. *The Sociology of Georg Simmel*, trans. and ed. Kurt Wolff. Glencoe, Ill.: Free Press.

_____. 1957. "Fashion". *American Journal of Sociology* 62:541–58

Sister C. 1973. Student's Paper 18 Nov.

Slesin, Suzanne. 1978. "Next: Urban-Cowboy Clothes". *Esquire* Sept.

Slusher, Howard. 1967. *Man, Sport and Existence*. Philadelphia: Lea & Febiger.

Smith, Betty. 1943. *A Tree Grows in Brooklyn*. New York: Harper.

Smith, Paul, and John Elting. 1978. "Field Artillery, U.S. Army, 1861–1865". *Military Collector and Historian* 30:180.

Snell, Joseph. 1980. "Kansas cow-town life was in part a comedy of errors". *Smithsonian* Feb.

Snowden, James. 1979. *The Folk Dress of Europe*. New York: Mayflower.

Sowers, J. Luther, and Ross Kimmel. 1979. "The Maryland Forces, 1756–1759". *Military Collector and Historian* 31:81.

Springhall, John. 1971. "The Boy Scouts, Class and Militarism in Relation to British Youth Movements, 1908–1930". *International Review of Social History* 16 (part 2): 125–58.

———. 1977. *Youth, Empire and Society: British Youth Movements, 1883–1940.* Hamden, Conn.: Archon.

Squire, Geoffrey. 1974. *Dress and Society, 1560–1970.* New York: Viking.

Stabiner, Karen. 1982. "Tapping the Homosexual Market". *New York Times Magazine* 2 May.

Stanton, Alfred, and Morris Schwartz. 1954. *The Mental Hospital.* New York: Basic Books.

Stern, Jane. 1975. *Trucker: A Portrait of the Last American Cowboy.* New York: McGraw Hill.

Stevenson, William. 1976. *A Man Called Intrepid.* New York: Ballantine.

Stewart, Edgar. 1955. *Custer's Luck.* Norman, Okla.: Univ. of Oklahoma Press.

Stoller, Robert. 1968. *Sex and Gender.* London: Hogarth.

Stone, Gregory. 1962. "Appearance and the Self". In *Human Behavior and Social Processes,* ed. Arnold Rose. Boston: Houghton Mifflin. 86–118.

———. 1970. "The Play of Little Children". In *Social Psychology Through Symbolic Interaction,* eds. Gregory Stone and Harvey Farberman. Waltham, Mass.: Xerox. 545–53.

Stone, Lawrence. 1967. *Crisis of the Aristocracy 1558–1641.* New York: Oxford.

Strange, Heather, and Joseph McCrory. 1974. "Bulls and Bears on the Cell Block". *Society* July/Aug.:51–59.

Strauss, Anselm. 1962. "Transformations of Identity". In *Human Behavior and Social Processes,* ed. Arnold Rose. Boston: Houghton Mifflin. 63–85.

Strauss, Leo. 1963. "How to Begin to Study the Guide of the Perplexed". In *The Guide of the Perplexed* by Moses Ben Maimonides. Chicago: Univ. of Chicago Press. xi–lvi.

Sturcke, Roger, and Anthony Gero. 1977. "33rd United States Colored Troops, 1st Regiment South Carolina Volunteer Infantry, 1862–1866". *Military Collector and Historian* 29:123.

Sudnow, David. 1967. *Studies in Social Interaction.* New York: Free Press.

Swain, Barbara. 1932. *Fools and Folly During the Middle Ages and the Renaissance.* New York: Columbia Univ. Press.

Taft, Robert. 1953. *Artists and Illustrators of the Old West: 1850–1900.* New York: Charles Scribner's Sons.

Talbott, John. 1976. "The Myth and Reality of the Paratrooper in the Algerian War". *Armed Forces and Society* 3:69–86.

Tallant, Robert. 1948. *Mardi Gras.* Garden City, N.Y.: Doubleday.

Tily, James. 1964. *The Uniforms of the United States Navy.* New York: Thomas Yoseloff.

Time. 1975. "Crossing Signals". 8 Sept.

———. 1978. "How to Be a Terrorist". 8 May.

———. 1979. "Sie Ritten Da'Lang, Podner". 8 June.

Todd, Frederick. 1955. *Cadet Gray.* New York: Sterling.

———. 1976. "The State Fencibles of New York: A Story of Regimentation". *Military Collector and Historian* 28:65–72.

Toennies, Ferdinand. 1957. *Community and Society,* trans. and ed. Charles Loomis. East Lansing, Mich.: Michigan State Univ. Press.

Trillin, Calvin. 1969. "Lower Bucks County, Pa., Buying and Selling Along Route 1". *New Yorker* 15 Nov.

———. 1971. *U.S. Journal*. New York: E.P. Dutton.

Turner, Ernest. 1956. *Gallant Gentlemen: A Portrait of the British Officer, 1600–1956*. London: Michael Joseph.

Turner, Victor. 1967. *The Forest of Symbols*. Ithaca, N.Y.: Cornell Univ. Press.

———. 1969. *The Ritual Process: Structure and Anti-Structure*. Chicago: Aldine.

———. 1974. *Dramas, Fields, and Metaphors: Symbolic Action in Human Society*. Ithaca, N.Y.: Cornell Univ. Press.

———. 1983. "Liminal to Liminoid, in Play, Flow and Ritual: An Essay in Comparative Symbology". In *Play, Games and Sports in Cultural Context*, eds. Janet Harris and Roberta Park. Champaign, Ill.: Human Kinetics. 123–64.

UKMD (United Kingdom Ministry of Defense). 1978. *Dress Regulations for Officers of the Army 1969*. Pamphlet No. 1, Amendment No. 7. HMSO.

USA (United States Army). 1981. *Army Regulations: Wear and Appearance of Army Uniforms and Insignia*. Dept. of the Army. Washington, D.C.: GPO.

USMC (United States Marine Corps). 1976. *Marine Corps Uniform Regulations*. Dept. of the Navy. Washington, D.C.: GPO.

USN (United States Navy). 1981. *Uniform Regulations*. Bureau of Naval Personnel, Dept. of the Navy. Washington, D.C.: GPO.

U.S. Travel Service. 1973. *Festival USA 1973*. Washington, D.C.: GPO.

University of Wyoming Museum. n.d. Brochure on Cowboy's Clothes, Tools and Work.

Unwin, George. 1938. *The Gilds and Companies of London*. 3rd ed. London: George Allen & Unwin.

U'Ren, Richard. 1975. "West Point Cadets, Codes and Careers". *Society* May/ June:22–29.

Utley, Robert. 1973. *Frontier Regulars: The United States Army and the Indian, 1866–1891*. New York: Macmillan.

Vagts, Alfred. 1959. *A History of Militarism: Civilian and Military*. Rev. ed. New York: Greenwich Editions (Meridian).

Vanderzwaag, Harold. 1972. *Toward a Philosophy of Sport*. Reading, Mass.: Addison-Wesley.

Van Maanen, John. 1973. "Observation on the Making of a Policeman". *Human Organization* 32:407–18.

Varron, A. 1940. "Children in Adult Dress". *Ciba Review* 3:1135–40.

———. 1941. "The Necktie as an Expression of Political Opinions". *Ciba Review* 4:1374–79.

Veblen, Thorstein. 1934. *The Theory of the Leisure Class*. New York: Modern Library.

Walzer, Michael. 1977. *Just and Unjust Wars*. New York: Basic Books.

Wamsley, Gary. 1972. "Contrasting Institutions of Air Force Socialization: Happenstance or Bellwether?". *American Journal of Sociology* 78:399–417.

Ward, Christopher. 1952. *The War of the Revolution*. 2 vols. New York: Macmillan.

Warren, Roland. 1946. "The Naval Reserve Officer: A Study in Assimilation". *American Sociological Review* 11:202–20.

Weber, Eugen. 1971. "Gymnastics and Sports in *Fin-de-Siècle* France: Opium of the Classes". *American Historical Review* 76:70–98.

Weber, Max. 1930. *The Protestant Ethic and the Spirit of Capitalism*. New York: Charles Scribner.

———. 1978. *Economy and Society*. 2 vols. Berkeley, Calif.: Univ. of California Press.

Webster's Ninth New Collegiate Dictionary. 1984.

Weinberg, Ian. 1967. *The English Public Schools.* New York: Atherton.

Welch, Charles, Jr. 1966. "'Oh Dem Golden Slippers': The Philadelphia Mummers Parade". *Journal of American Folklore* 79:523–36.

Wells, Tom. 1971. *The Confederate Navy: A Study in Organization.* University, Ala.: Univ. of Alabama Press.

Welsford, Enid. 1966. *The Fool: His Social and Literary History.* Gloucester, Mass.: Peter Smith.

Whitestone, Debra. 1983. (Under supervision of Prof. Leonard Schlesinger.) "People Express". Case Study. Harvard Business School.

Wilkinson, Paul. 1969. "English Youth Movements, 1908–1930". *Journal of Contemporary History* April:7–23.

Willeford, William. 1969. *The Fool and His Scepter: A Study in Clowns and Jesters and Their Audiences.* Evanston, Ill.: Northwestern Univ. Press.

Williams, Loretta. 1980. *Black Freemasonry and Middle-Class Realities.* Columbia, Mo.: Univ. of Missouri Press.

Willis, Paul. 1978. *Profane Culture.* London: Routledge & Kegan Paul.

Wills, Garry. 1972. "The Making of the Yippie Culture". In *Side-Saddle on the Golden Calf,* ed. George Lewis. Pacific Palisades, Calif.: Goodyear. 343–58.

Wise, Terrence. 1978. *Military Flags of the World 1618–1900.* New York: Arco.

Wissler, Clark. 1945. *Indians of the United States.* New York: Doubleday & Doran.

Withington, Robert. 1918. *English Pageantry.* Vol. 1. Cambridge, Mass.: Harvard Univ. Press.

Woodham-Smith, Cecil. 1953. *The Reason Why.* New York: McGraw Hill.

Young, Michael, and Peter Willmott. 1962. *Family and Kinship in East London.* Baltimore: Pelican.

Young, Peter. 1967. *The British Army.* London: William Kimber.

Young, Wayland. 1970. "Prostitution". In *Observations of Deviance,* ed. Jack Douglas. New York: Random House. 64–85.

Younger, Carlton. 1968. *Ireland's Civil War.* London: Frederick Muller.

Zahn, Gordon. 1969. *The Military Chaplaincy: A Study of Role Tensions in the Royal Air Force.* Buffalo, N.Y.: Univ. of Toronto Press.

Zborowski, Mark, and Elizabeth Herzog. 1962. *Life Is with People: The Culture of the Shtetl.* New York: Schocken.

Zimbardo, Philip. 1972. "Pathology of Imprisonment". *Society* April:161–63.

Zumwalt, Elmo. 1976. *On Watch.* New York: Quadrangle.

Zweig, Ferdynand. 1952. *The British Worker.* Middlesex, England: Penguin.

Index

Bureaucracy (*continued*)
symbolism, 45; and uniforms, 2–3,
15, 101, 112–13; values, 113, 155.
See also Control; Quasi uniforms
Bureaucratic professionals, 141 n.1, 150–
51
Bureaucratic role ideology, 155–56

Career apparel, 144, 165 nn.2, 3, 204–5.
See also Occupational clothing
Castro, Fidel, 140
Ceremonies and ceremonial dress, 25,
45, 180, 190; in military, 71, 73–74,
85–86, 104, 107–8, 113, 116; symbolism, 28 n.3, 60–61, 101
Charity dress, 20
Chevalier, 105, 125
Chivalry, 19, 47 n.9, 111, 132. *See also*
Romanticism, nostalgia for past
CIA, 61 n.4. *See also* Signs, types: subtle cues
Class, 26, 56, 72, 142 n.12; attitude
toward military, 92–94, 106–7, 112;
class basis of military branches, 94,
98–99, 102 n.10; and costume, 187,
189–90, 196, 198–99; economic basis
of clothing, 57, 58–59, 114; and leisure dress, 170–72, 172–74, 175–77;
and livery, 112, 132–34; and military
dress, 12, 15, 78, 79, 86, 91–94,
109–10, 132–34; mobility and dress,
54, 57, 172–74, 189–90; and occupational dress, 145, 149, 153, 165 n.8;
signs, 9, 11–12, 23–24, 32, 44, 112,
115; and values, 106–7, 175–77, 206–
7, 207–8, 216 n.9. *See also* Youth
and children, general socialization
Clothing engineering, 215
Clowns, fools, and jesters, 191, 205,
208
Cody, William ("Buffalo Bill"), 127
n.13
Cognitive categories. *See* Symbols as
cognitive and perceptive categories
Comic strip deities, 188–89
Communitas, 190. *See also* Liminality
Conflict, 87–89, 155, 164, 200, 207

Conformity, 25, 85, 99–101, 119; as
symbol, 50, 67–69, 119
Conspicuous and vicarious consumption,
34, 39, 44, 135, 171–72. *See also*
Status, expressive
Continental uniforms: army, 3, 31, 104,
110, 123, 206; navy, 126 n.4
Control, 2–3, 50, 59; costumes, 189–93,
196–98, 207–8; through interaction,
71–75; leisure, 168–69, 174, 207–8;
through membership definition, 69–71;
and power, 39–40; quasi uniforms,
149–51; social contexts, 75–77, 196–
98; through toleration of deviation,
79–80; uniforms, 42, 65, 141 n.1; and
witnessing, 80–81. *See also* Bureaucracy and bureaucratization; Deviation
from uniform norms; Power;
Witnessing
Costumes, 201 n.2; change of identity,
189–93, 193–94; change of interaction, 4, 18, 183–84, 189–93, 195;
characteristics, 184–89; class, 198–99;
community interaction, 196, 198, 199,
200; controls, 183, 196–98; ludic
function, 193–94; as protest, 193–94,
199–200, 212–13, 217 n.12; social
change, 199–200, 212–13, 217 n.12;
types, 185–89. *See also* Liminality;
Nudity; Rites of passage; Status,
reversal
Counterculture, 106, 166 n.12; long hair,
symbolism, 31, 124; ludic use of symbols, 181 n.7, 185, 194; use of costume, 184, 185, 186, 194. *See also*
Hippies
Cowboys: as abstraction of symbols, 26;
actual dress, 122, 123, 127 n.14, 144;
adoption by truckers, 124–25; differential use as symbol, 123–25; fictitious
symbolism, 13, 103, 127 n.13, 128
nn.19, 20; free associations, 105, 121;
function as symbol, 125; as ideology,
122–23; separation from outsiders,
122, 124, 148
Cracker barrel philosophy, 186. *See also*
Status, reversal

in, 151, 153–58; role set, peers in,
161–62; role set, public in, 159–61;
role set, superiors in, 151–52; role set
of wearers, 153–55
Queen Anne, 60
Queen Elizabeth I, 111, 134
Queen Elizabeth II, 53

Racial symbols. *See* Minorities
Random distribution of sartorial signs,
53, 62 n.5
Rationality, 165 n.4, 175–77, 206–7,
216 n.9; substantive vs. functional,
80–81
Rebeccas, and costumed protest, 196,
200, 212
Redcaps, as urban guide, 146–47, 158
Reference groups, 52, 87, 91–92, 152,
156, 162. *See also* Signs, types: subtle
cues
Remington, Frederick, 26, 128
Responsibility, sartorial designation of:
costumes, 4, 191–93, 195; and eco-
nomics, 59–60; leisure clothing, 168–
69, 208–9; quasi uniforms, 148, 161;
uniforms, 67–69, 78, 82, 106. *See
also* Internalization of beliefs; Profes-
sional role ideology; Witnessing
Retainers. *See* Livery; Patrimonialism;
Sartorial honorifics; Status, expressive
Rickover, Adm. Hyman, 70
Ridgeway, Gen. Mathew, 32
Rifleman, 105, 108–110, 123. *See also*
Hunting shirt
Rites of passage, 24, 149, 190, 199, 213
Ritualistic use of clothing, 60–61, 176,
201; costume, 184, 187, 198, 213;
leisure clothes, 169; rites of rebellion,
183, 199–200; uniforms, 46, 118–19.
See also Death and mourning; Rites of
passage
Role reversal, 183–87, 194, 199
Roles: changes through leisure clothing,
177–80; role distancing and uniforms,
88–91; role set of quasi uniforms,
151–53; role set of uniforms, 38, 70–
71, 103–4, 119; role stereotypes, 103–
6, 164. *See also* Bureaucratic role ide-

ology; Others, interaction with; Profes-
sional role ideology
Romanticism, nostalgia for past, 15, 18,
28 n.10, 74, 187–88
Roosevelt, Theodore, 26, 121, 170
Rubin, Jerry, 106

Sadat, Anwar, 52
Salvation Army: use of metaphor, 16, 33;
witnessing, 51, 160–61
Santa Claus, 184, 192
Sartorial dissimulation, 34–35, 54–57,
73, 161. *See also* Signs, social contexts: safety
Sartorial honorifics: statuses, 19, 29
n.12, 43, 44; symbols, 19, 29 n.15,
79, 109, 206–7, 216 n.8, 217 n.19;
uniformity of appearance, 115
Sartorial stereotypes: sources, 108–16;
types, 103–8, 111; and verbal stereotypes, 164
Self: costumed interaction, 185, 189–93;
leisure interaction, 168–69, 177–78;
location of true self, 57, 58, 154, 168–
69, 185; nonconformity, 85, 97–98,
155; quasi-uniformed interaction, 119,
153–55, 157; self as audience, 49, 57–
58; self and sartorial layers, 54–57,
58; symbols define self, 22, 23–25,
41, 119, 138, 153, 155, 157; uniformed interaction, 74. *See also* Control; Liminality; Looking glass self;
Others, interaction with; Professional
role ideology; Socialization
Semiotics, 4, 60, 62 n.9
Separation and reintegration, 75–77, 79,
95–98, 151, 157, 162. *See also* Control; Status, separation
Service academies. *See* Symbols, repositories of
Sexuality and sartorial symbols, 14, 22–
23, 40–41, 83 n.3, 105, 120, 158, 193
Shaka, 76
Sherman, Gen. William, 86
Signals: defined, 9; difference from symbols, 9–11, 28 n.4; in illiterate con-
texts, 10. *See also* Signs; Symbols;
Urban context of signs

About the Author

NATHAN JOSEPH, Associate Professor of Sociology, Herbert H. Lehman College, has done research in communication and political socialization, and has published in the areas of public health education and the sociology of uniforms.